W9-BBE-273

the Jew within American Society

the Jew

within American Society

A Study in Ethnic Individuality

by C. Bezalel Sherman

DETROIT · WAYNE STATE UNIVERSITY PRESS · 1961

Grateful acknowledgment is made
to the Morris and Emma Schaver
Publication Fund for Jewish Studies
for financial assistance that makes
possible the publication of this
volume.

Foreword

A vast literature has been created on the subject of minorities in the United States, but we are still waiting for a clear-cut and generally accepted definition of what constitutes a minority in this country. According to the definition of some population experts, the United States is a land without an ethnic majority group, while the definition of others would lead to the conclusion that no minority groups exist here. A case could be made out for either view. Were we to break up the majority group into its component parts, it would cease to be a majority; were we, on the other hand, to compare a minority group with each one of the parts comprising the majority, the former would then no longer appear as a minority. And yet we know that America has from the beginning struggled with the serious social problems growing out of the relations between majority and minority groups and has still to find a solution for them.

Some historians and sociologists have divided the minorities into two basic categories: racial groups and immigrant groups—with the former doomed to a perpetual minority status, and the latter expected to become part of the majority after shedding the last vestiges of their "foreign" heritage and completely losing their ethnic individuality.

Whatever merit this division has when applied to other groups is lost in relation to the Jews who, although of the white race and overwhelmingly non-immigrants, nevertheless display no disposition to dissolve as a distinctive group.

As a matter of fact, the Jews defy categorization as an entity. Are they a religious fellowship, an historical continuum, a cultural group with peculiar racial traits, or a people? They would seem to be all of these and more. This is what distinguishes them from all other ethnic groups in the United States and makes their position as a sub-community * of the larger American society so exceptional. To appraise this position correctly, the student has therefore to address himself not only to that which the Jews have in common with the rest of the population but also to that which sets them apart from the rest of the population. In doing so, he should avoid the common mistake of comparing the Jewish group with the total non-Jewish population, for the latter is divided into geographic regions, ethnic communities, economic blocs, religious denominations, racial strands, and national origins. Each one of these groupings, conditioned by divergent interests and varying historical development, stands in a specific relationship to the country as a whole in respect to cultural standards, economic attainment and social attitudes. Hence it becomes necessary first to establish whether there are certain laws which govern the development of all groups in this country, and then to see how these laws affect each group separately and the Jewish group in particular. This we shall try to do in the present work by showing wherein the adjustment of the Jews parallels that of other groups and wherein, and why, it deviates from the general patterns, i.e., wherein the Jewish group shares the experience of other ethnic groups and wherein it represents something original in the American social system. This ambivalence in the position of the Jews has been largely overlooked in studies of the American Jewish community.

Both American society as a whole and the various groups comprising it—including the Jews, individually—have strongly felt the effects of what will be presented in the following chapters as the failure of moral

---

* The term "sub-community" probably more accurately describes the status of the Jewish group, but I find it more convenient and less confusing to use the term "community" throughout the following pages.

advancement to keep pace with the technological progress of the American people, or, to put it another way, the lag that has arisen between culture and civilization. The terms "culture" and "civilization" have a wide significance depending upon the particular intellectual discipline and intent of the user. They lack, as do all such general terms, a scientifically limitable denotation. As applied here, "culture" represents the sum total of religious beliefs, ethical and esthetic values, philosophical systems and psychological attitudes comprising the spiritual tradition of a people; the term "civilization" refers to the sum total of a people's material acquisitions, techniques for mastery of the physical environment, socio-economic processes and their concrete manifestations in standards of living and class stratifications. Politics is considered as looking both ways, being the meeting point, often the battle ground, of culture and civilization.

A word of explanation about the use of the term "ethnic group," which is the key to this work, is in order. Many meanings are attached to this term by social scientists. In this book the term is applied to groups who possess a culture of their own, traditional means of expressing it, and whose nationality contours are clearly discernible. According to this definition, the Negroes are not an ethnic group whereas the Chinese are. By the same token Catholics or Protestants would not, on the basis of religious identification alone, constitute ethnic groups—they would qualify as such only if they operated within a communal framework that was the direct outgrowth of their national origin. Only in relation to the Jews, in whose collective existence religion, peoplehood, historical background, and common destiny are inextricably bound up, is the term "ethnic" relevant in all of its meanings.

The drama, which in less than a century saw the Jews in the United States expand from an insignificant community representing a small fraction of the Jewish people into the largest community in Jewish history, accounting for nearly half of the total number of Jews in the world, was played on a stage set by the processes that directed the development of the country at large. These processes will be analyzed in the first two chapters, which are based on a thorough examination of the pubished material on immigration and minority problems in the United States. The subsequent chapters will be devoted to a review of the drama itself. The acts of this drama are of uneven length, with the most important one, beginning with the 1880's, still being performed.

Insofar as this book deals with developments since the turn of the century, the most decisive chapter in American Jewish history, extant literature is supplemented and controlled by personal experience. During the last thirty years, I have spent no less than three months out of each year in travel and observation. Since I have visited every Jewish community of any significance many times and at varying intervals, I have had the opportunity to see firsthand the changes Jewish life has been undergoing since World War I. The usual visit to a community consisted of calls upon Jewish institutions, conversations with Jewish leaders, interviews with rabbis and communal functionaries, attendance at Jewish meetings, and the seeking out of old Jewish settlers with a view to getting their family histories. The impressions thus gained and the facts disclosed were checked against the experience of other travelers and in the light of printed material where available.

Much information concerning the Jews was taken from the United States Government censuses. The reports of such central agencies as the Council of Jewish Federations and Welfare Funds, the National Jewish Welfare Board, the American Association for Jewish Education, the United Jewish Appeal, and the synagog bodies have proved of inestimable value as sources of information. The Yiddish and the English-Jewish press and the American Jewish Year Books were used consistently in order to keep abreast of current Jewish events, and the reports of the Anti-Defamation League of B'nai B'rith, the American Jewish Committee, the American Jewish Congress, the National Community Relations Advisory Council, and the local Jewish community councils supplied data on relations between Jews and their Gentile neighbors. The flow of material from the Vocational Service Bureau of B'nai B'rith and the Jewish Occupational Council registered trends in employment, and meetings with trade union leaders shed further light on Jewish occupational tendencies.

Throughout the years I have found no better way of keeping a finger on the pulse of Jewish communal activities than attending—as delegate, observer or correspondent—the conventions and conferences of the major Jewish organizations. I appeared at most of them in recent years, and on their screens I watched the changing panorama of American Jewish life unfold itself in all of its dimensions.

Neither America nor the Jew has been wholly on the receiving end or wholly on the giving end in the casting of the Jewish community as an integral part of the American nation and as a segment of the Jewish people. There has been a dynamic give and take, and reciprocal influences have been constantly at play in the process. This is what makes the evolution of the Jewish settlement in this country so significant and fascinating a page in the annals of both the United States and the Jewish people.

C. BEZALEL SHERMAN

New York City, October, 1960

Preface

This book has grown out of ideas and theses which I have developed in numerous magazine articles and pamphlets over the years and which I first set forth at length in a Yiddish book, *Yiden un Andere Etnishe Grupes in di Faraynikte Shtatn* (*Jews and Other Ethnic Groups in the United States*), published by Unser Weg, New York, in 1948. A Hebrew version of this book was brought out in Tel Aviv, Israel, in 1954 by *Am Oved*, publishing house of the *Histadrut* (Israeli Federation of Labor). Since that time new material has become available which has enabled me to amplify and to extend the theme of American Jewish individuality suggested in my earlier work.

My work has been made easier by the friendly advice and encouragement I have received from a number of Jewish scholars and community leaders. I have sought their criticism, intellectual challenges and opposing views whenever in need of clarfying a thought, crystallizing an idea or verifying a little-known fact. Their kind response has helped me avoid errors I would otherwise have made.

The assistance I have received from Mr. Nathan Goldberg, Professor of Sociology, Yeshiva University, New York, in the compiling of statistical data has been of inestimable value. I am in debt to Mr. Moshe

Decter for technical help in preparing the manuscript. Mrs. Chanah Mloteck deserves my special thanks for typing the manuscript and arranging the index.

I should like to express appreciation to Dr. Harold Basilius, Director of the Wayne State University Press, for the special interest he has shown in my work and for his guidance of the manuscript through the process of publication. I am deeply appreciative of the contribution Mrs. Barbara C. Woodward, Assistant Editor, has made to the book. Her interest in this work has gone for beyond the call of duty as editor, and her perceptive comments and constructive suggestions have made this a better book than it would have been.

I want to express thanks to the Herzl Institute in New York, and to its president, Dr. Emanuel Neumann, for the financial aid they have given me to carry on the necessary research, and to Mr. Alexander Shapiro of Boston for helping defray the cost of clerical service.

It has not been given to my wife, Dora, who passed away on June 1, 1960, to see this work in print, but without her patient and understanding cooperation this book could not have been written.

C. B. S.

Contents

Contents

List of Tables

1 Minorities and the Dominant Group in the United States

Nearly three and one-half centuries—divided into two periods of roughly equal length—have gone by since the foundations were laid for the settlement out of which arose the United States of America. The colonial period ended with the Declaration of Independence, which also signalled the beginning of the second period. Some American historians have been wont to consider all the white persons who came to this country before the Revolutionary War as "settlers" and all post-Revolutionary arrivals as "immigrants." Unless otherwise specified the term "settlers" will be used in this work to denote the English of the colonial period.

The population of the original thirteen colonies toward the end of the first period was around 3,000,000; in the 180 years that followed, the population of the United States multiplied 55 times. By 1950 the more than 10,000,000 foreign-born inhabitants constituted a population that was three times the size of the entire population of the Republic at the time it was founded. In the course of the intervening years, more than 40,000,000 immigrants entered the country.

They came from every corner of the world, were recruited from every nation, race and religion, spoke every language, and represented

I

every social level and economic class. Among them were people of the highest culture and illiterates, idealists and former criminals, god-seekers and adventurists. But the vast majority of the immigrants were ordinary people whom economic need and political and religious persecutions had driven from their homelands. The selfsame factors had earlier brought the settlers here.

The settlers themselves had not all come from the same country, nor did they all belong to one nation nor speak one language. A few decades before the English took New Amsterdam from the Dutch, there were to be found in and around the city fully eighteen language groups. In the middle of the eighteenth century New England had its Scotch-Irish on the frontier, its Huguenots in the larger cities, and an important Jewish colony at Newport, Rhode Island.[1] The dominant political and cultural institutions were indeed English, but the influence of the non-English-speaking immigrants was not negligible. At the time of the Revolution, twenty-five German newspapers appeared in the colonies. The first French newspaper was published in 1789. At the beginning of the eighteenth century the population of Philadelphia included Englishmen, Dutchmen, Germans, Frenchmen, Scandinavians, and other national groups. And there were Jewish synagogs in five American cities at the time of the Revolution.

Nevertheless, the population was never again as homogeneous as it was toward the end of the colonial period. Over 80 percent of the population stemmed from England, another 7 percent from Scotland. Nine-tenths of the population came from English-speaking countries, and some 98 percent professed the Protestant faith. The picture was an altogether different one in 1950. A majority of the white population of the United States consisted of immigrants and their offspring, and the descendants of the settlers were in the minority. The Anglo-Saxon elements comprised less than a third of the population. According to the 1940 census, 22,000,000 persons—nearly 17 percent of the American people—signified a language other than English as their mother tongue.[2]

In other words, while the relative number of English-speaking immigrants was steadily declining and that of non-English-speaking immigrants steadily rising, while the ethnic, racial, and religious physiognomy of the American population was undergoing a fundamental change, the English language, the linguistic instrument of American culture, succeeded not only in maintaining its hold but in expanding its proportionate sway. Thus, at the very time when the American people were moving farther from the ethnic homogeneity of the colonial period, they increasingly approached linguistic uniformity. In any study of ethnic minorities in the United States, the question arises whether linguistic uniformity stems from the disappearance of group individuality on the part of the non-Anglo-Saxon immigrants, or whether the immigrants merely adapt themselves to a new linguistic instrument for the expression of their old culture values. This is a key question involved in dealing with minorities in America.

Minority problems in the United States are entirely different from minority problems in other parts of the world. Elsewhere, the term "minorities" is applied to ethnic groups which, though concentrated in specific geographic areas and possessing their own cultures and histories, live under the political rule of other nations. These minorities constantly aspire to free themselves from foreign domination and to attain independence. As long as they are forced to remain minorities, they generally demand the right to conduct their collective life in their own way and in consonance with their own historical development.

In Europe and other continents, consequently, minority problems are problems of national self-determination. National conflicts arise from the political, economic, social and cultural differences between minorities and majorities. In the United States, such problems are unknown and national conflicts are nonexistent. In fact, the unique quality of American political development is precisely that the country has avoided national conflicts among the multitude of ethnic groups that live here. To the extent that conflicts among them did occur in the past —and they were not absent—the battle-cry was not the right of national self-determination. With the exception of a few isolated, short-lived attempts, no ethnic group has ever sought to organize itself as a separate political entity within the framework of the American state; no ethnic group has ever aspired to the status of a national minority. Gunnar Myrdal makes the penetrating observation that "the minority peoples of the United States are fighting for status in the larger society; the minorities of Europe are mainly fighting for independence from it." [3]

3

It is understandable, therefore, that a proper definition of ethnic "minority" in the United States is hard to come by. R. A. Schermerhorn defines a majority or dominant group as "that group whose historical language, traditions, customs, and ideology are normative for the society: their pre-eminence is enforced by the folkways or by law, and in time these elements attain the position of cultural presupposition." [4] It follows, therefore, that minorities "are subgroups within a culture which are distinguishable from the dominant group by reason of difference in physiognomy, language, customs, or culture-patterns (including any combination of these factors). Such subgroups are regarded as inherently different and 'not belonging' to the dominant group; for this reason they are consciously or unconsciously excluded from full participation in the life of the culture." [5] Francis J. Brown proposes the following formula: Minorities are "individuals and groups that differ or are assumed to differ from their dominant social groups and that have developed, in varying degree, an attitude of mind which gives them a feeling of greater social security within their own groups than they have in their relation to the dominant group." [6] Brown's definition should be amended to include the component of majority prejudice against the minority. A minority is such not merely because it is different from the majority, but also, and perhaps chiefly, because in the process of its integration into the general life of the country it encounters resistance from the dominant group. The latter need not indeed constitute a majority numerically. We have already noted that people of Anglo-Saxon descent are today far from representing an absolute majority in the United States; nevertheless, they are unquestionably the dominant ethnic group.

Ethnic minorities in the United States have been the subject of intensive survey and research. In the study of the Jewish minority contemplated here, we shall find an invaluable frame of reference in the results of these investigations. Thus, we shall first discuss the characteristics of the dominant group and the circumstances of American life which gave a particular direction to the history of European ethnic minorities in America. In the following chapter we shall briefly analyze the social forces tending to preserve the identity of the ethnic minority within the larger community and those leading to the disappearance of the minority as a distinct group.

4

CULTURE AND CIVILIZATION

Englishmen became the pioneers of the American settlement because they did not come here to turn absentee landlords looking for an opportunity to exploit cheap native labor. Material interests alone did not impel the Pilgrims to seek the shores of a strange and wild continent. They were also borne aloft by a religious passion—and this is perhaps the chief difference between the Puritans who came from England and the settlers from other lands. The latter, even when they came with the intention of making the new land their home, were moved by no social objective or spiritual ideal; they consequently failed to inject into their work conscious social purposes. The Puritans, having suffered religious persecution at home, sought to create here a society in keeping with the religious views to which they had found it impossible to give full expression in England. They created a theocracy, a religious state whose impact is still strongly felt in American social life.

Here can be discerned the first great contradiction in American development. Whereas in England the Puritans themselves were in opposition and refused to abide by the rules of the majority, in the colonies they introduced, and maintained for a long time, an iron discipline against dissenters. They were themselves orthodox and did not hesitate to use police power against other religious groups and heretics. Regimentation was not restricted to the church; it extended to every aspect of social and cultural life and was intended to maintain the mores and attitudes the Puritans had brought with them from their motherland. While in respect of their physical needs the settlers embarked upon untrod ways and undertook new means, in their spiritual life they followed the traditional paths originally laid out in England; in other words, they built a new civilization but they retained the old culture.

The settlers from England were compelled to build a new civilization because, on the purely physical level, they found in this land nothing which they could continue. Alone they had to build a new life, and alone they had to produce the raw materials needed for the venture. Their background from the motherland helped them but little. The England from which they had departed was a highly developed country with crystallized social forms; America was an economic desert and a social no-man's-land. With all the backing of powerful trading companies and all the support of their home governments, the settlers in the main had to rely on their own resources.

The conquest of America required great determination and initiative. An unfriendly nature had to be tamed, barren land had to be cultivated, thousands of highway miles had to be laid through the wilderness, the resistance of the Indians had to be broken—often enough with fire and sword. The weak fell by the wayside, but even the strongest were able to pursue their tasks only with the greatest of sacrifices. Their utter concentration upon the construction of a new home for themselves reflected an incomparable pioneering spirit that was in no small measure nurtured by the religious zeal which brought them to this side of the Atlantic.

Religion was indubitably their most decisive spiritual need—but no new cultural values had to be created for the satisfaction of that need. In fact, this merely required the application on American soil of mental tools already forged in Europe. With one difference, however: in Europe *other* sects had used those tools against the Puritans; in the colonies the *Puritans* used the same tools against other sects.

In these circumstances the settlers could not build a new culture; they could not spare the energy for it, and they felt no particular need to do so. Nor did they desire to form a new social order: they were quite content with harnessing the social forms that prevailed in England to serve their specific purposes here. Indeed, in their homeland they had belonged to the underprivileged classes, chiefly the petty bourgeoisie, and had few prospects of advancing because the higher levels of the socio-economic ladder were occupied by their betters; in the colonies, on the other hand, they themselves built that ladder, and no one stood in their way.

Still less did the settlers desire political reforms. Charles E. Merriam observes that what the Puritans wanted to create was not so much a state as a church. This—not because, as Merriam sees it, political ends were of secondary consideration for the Puritans, but rather because they simply did not aspire to any political innovations.

Nor did the Revolution resolve the contradiction between a new civilization and an old culture. It gave the colonies political independence; but culturally they remained for nearly a century after the

6

Revolution a province of England. However, the Revolution opened the sluice-gates to an extraordinary commercial expansion and ushered in the period of the moving frontier. The frontier, as Frederick J. Turner defined it, was "the meeting point between savagery and civilization." [7]

The frontiersmen had no accumulated experience to draw upon: they had to create their reality alone—and often enough with gun in hand. Only men of unparalleled intrepidity, unlimited self-confidence, adventurous spirit, and readiness to make enormous sacrifices could have undertaken to hew out new paths in the West under the conditions prevailing in the early and mid-nineteenth century.

Not always were the frontiersmen able to overcome the physical hardships they encountered. Nor could they stop to consider the cost in terms of cultural values. Education had nothing to offer them, and to the very limited extent that they even thought of it, they viewed it with disdainful indifference. The frontier, wrote Howard K. Beale,

> . . . had no reverence for the wisdom of the past. Experience with the civilized world was unnecessary. Education and cultivation were not assets but handicaps among the crudities of new settlements. The frontier worshipped practicality. Learning was impractical. What was worse, it was effeminate. Men's place was fighting Indians, hunting, felling trees, working fields.[8]

The frontiersman accelerated the technical progress of the United States while delaying for a time cultural advancement. The rapid development of industry and capitalism in America had a similar effect.

Vernon Parrington characterizes the three decades following the Revolution as a period in which the old America was in the process of dying. The new America that was arising was "a shifting, restless world, youthfully optimistic, eager to better itself, bent on finding easier roads to wealth than the plodding path of natural increase. It conceived of human nature as acquisitive, and accounting acquisitiveness a cardinal virtue, it set out to inquire what opportunities awaited it in the unexploited resources of the continent." [9]

Although in the second quarter of the nineteenth century the majority of the population of the United States was still overwhelmingly rural, industrialization was sweeping the North from one end to the

7

other with the force of a volcanic eruption. As the Beards describe that period:

> . . . inventors were altering the face of the earth and the sea; builders of factories and railroads were striding forward in seven league boots followed by their swelling army of industrial workers; steamships were beginning to drive sailing vessels from the deep; and packages of securities in strong boxes were growing bulkier day by day.[10]

In such an atmosphere, capital had little patience for moral scruples. It could not stand still and wait for culture to catch up with civilization and come abreast of technology. Industrialists could not occupy themselves with cultural affairs, and they cared little for the spiritual impulses of their workers, especially of the immigrants who, during this period, began to arrive in the United States in large numbers.

After the Civil War, technical development propelled the United States into incomparable material progress. Natural disasters, social dislocations, economic reverses, political upheavals, and wars slowed up this progress from time to time, but never did it come to a full stop. Inventive genius accompanied America at every step—indeed, it went ahead and pulled the country with it—but always in a utilitarian direction. And throughout, those aspects of creativity that could not be translated into immediate practical uses lagged behind, giving a twist of one-sidedness to America's march along the road of social progress. Civilization was at the head of the column, culture in the rear.

How wide was the gap created by the failure of social morality to keep pace with the industrial revolution is best demonstrated by the Negro problem. Characterizing this problem as the "American Dilemma," Gunnar Myrdal defines it as an incessant struggle between the democratic principles and Christian morality of the American credo on the one side, and mores and customs which have their roots in prejudices, predatory interests, economic lust, jealousies, status aspirations, caste divisions, envies and mistrusts on the other side. As the classical minority in the United States, the Negroes of our days suffer less from legal disabilities than from unavailability of means to give effect to the legal rights they do possess under the American Constitution.

THE "TYRANNY OF THE MAJORITY"

From the "cultural lag" which we have described comes the contradiction to be observed in American social attitudes: the same America that stands in awe of the exceptional man who has attained material success mistrusts the exceptional man who diverges from the spiritual norm. The America that glories in the individual achievements of its pioneers and builders is still in large measure guided by what Alexis de Tocqueville called a "tyranny of the majority" in its cultural life.[11]

The frontiersman avoided seeking aid and support from outsiders; least of all did he seek it from the government. His social dissatisfaction was consequently expressed not in mass protest but in individual action and in mistrust of otherness. His faith in his own powers was the foundation of his personal political equality; the same faith shackled his spiritual individuality. It fortified the tyranny of the majority—a tyranny far more oppressive, according to De Tocqueville, than the tyranny of kings, precisely because it is not predicated upon legal processes. The authority of a monarch is only physical and has no dominion over men's wills. A majority, on the other hand, possesses a power that "acts upon the will as well as upon the actions of men." It is possible to take a stand in opposition to kings; the tyranny of the majority not only deprives the minority of the will to oppose accepted patterns of life, but "represses . . . all controversy" as well.[12]

The tyranny of the majority is to be observed in all phases of American cultural life: in politics, in recreation, even in American literary taste. In the area of religion, it may take the form of intolerance and bigotry.

In Puritan America, the church prohibited any form of recreation that was not intimately connected with religion. The church not only determined the forms of recreation—it provided the recreation itself. For the frontiersman, religion was not only a spiritual instrument regulating his relations with his God; it also provided the only festive relief from his hard daily grind. Even before the new settlements were large enough to sustain churches of their own, there appeared among them missionaries and circuit-riding preachers who in addition to preaching performed several other functions of value. In the first

9

place, they tried to set up moral boundaries within the geographical expansion. As noted previously, the frontiersman paid small attention to the laws of the government; the sanctions of religion were virtually the only authority he recognized; and the missionaries and preachers embodied that authority. They were also the first bearers of culture and education in the newly-occupied territories; they instructed the children in reading, writing and the duties of citizenship. Last, but not least, they brought to the frontiersman a religious ecstacy which was also his greatest form of entertainment.

As a result of the physical exhaustion and nervous strain induced by his mode of life, and because of the primitiveness of his esthetic taste, the frontiersman was able to derive his best enjoyment from crude emotional experience. A religion of carefully modulated manners and settled liturgy would scarcely have satisfied him. He looked for a religion into which he could pour his untapped psychical force and through which he could be raised to the heights of his heated fantasies. A dedicated individualist, he sought in religion fusion with numbers of like-feeling persons. He wanted to taste the sensation of immersing himself in a sea of people and of being freely wafted on the emotional waves of that sea. He found that sensation in Evangelicalism.

Evangelicalism transported the individual from his own hard reality to the spiritual surcease derived from an enflamed mass of humans. It was a democratic religion, for it spoke not to the highest social levels but to plain folks. It was authentically American, in the spirit of the tyranny of the majority, in that it appealed to the "herd" instinct. Evangelical services were not merely religious worship with their mass spectacles, "revivals" and "roads to redemption"—they were also forms of entertainment. And this is precisely why Evangelicalism had in many ways a retarding cultural effect: it injected spiritual intolerance into recreation, thus coming into conflict with its own democratic character. In the words of Beale: "The very religious devotion and enthusiasm of the evangelical sects have tended to make them intolerant of those who differ from them." [13]

The mass ecstasy that virtually overwhelms the participant is perhaps the most striking element in all the national forms of recreation in the United States. In baseball, football, wrestling, boxing, horse-racing, and similar sports, the reaction of the crowd is no less a part of the entertainment than the roles of the players. Without this reaction it would be difficult for the protagonists to retain the interest of the onlookers. There is in the mass nature of the recreation an equalizing and levelling element through which the individual is subsumed within the group.

The same levelling element was discernible in the literary tastes of the American people. It will be remembered that for a long time American literature was merely a by-product of English culture. American literature thus reflected not the reality of life on these shores, but a foreign unreality. American entertainment has largely remained weighted by old traditions and outmoded tastes to this very day. The standardization of amusement, an outgrowth of the tyranny of the majority, has prevailed in the age of television.

The tyranny of the majority, the stress on utilitarianism, combining with other circumstances in American life—unlimited opportunities for men of ability and initiative, the universal suffrage which made one man's vote as weighty as another's, optimistic faith in one's own powers, the unceasing migrations and continuous flux—prevented the development of class consciousness in the average American. The American never saw himself as a member of a specific economic group whose interests must always conflict with those of another economic group. The frontiersman's social outlook was forged by his participation in the conquest of a continent. V. F. Calverton describes the process in vivid terms:

> The Western frontiersmen advanced into the wilderness as equals, fought as equals, and established their communities upon an equalitarian basis. Class distinctions could have little meaning in an environment that demanded individual initiative, energy, strength, courage, and a willingness to work rather than willingness to live on the work of others. Society took on a fluidity which it had never experienced before and will never experience again. Individuals found themselves for the first time in their lives unfettered by class or rank, unencumbered by the cultural and economic vestiges of the past.[14]

As for the urban workers of the East Coast, they never thought of themselves as an independent economic layer, but as partners with the owners in the industrial processes. This was most clearly reflected in their political activities. It is one of the paradoxes in the development of American society that the very social mobility of the population and the unceasing flux of the economy led to a kind of political stagnation. For so long as Americans could without particular difficulty shift from one social status to a higher one, they wanted no governmental intervention into private business and no political reforms to disturb the status quo. But there have also been abnormal times in the United States when the governmental program conflicted sharply with the interest of particular sectors of the population—the workers, the lower middle classes or the farmers. At such times the latter groups became keenly aware that the principle of governmental non-interference with "free enterprise" played into the hands of the trusts and large banks. This awareness gave rise to "populist" movements which took the form of either third parties or opposition blocs within the two major parties.

Because of its rural, agrarian and lower middle-class base, the populist social horizon was narrow; because of its individualistic philosophy, a legacy from the frontier, it was intolerant of cultural change. Populists were for the most part anti-foreign and anti-immigrationist. Almost all movements of an "anti-alien" nature, including anti-Semitism, have struck a populist note and found their greatest response among adherents of populism.

The swift technological growth of the United States created a demand for hundreds of new types of qualified laborers. While the industrial machine was swallowing workers with no regard for their individuality, it also threw up layers of employees who gradually rose from the status of wage-earners to membership in the middle classes. This group was the bridge between industry and finance, on the one side, and between producers and consumers, on the other. Concurrently, a continuous process of social change was going on in the workshops and factories. Cheap labor was constantly being infused from the outside; inside, workers were moving from poorly-paid to better-paid positions. Not only were the latter's wages higher and their work easier, but they also gained a privileged status vis-à-vis the workers on the lower levels.

The new technological functions were constantly on the increase. The professions, the white-collar occupations, the executive and administrative positions, as well as skilled labor, recruited their man-

12

power from elements that possessed a better-than-average education and greater social prestige. The top levels among these socio-conomic groups were occupied by the early arrivals who, because they had come here first, were on the ground floor at the beginning of every enterprise and process.

The late-comers could operate only within the framework shaped by the dominant elements, who synthesized their moral conceptions with their practical needs. It was not without reason that a European visitor to the United States remarked that nowhere else had he seen people with such hard heads and soft hearts.

This hardheaded softheartedness made itself felt in the attitude of the early arrivals to the late-comers. There was in that attitude both a desire to help underprivileged immigrants fleeing from poverty and oppression, and a determination to build up labor reserves with sufficient capacity to meet all the requirements of an evergrowing machine economy. The immigrants were of course expected to shed their own ethnic individuality and accept the established cultural and social standards with dispatch and without protest.

Wherever cultural standardization exists, there must needs be someone who creates the standard and has an interest in its perpetuation. In the United States the role of Procrustes has been played by the Anglo-Saxon Protestant elements. They have constituted the country's social aristocracy and dictated its national direction. They have molded public opinion; from their ranks have come the most influential intelligentsia; and it was they who set the tone of entertainment and recreation. All other elements had, as time went on, to adapt themselves to this group; and the entire subsequent development of the United States was such as to fortify the privileged position of the descendants of the original English settlers.

Had they remained in one place, their influence would not have been so decisive. But it was they who also produced the frontiersman, who spread their commanding status from one end of the vast country to the other. They were, in addition, a healthy and fertile stock and reproduced at an incredibly swift rate. In the early periods, the country's population doubled every twenty-five years. How small a role in this increase was played by immigration can be seen from statistics compiled by Edward Jarvis in 1877. From 1790 to 1800,

13

44,282 immigrants entered the country; in the same period, the natural growth of the white population was 1,090,158. For the decade 1800 to 1810, the corresponding figures were 52,443 and 1,503,179. The comparable figures for the following decade were 80,100 and 1,924,148; in the next decade, 139,005 and 2,532,032.[15] It was only in the latter part of the nineteenth century, when the country's cultural foundations and life-rhythm were clearly formed and fixed, that the fertility and birthrate of the Anglo-Saxon elements diminished. Immigration was at no time greater than the natural increase, however, and the native population could always without difficulty assimilate the new elements culturally.

In these circumstances, it would have been exceedingly difficult for the non-English-speaking groups to maintain their ethnic identity even if they had not met other obstacles. But as we shall see, other obstacles existed aplenty, and as a result the country which Turner characterized as a nation of nations entirely avoided minority conflicts based on nationality.

Some one hundred years ago, Marcus L. Hansen relates, three ships left the port of Hamburg loaded with German passengers. The first sailed for New Orleans (its passengers ultimately settled in Missouri); the second went to Rio de Janeiro, and the third to Australia. Here is what happened to these three groups as described by Hansen:

In Brazil the descendants of the German passengers "think German, vote German. They constitute a Teutonic state in the Brazilian federation." In Australia the descendants still constitute "a community which retained its German individuality with much more tenacity than did that of their Missouri compatriots, and this in spite of the fact that in Australia they were surrounded by an atmosphere more thoroughly Anglo-Saxon."[16] Only in the United States have the descendants of the German passengers become fully integrated with the larger community. Here, in a nutshell, we have the history of immigration in this country.

2 Isolation and Assimilation: Conflicting Tendencies

Every ethnic minority is subjected to two conflicting tendencies, the isolating and the assimilating. Ber Borochov defines the isolating tendencies as the sum total of those factors, both of a positive internal character and of a negative external character, which impede the absorption of the minority within the majority.[1] The assimilating tendencies consist of those economic and cultural factors that create for the minority the necessity and the will to dissolve within the majority. National minorities are constantly in turmoil as the result of the clash of tendencies within their social framework, and except where the majority absolutely refuses to absorb the minority, or where the minority is a territorially constituted political entity, the assimilatory tendencies always prevail.

Aside from rejection by the majority, many factors function to isolate members of an ethnic minority who have emigrated from their homelands, and strengthen their will to preserve their group identity in the land of their immigration. Among these factors are conditions in the homeland, ideological commitments—religious, political, and social—and the methods by which the minority group accommodates itself to life in the new land.

A variety of processes operate as assimilating tendencies on all ethnic groups in this country. Donald R. Taft's *Human Migration* places them in three categories: (1) economic opportunity, (2) utilitarianism, and (3) democracy.[2] In addition to general processes, there are also factors specific to the unique national character of the various immigrant groups which evoke greater or lesser resistance to assimilatory tendencies.

ISOLATING FACTORS

Majority Attitudes. From the very beginning of the American settlement, there were elements that viewed immigration and immigrants with mistrust and antagonism, notwithstanding the extraordinary contribution to America's development made by the newcomers. Anti-immigrationists offered a variety of supporting arguments for their demand of a closed-door policy, all characterized by one consistent motif: further immigration would threaten the country's stabilized social and economic order. This attitude was directed against all ethnic groups, including Englishmen, and at all times, with varying intensity. As American history approached our own time, anti-immigrationists reaped increasing success.

All the anti-immigration arguments and motivations of the twentieth century—racial, hygienic, economic, political—were already current in the eighteenth and early nineteenth centuries. At that time the arguments were cited against the immigration of English, Germans, Scandinavians, and other "Nordic" Protestants of the "old" immigration. In mid-century they would be used with particular bitterness against the Irish Catholic minority, and later against the "new" immigrants pouring in from eastern and southern Europe beginning in the 1860's.[3]

Objections to immigration constantly stress the immigrants' poverty, their ignorance of English, their "otherness" in general, the menace they present to the health and the economic well-being of the community, their responsibility for increase in crime and the consequent social burden. But despite strong anti-immigrationist sentiment, this country, except in periods of economic crisis, welcomed immigration because a larger population was needed to fill the demands of agriculture and of burgeoning industry. America wanted immigration but disliked immigrants.

Prejudice against the immigrants was to be found in both urban and rural areas of their place of settlement. However, the early agrarian immigrants settled in sparsely populated areas; and for this reason conflicts rarely arose between them and the native population. Although anti-immigrationist sentiment hardened as the proportion of urban immigrants increased, conflicts did not assume serious proportions as long as the immigrant population did not differ greatly from the majority in economic, social, or cultural terms, except for the language of those who did not speak English. Because the "old" immigration from Northern Europe was largely Protestant, the explosive element of religious "otherness" was not present.

It was present in relation to the Irish Catholics who in the middle of the nineteenth century became a "minority" here in the full sense of our definition. Although contemporary reports emphasize the social and economic problem presented by the mass immigration of poverty-stricken Irish peasants and farm laborers to large American cities at a time of social and political unrest, the overt hostility of nativist elements centered largely about the religious "alienism" of the Irish. There were riots, destruction of Catholic church property, publication of slanderous anti-Catholic literature, attempts to restrict the right of Catholics to hold public office, and to make the legal process of their naturalization difficult in order to exclude them from political influence.

Open rejection by the dominant majority, along with the social and economic gulf between the Irish immigrant and the native Protestant population, tended to prolong the cohesion of the Irish as an ethnic island apart from the larger community. Herein they exemplify a tendency to be observed among all ethnic groups—the more a group diverges from the majority, the less friendliness it encounters and the more durable its group identity.

Eastern and southern Europeans migrating to America in the later years of the nineteenth century—the so-called "new" immigration—did not, for the most part, come here possessed of ambitions to maintain national separateness. Although they were by no means poured from one mold and were sharply divided among themselves in religion, tradition, social status, historical experience, and economic development, American nativism nevertheless classified them all as foreigners

17

and unwelcome. At the time of their arrival, the country's prevailing mode of life was far more stabilized than it had been during the "old" immigration. This explains the greater impatience of the American majority with "strangers" and its standard intolerance of non-conformists.

During the twentieth century, the state of the American economy itself has fostered anti-immigration attitudes. The migration of native Negro workers to the northern industrial states lowered the demand for cheap foreign labor; a steadily increasing industrial reserve army came into being as the result of technological improvements and the consequent increase in the productivity of the individual worker; organized labor, steadily gaining in numbers and political influence since the turn of the century, adhered to the theory that immigration depressed the standard of living.

The "new" immigrants did not seek the status of ethnic minorities; it was thrust upon them as it had been thrust upon the Irish Catholics. They had little opportunity to settle on the land. In the cities, the new immigrants were forced to live in the poorest and most neglected sections and were blamed at the same time for locking themselves up in narrow, dirty ghettos. The America which rejected them could not at the same time forgive them their slow assimilation. The America which brought no order or plan into the integration-processes of the immigrants, leaving them to their own devices or to the mercy of exploiters and swindlers, spun out race theories on the prevalence of crime among aliens when an immigrant happened to be the culprit before the law.

Many "new" immigrants came from countries where illiteracy was common and sanitation at a most primitive level. They had never set eyes on a machine in their native lands; here they were cast into an industrial cauldron and left to make their own way. This increased the dependence of the immigrants on each other. The more frustrating their contact with the outside world, the more they clove together. The more difficult they found it to absorb American culture, the more they cherished their own language. The more rejected they felt in the United States, the more heart-warming they found the memories of the towns and villages they left behind. It is no wonder then that until World War I—and in large measure even thereafter—

the foreign-language press was full of news items about the old countries and rarely touched on American national problems. It is not even surprising that a number of ethnic groups created a more extensive press here than they had possessed in their native lands. At home, they could easily dispense with a newspaper; here, it was an absolute necessity. And this accounts for the paradoxical fact that a great number of immigrants first learned to read and write their native tongues in America. Furthermore, masses of Italians, Poles and others of the "new" immigration developed here a sense of national solidarity which they had wholly lacked at home. There, their loyalty was extended to the region, not to the country; to neighbors, not to the nation. Only in America did they come to feel that they belonged to a national entity. As Caroline Ware suggests:

. . . the mass of peasant immigrants did not bring with them a national consciousness, for nationalism, on the whole, has been a product of the middle classes, while the peasant has known only his family and his village.[4]

The brutally uncompromising demand that the immigrants fully assimilate overnight produced, for a time, the opposite effect: it strengthened their nationalist ties with the countries of their origin.

Other negative factors besides the attitude of nativist Americans and the pressure of mechanical Americanization tended to isolate particular groups. Italian immigrants, for example, were for a long time frightened by America. They felt alien here—and this strengthened their ties to the homeland, making them "more aggressively Italian in the United States than they had ever been in Italy."[5] Many of them were "birds of passage," immigrants who came here to earn and put by a few dollars, only to return to their homeland. It was natural for such immigrants not to conceive of integration with the American environment. But even those who came with their families to settle here were unable, because of the unfriendly atmosphere and their own ignorance, to become psychologically and spiritually rooted in America. For a long time they were the most exploited of workers. Socially, they were among the lowest strata of white society; and culturally, they were among the most backward white elements in the country. They remained an isolated colony because they were slow in erecting a bridge to the outside world, and the outside world sought no path to them.

Conditions in the Homeland. Circumstances in the homelands of the immigrants contributed greatly to the extent of group cohesion in the United States. The history of minorities in America shows that groups springing from nationally or religiously oppressed peoples retain their cohesiveness in this country for a longer period than those from independent or dominating nations.

Immigrants from the south of Ireland belonged to a greatly oppressed people. They carried with them the bitter consciousness of national grievance, driven as they were from their beloved homeland by desperate economic need and political persecution caused by foreign rule. Coming here determined to use this country as a base from which to carry forward their fight for Irish independence, they found this country dominated by descendants of the hated English. Exploited and maltreated shamefully here, the Irish were not given a chance to forget, even if they had wanted to, the injustice committed against them by the English in Ireland.[6] Painful experiences in their new home flowed together with painful memories from their mother country and reinforced the Irish hatred of England and the English, which was one of the most significant factors in cementing Irish solidarity in the United States. The persistence of this hatred as a communal bond well into twentieth century explains why the Irish, although chronologically of an "old" immigration, are in their relation to the dominant group closer to the "new" immigrants. With the establishment of the Irish Free State, concern of the Irish in the United States for the welfare of the homeland has grown progressively weaker.

The "new" immigration included many groups from subjugated lands, who, like the Irish, carried on campaigns in this country for the liberation of their peoples—and thus solidified their ethnic cohesion here. Czechs, Poles, Ruthenians, Yugoslavs and others gained the opportunity, for the first time, of supporting their national struggles openly. Thus two sources nourished their nationalism: their rejection in America, and inner ties to their own oppressed peoples.

The Church. The positive forces making for cohesion in the ethnic minority can most clearly be seen operative in the history of some of the older immigrant groups. With the early Pennsylvania Dutch settlers, as with the German immigrants later, religion was a strong positive cultural factor in maintaining group cohesiveness. Arriving in the seventeenth and eighteenth centuries, when there was plenty of cheap, arable land available, the Pennsylvania Dutch were for a long time able to live a self-contained existence. They established German islands in the midst of an Anglo-Saxon sea and held off the engulfing waves of that sea longer than any other non-English-speaking group. The spiritual center of these islands was the church—Amish, Mennonite, Lutheran, Reformed, or Moravian. Although their patriotism was centered entirely on their new home and they had virtually no bonds to the land of their origin, the Pennsylvania Dutch nevertheless remained true to their version of the German tongue longer than the German nationalists, who came to America in the 1830's and 40's, adhered to their native language.[7]

The social life of the Pennsylvania Dutch was a balanced one, and the equilibrium was kept free from outside disturbance chiefly through the influence of the church. They were not merely Protestants but members of specific sects in which they were the majority. Their church functioned therefore within a more or less restricted ethnic environment whose cultural needs were co-extensive with its religious interests. In religio-ethnic restrictedness, the Pennsylvania Dutch were close to the Jews.

The church maintained its enduring influence among the Pennsylvania Dutch because it was rooted in their mode of economic life, and this mode, in turn, was capable of perpetuation only within specific cultural settings. "The Pennsylvania German farmer," writes Arthur D. Graeff, "sensed correctly that his cultural patterns rested on a foundation of language, religion, and agrarian mores." [8] His economic situation was stable, and he preferred not to upset it through innovations. As early as 1786 the Lutheran church incorporated the following prayer into its liturgy:

> . . . since it has pleased Thee, chiefly by means of the Germans, to transform this state into a blooming garden, and the desert into a pleasant pasturage, help us not to deny our nation, but to endeavor that our youth may be so educated that German schools and churches not only be sustained but may attain a still more flourishing condition.[9]

Although the cultural level of these Pennsylvania farmers was not particularly high, they maintained parochial schools for the elementary education of their children and protested vehemently against the establishment of public schools, which they correctly interpreted as a threat to their religious and economic order.[10]

Many other examples of the church as a positive force in prolonging ethnic identity may be found among the northern European Protestants, both settlers and immigrants.[11] For nearly a century and a half the Dutch Reformed church (founded in 1628) forbade the use of English in a sermon; and among the newcomers from Holland in the middle and later parts of the nineteenth century there were many who deliberately shut themselves off from contact with non-Dutch elements in order to preserve their customs and religious traditions. Norwegians, divided into many denominations within Lutheranism, established their own parochial schools on the elementary, high school and even college levels.

Reference has already been made to the place religion occupied in the life of the Irish. The Catholic church and the Irish are inseparable in the United States but, oddly enough, their very strength within the Catholic community tended to weaken Irish ethnic integrity. As the leaders of the Catholic church, their religious demands included the spiritual needs of Catholics of other ethnic origins, and their institutions served the interests of all Catholic groups.[12] Their parochial schools, because the language of instruction in them was English, were not the ethnocentric factor which Catholic parochial schools were for the Poles and the French-Canadians, for example.[13] For the newer immigrants the parochial school became for a time the most important instrument for the retention of the national language.[14]

As with the "old" immigrants and settlers, the central point in the social life of the "new" immigrants was the church. And the more backward, in an educational sense, an ethnic group was, the more influential was the role played by organized religion in its existence. The church was a piece of the old country transported to the new land, the storehouse not only of the familiar catechism and religious modes, but of the old political atmosphere and social traditions as well. The church made its greatest impact on those who were most attuned to those traditions. Often enough, foreign governments sought to exploit religion in order to maintain some hold on the immigrants, and they therefore aided the churches in a variety of ways. As a consequence, a reactionary spirit that ran counter to the American democratic temper frequently prevailed in the ethnic churches, thus reinforcing the barriers between the immigrants and native America. The clerical leaders of the immigrants feared the impact of New World ideas, and the natives in turn viewed the immigrants as subverters of the American way of life.

Social and Political Beliefs. Another positive factor in the preservation of group identity is the possession by the group of common political and social beliefs about which cultural activities center.

Many nineteenth-century German immigrants to America, for example, came here with crystallized political and social convictions and a not-unjustified belief that their culture was superior to that of the Americans.[15] After the German revolutions of 1830 and 1848, political refugees of great intelligence and moral stature were active leaders in the German community here. Some, hoping for a speedy return to the homeland, devoted themselves to the welfare of revolutionaries in Germany and to the task of uniting refugees here.[16] Others threw themselves with extraordinary energy into efforts to create centers of German culture: press, theater, choral societies, sports-clubs, dramatic groups, kindergartens, schools, etc. The radical ideology of some of these German refugees resulted in the founding of societies of workingmen and an extensive German language press. The Germans were the pioneers of socialism in the United States, and socialist newspapers in the German language antedated their English counterparts.[17]

Although the ideologically committed Germans founded no state, they established centers of German group life which have not altogether lost their effectiveness to this day as factors of group cohesion. In the same way, nonreligious immigrants of the "new" immigration established secular ethnic institutions. Aside from the Jews, to be discussed later, the Czechs accomplished most in this field.

Whether group life was stimulated by the conscious effort to preserve valued beliefs and ways of living or was determined by external circumstances, the immigrant neighborhoods produced a variety of social and cultural activities. Press, literature, theater, fraternal societies, mutual aid associations, churches, schools, philanthropic

23

exercises and social services filled needs in the lives of the immigrants and at the same time formed repositories of the culture which they had brought from overseas, tending to preserve their identity as ethnic groups.

ASSIMILATING FACTORS

Study of the history of European ethnic groups in America suggests that their rich and varied social and cultural activity was a transitory phase of their life in America. Full-blown ethnic identity was the rule only when the immigrant generation predominated and when its masses still spoke their own language. Group cohesion among their children was considerably diminished and dissolved almost completely among their descendants.

By the end of the nineteenth century, for example, even the Pennsylvania Dutch no longer possessed a single elementary school in which German was the language of instruction. Among other groups linguistic assimilation proceeded more rapidly. Little is left of the secular German and Czech cultural movements that played so important a role before World War I. Foreign-language social life is disappearing; hardly anything remains of the professional non-English theater. The foreign press, though still extensive, is losing both newspapers and readers.[18] No foreign-language group, with the exception of the Spanish-speaking group, has been able, through fresh immigration, to make up for the eroding effects of English.[19]

The forces which tend to promote the assimilation of the ethnic minority within the larger community have been summed up as economic opportunity, utilitarianism, and democracy.[20] We shall survey them in a more detailed classification, based on the specific ways in which the forces of assimilation work themselves out concretely in the lives of immigrant groups: economic integration, education, political activity, recreation, and intermarriage.

Economic Integration. The settlers, in achieving economic integration within their new environment, had to combat material forces; the immigrants, particularly the later ones, had to cope with a society as well. Integration into American conditions thus required greater expenditures of energy on the part of the immigrants than on the part of the early settlers.

Numerically, the German elements were second only to the American elements of English origin. Economically, they rose to the level of the Anglo-Saxon "aristocracy." They were, however, never the first to settle a state, nor did they ever become a majority in any established state. Because they arrived after the socio-cultural foundation was already firm enough to support the tyranny of the majority, the problem of accommodation confronted them, not the English-speaking group.

The agrarian Irish Catholic immigrants had to undergo a course of radical transformation, within an unfriendly environment, that forced them to begin at the lowest rung of the industrial ladder. Like all other underprivileged immigrants, they had to adjust to what Herman Feldman describes as the "established tradition" that newcomers start at the bottom with unskilled work no matter what their qualifications for better jobs may be.[21]

In one important respect the accommodation of the Irish to the demands of the new life in the United States was easier than that of other immigrants who also had to contend with the "established tradition": because English was their mother tongue, the learning of a language was not added to the burdens which the Irish bore. Because they did not come to the United States in possession of the tools for the creation of a separate culture, and because they spoke English, they formed no language group and were consequently able to yield more readily to the process of economic transplantation.

Speaking English, it was possible for them to take advantage more quickly of economic opportunities, notwithstanding all the social disabilities to which they were subjected. At a time of enormous upsurge for the young capitalism, the Irish could not be held too long at the lowest economic levels; and soon there were among them elements that began the successful upward climb. The immigrant mass began to be socially differentiated; and along with this differentiation there developed, on the one hand, a greater rootedness in the United States and, on the other hand, a diminution of Irish ethnic solidarity. The split between the "shanty Irish" and the "lace-curtain Irish" appeared early in their sojourn here.

25

Most of the "new" immigrants, like the Irish before them, remained in the cities and had to accommodate themselves to an urban economy. During the period of the "new" immigration, mass production became the basis of American manufacturing. This entailed industrial standardization, atomization of work, and the downgrading of the craftsman. It was a process that had a mechanizing effect on the psyche of the American people. According to Stuart Chase, there were three stages in the development of the factory machine:

In the first stage, the machine increases the power of the skilled workman and raises his productivity, while leaving the character of his job little altered. In the second stage, the work process is atomized. The machine requires only unskilled or semi-skilled workers who do nothing but repeat their particular monotonous motions in the process of production. In the third stage, the machine dispenses entirely with unskilled labor and fulfills that function itself.[22]

The "new" immigrant workers were mainly identified with the second stage, which Chase calls the robot phase. While it actually constituted economic and social progress in comparison with the work involved in shouldering heavy loads, digging ditches, splitting rocks, clearing roadways, etc., the robot phase was not conducive to original creativity.

Mastery of English represented for all non-English-speaking immigrants the first step in the direction of economic advancement, and concomitantly, the first act of assimilation. Every further step in the same direction was bound up with greater "at-homeness" in American culture and a more intimate accommodation to prevailing customs and behavior; by the same token, every such step was one more move away from the immigrants' ethnic groups. Economic progress implied not only material improvement; it meant also higher social and political prestige. At the first opportunity, the immigrant left the ghetto and moved to a better part of town. And what he had begun his children pursued, and at a quicker tempo. Economic progress led to upward residential mobility, and that, in turn, to ethnic group decomposition.

In order to prevent accidents at work, employers were often forced to initiate classes in English for their foreign workers. This, however, did not keep the former from introducing into their shops a "balance of nationalities," a system designed to prevent the rise to dominance of a group of workers of a particular race or nationality. The unmistakable motivation behind this system was stated by William M. Leiserson:

> . . . racial animosities and lack of a common language kept the employees divided, and concerted action for higher wages or shorter hours, such as were common among native-born skilled workmen, could thus be averted.[23]

American trade unions, far more than any other urban voluntary association, mirror the various stages through which foreign-born laborers—comprising the vast majority of adult immigrants—have passed on their way to economic stability. Unions, like those of the mine, steel and textile workers, appointed organizers who could speak the required foreign languages; they also put out foreign-language union literature and newspapers. A number of unions even organized ethnic locals, a very few of which continue in existence to this day. Anti-union forces exploited this fact in order to discredit labor organizations as imported European institutions which tended to undermine the foundations of American democracy, while the unions, largely the product of immigration, soon placed themselves, as mentioned before, in the forefront of the fight against further immigration into the United States.

The unions would have been unable to make any headway at all, and would have been internally disrupted from the outset, had they not set as their first and most pressing task the integration of their members of various races, faiths and nationalities into one economic bloc. They thus evolved into one of the most effective assimilating forces. John R. Commons, in *Races and Immigrants in America,* wrote that in the large urban centers the unions were the most important Americanizing factor in the lives of the immigrant workers.

Leiserson evaluates the Americanizing role of the trade unions with this astute comment:

> . . . a trade union needs to engage in no Americanizing or proselytizing campaigns to make Americans of immigrant workmen. If it is efficient and successful as a union, it unites all the workers in the industry and imperceptibly fuses native and foreign born into a common folk.

27

A union, in essence, is more than a mere professional organization, Leiserson continues:

> . . . the union [has] not only assured him [the worker] an American standard of living, so he can bring over his family and educate his children American fashion, but it has also furnished him a practical school in citizenship, giving him practice in voting, elections, and law-making . . . obedience to the agreements of the union and the employers, which are the laws of his industry, and introducing him to judicial processes and methods through the arbitration procedure which the agreement has established. The union is a miniature republic, training him for American citizenship by teaching him American democratic methods of dealing with the problems of his work and wages, the things of most vital interest to him.[24]

But not all immigrants were workers, and not all immigrant workers were union members. Problems of work and wages transcended the boundaries of the alien colony and had the effect of weakening ethnic barriers. Here, we approach a very significant aspect of economic integration, one that has had the most far-reaching influence on the relations between ethnic groups and the American population as a whole.

As soon as a measure of economic accommodation was achieved, class divisions and social differentiations began to appear among the ethnic groups. When the immigrants first arrived here, they found themselves, for the most part, on the same impoverished socio-economic level—even those who in the old country belonged to the propertied and middle classes. After they had been here for a while, changes occurred in their financial conditions, from which emerged different economic groups with particular interests to advance and defend. And these interests undermined the foundations of ethnic structure.

It sometimes happens that social stratifications crystallize within the framework of the ethnic colony itself. This occurs when the production process, and the divergent elements participating in it, all operate within the same ethnic setting. Such a phenomenon, however, is rare—it appears more among Jews than any other ethnic group; when it does occur, the ethnic group becomes the arena for social conflicts that disrupt internal unity. But this unity is damaged even more when economic conflicts spread beyond the confines of the ethnic colony. Members of an ethnic group have more in common economically with persons of the same economic status from another ethnic group than with persons of conflicting economic interests and different social class within their own ethnic group. Polish members of a union share more economic interests with German members of the same union than with Polish employers. And Italian farmers have more in common with Scandinavian farmers than with Italian tailors. The more an ethnic group is economically divided, the less its organic integrity.

Economic processes leave an imprint on all other aspects of social life among immigrants. As soon as they arrive here, their old categories of prestige begin to break down. When one is shoveling snow or digging canals or working in a sweatshop, one has greater concerns than preserving the old patterns of social status. But after a person has worked his way up the ladder and can afford to live a little better, move to a nicer neighborhood and make his way into the organizations and leisure institutions of "authentic Americans," he begins to look down upon later arrivals of his own ethnic group. German-Jewish Americans snub Jews from Poland less because of geographical origin than socio-economic stratification. Because of the same divisions, the "lace-curtain" Irish prefer not to have anything to do with the "shanty" Irish. Not all segments of an ethnic group are evenly established in American economic life, and the results are similarly uneven.

So much for economic integration in the urban centers. The same tendencies are to be discerned in rural areas and on the farms. It is frequently assumed that assimilation proceeds at a more leisurely pace on the land than in industry. This, as we have seen, was true many years ago, but the reverse has actually been the case in more recent times. The reasons are readily apparent. With the exception of particular ethnic concentrations, such as the Pennsylvania Dutch, agrarian settlement lacked the compactness of ethnic group life in the cities. Furthermore, the agricultural element was more deeply affected by the psychology of individual possession than by the tradition of collective cooperation.

It should not be forgotten that the technological revolution did not bypass agriculture. The farm today is no longer the isolated institution it used to be. Modern communications bring even the most remote farm close to the city; rural areas are largely urbanized in a cultural sense. Farm children, no less than city children, are obliged to attend public school. The farm population sees the same films, hears the same radio programs, watches the same television shows, and reads the same syndicated columns as does the urban population. Communication is exclusively in English, and it affects non-English-speaking farmers equally with English-speaking farmers. But the immigrant farmer misses the opportunities available to his ethnic confrère in the city to read newspapers in his mother tongue, send his children to parochial or supplementary schools where his language is taught, converse with neighbors in his own vernacular, and generally to circulate in his own ethnic sphere. The immigrant farmer therefore succumbs more quickly to the influence of the native culture. The time is long since past when agricultural immigrants could achieve accommodation through isolation.

The Pennsylvania Dutch, though they succeeded in retaining their ethnic compactness and cultural identity longer than other groups, lost their linguistic integrity under the impact of inescapable circumstances. The rural Little Holland created years ago in Michigan is in process of dissolution. Colonies established by Danes, Czechs, Poles and members of other groups with a view to creating centers of their respective cultures quickly lost their ethnic character even in the rare cases when they turned out to be successful economic ventures.[25] The fact is that the ethnic farm population is decreasing at an even faster rate than the general farm population in the country.

Education. The most important instrument in the assimilation of the minority group is the school, which is universally obligatory until a minimum age. The effect of the school on the child's psyche is twofold. In the first place, the school removes him for the greater part of each weekday from the cultural sphere of his home and from physical contact with his parents; that is, it removes him from the area of ethnic influence. In the second place, the school brings the child into an atmosphere of American national unity. In this atmosphere the child fears he is not fully discharging his patriotic duties to America if he speaks a language other than English. Foreign languages are not taught in the elementary grades, and in the upper grades they are learned without any relation to the student's ethnic origins. This is especially true of children of the "new" immigrants. Rarely will one find an Italian, Czech, Polish or Russian child choosing his own tongue for foreign-language study in school. Despite the fact that a million and three-quarter persons listed Yiddish as their mother tongue in the 1940 census, there was not one high school in the country where Yiddish was taught as a foreign language, and only a few universities have instituted the study of Yiddish for credit, and that, only since 1947.[26]

The monolithic reign of the English language is the alpha and omega of the public school system in the United States. The religious schools, which once were and to a slight degree remain linguistic islands, are on their way to losing their ethnic character and are tending increasingly to reflect the expanding power of their churches rather than the cohesive force of their ethnic groups.

The Catholic parochial schools will serve as an example since they possess a far broader scope than similar schools of other denominations. Catholic schools are ceasing to be ethnic schools. With the rising aspirations of the Church to become the majority religion in America, its interest in ethnic separateness declines. As a result, foreign languages have been almost entirely eliminated from Catholic elementary schools, and they occupy a much smaller place than formerly in the curriculum of the secondary schools. Moreover, Catholic secondary schools are slowly being removed from the jurisdiction of individual parishes and are increasingly assuming the character of city-wide institutions.[27] How small a place ethnic considerations now occupy in the curriculum of these central high schools is indicated by a study of the foreign languages which were taught there in the years 1930–49. These followed closely the program of the public high schools, with Spanish, French, and German in addition to classical Latin and Greek. Only six schools had courses in Polish—the language of the ethnic group with the largest number of Catholic parochial schools.[28]

The tendency on the part of the Church to transform its school system into a religious one, with no ethnic implications, has intensified in the last twenty-five years. Of the Irish parochial schools in Yankee City, we find

31

. . . The school, like the church, is no longer ethnic in both a national and religious sense, but in the religious sense alone. The ethnicity of the school and church consists in their Catholicity, which continues to organize the group as a distinctive community.[29]

At one time, the Catholic church was one of the most important instrumentalities in cementing the ethnic colonies; today, these colonies are a hindrance to the Church, for they give Catholicism a foreign coloration and an identification with minorities. Protestant parochial schools realized this effect at an even earlier date. Not only the public school system, but also the religious schools hasten the assimilation of the ethnic groups.

Political Activity. Nowhere in the world has an ethnic group developed into a national minority without political action, while at no time has a minority in the United States attempted to organize itself into a separate and independent political party. Other causes aside, the tyranny of the majority would never have tolerated such a move. The affiliation of minorities in the United States with the national parties is an important assimilatory factor, although these parties frequently enough play on the religious feelings and sentimental attachments of ethnic groups.

The political activity of the Irish, although it first served to strengthen their group integrity, served also to integrate them into American life. Excluded from political life in their homeland, they brought to their new home the dream of achieving political influence. To this end they were aided by the bosses of the major political parties, who saw in them potential voters. James Bryce, in *The American Commonwealth*, observes that, in a certain sense, the political bosses were all that stood between the lowly classes and their total deprivation of rights by the dominant groups. Since the poorest citizen's vote weighed as much as that of the richest, and since the bosses could more easily manipulate the votes of the poor, it was in their interest to pose as the friends of the underprivileged. The bosses were the only persons of power to whom the pauperized Irish could turn when they first set foot on American soil.

Because the Federalist party consistently served the interests of property-owners, business, and industry, it was unable to attract the

Irish immigrants. The Democratic party, with greater appeal to the workers and lower middle classes, was friendlier to new arrivals, and the Irish flocked to it in great numbers.[30] In cities where they managed to become a political force, they gained control over the police and fire departments and other municipal functions. Thenceforth, they used their political influence to speed the process of entering better-paid trades and professions. The places of "black laborers," which they had evacuated, were then taken by immigrants from other countries, toward whom the Irish adopted an attitude no more compassionate than that which the native Americans had previously displayed toward them. And the very fact that there were later immigrants to whom the Irish could feel superior strengthened their attachment to America and sped their integration into American life.

The Germans who came here at the end of the seventeenth century and during the first quarter of the eighteenth, including the Pennsylvania Dutch, were little interested in politics; by contrast, the later German immigrants threw themselves into political life. So long as their political action stemmed from the social views which they had brought over from abroad, they remained separated from the others, and this fortified the isolating tendencies operating among the Germans. As soon as the political ideology took on the coloration of American realities, however, it was transformed into an assimilating tendency. A number of attempts were made to organize a collective German vote in political elections, but even the ethnocentric Germans at no time sought to form their own political party, preferring to work through the existing parties.

Socialist philosophy dictated the creation of German trade unions, but the very existence of these unions depended upon their not remaining within an exclusive ethnic context. The dialectics of the situation are even more sharply brought out in reference to the political activities of the German socialists. These activities initially set them apart from the mainstream of American labor, but precisely because they wanted those activities to be productive, they had to break out of their isolation. They could not achieve socialism in an exclusive German community, functioning within a capitalist encirclement, and were thus driven to extend their political operations to embrace the country as a whole—a process that hastened their assimilation.

33

Writing in 1890, Richmond Mayo-Smith observed that "the exercise of political rights . . . gives [the immigrants] a higher position than they were accustomed to at home, and this naturally attaches them to the new country." [31] In America, many immigrants, for the first time in their lives, join the possessing classes; but until they arrive at this point, they are good material for radical movements. It is characteristic of the immigrant radical that he enters American political life even before attaining citizenship. His political activity, we have seen, has both an assimilating and an isolating effect. Radicals are a minority in every immigrant group; but the "bosses" of the major political parties have their eye on the majority and seek to attract them into the great body of voters. Bryce describes a scene of the 1880's which he witnessed in an American court, where new citizens were being sworn in:

> Droves of squalid men, who looked as if they had just emerged from the emigrant ship, and had perhaps done so only a few weeks before . . . were brought up to a magistrate by the ward agent of the party which had captured them, declared their allegiance to the United States, and were forthwith placed on the roll. [32]

Citizenship gave them a share in America. Whatever the majority attitude may have been toward the immigrant, however heated the incitements against him, and no matter how lowly and rejected he was —on the election scales he weighed, after naturalization, just as much as the native American. There were many places he was not allowed to enter and many things he was not permitted to do—but with his vote he acquired a say in the administration of the country. Because he acquired, too, a sense of "belonging," his own self-image was no longer that of a stranger.

There is yet one more reason that no ethnic political parties were created in the United States. The overwhelming majority of immigrants did not become citizens in the manner described by Bryce. Most of them had to fulfill all the requirements of the law. They became citizens only after a minimum of five years' residence in the country, i.e., after they had already achieved a certain modicum of economic adjustment and were on the way to occupying a more respectable place in the social structure. By the time they received the right to vote, they had hewed out concrete economic interests which they desired to defend with their political activity. On the whole, these interests were no longer bound up with the ethnic atmosphere. Citizenship papers were an exit visa from the ethnic group and an admission ticket to the American nation.

After an immigrant achieves a measure of economic stabilization, becomes a citizen, and moves into a more pleasant home, he slowly begins to gravitate toward his neighbors and co-workers of other national origins. The points of contact outside his own ethnic world steadily increase. He becomes active in general patriotic and civic activities and joins organizations of mixed memberships. He gradually acquires a community interest that supersedes the ghetto needs. Even religious barriers are often weakened in the general socialization—this is truer of the second generation than of the immigrant, and truer still of the third than of the second generation. And so arise the various non-sectarian organizations and institutions active in the American community. Most local philanthropic institutions of all religious denominations are united in community chests and receive their budgets from general, city-wide campaigns in which the various religious groups participate in an organized fashion.

Although American democracy is replete with contradictions and not all segments of the population benefit from it equally, no one is completely shut out. Even those over whom the American Constitution does not spread its protective wings have the feeling that they are integral parts of the American democratic processes. American democracy undermines the cohesion of ethnic minorities through political activity. As W. Lloyd Warner and Leo Srole observe:

> Paradoxically, the force of American equalitarianism, which attempts to make all men American and alike, and the force of our class order, which creates differences among ethnic peoples, have combined to dissolve our ethnic groups.[33]

Recreation. The role of recreation in forming the American nation is incalculable. We have spoken of the tyranny of the majority; through entertainment forms, this tyranny becomes a pleasurable experience for all.

Some of this entertainment is in the form of the religious revivals discussed earlier; they evoke a burning ecstasy that inflames the

35

participants and onlookers. When large numbers are under the influence of this ecstasy, nothing exists for them outside this consuming emotional experience. Color differences disappear, ethnic divisions and class lines are obliterated—only the fiery mass exists. Such scenes can be observed at baseball games, horse races, boxing matches, football contests, etc. Warner and Srole quote from an editorial in a Yankee City newspaper: ". . . when you talk about the melting pot of America, the game of football comes nearer to filling the bill as melter than any other movement." [34]

The individual becomes lost within the crowd through mass entertainment; but even those forms of entertainment and recreation in which individuality remains intact have, in the United States, a tendency to blunt group differences. It is sufficient to mention literature and the press, the movies and the theater, automobiles, radio and television. According to a study made by Nettie P. McGill and Ellen N. Matthews, the entertainment of more than half of New York City's youth consists of reading, attending the theater and the movies, listening to the radio, athletic activities, and visiting with friends.[35] With the exception of the last, and that only in part, each of these forms of entertainment tends to dissolve group distinction. Amusement patterns in New York are followed in little Middletown, as Robert S. and Helen M. Lynd discovered, and throughout America.

The immigrant's child, let alone his grandchild, does not read the ethnic press; but he does read American newspapers and periodicals and enjoys the "funnies" no less than the child of the native American. The automobile has provided the immigrant with the opportunity of leaving the filthy ghetto and enjoying the American countryside. Sitting at the wheel of his car, the immigrant feels that not only the roof of his dwelling but the asphalt on the highway is his, too.

The tremendous impact of the movies on the American psyche was noted by the Lynds during their first visit to Middletown in 1929 and their observations were confirmed by what they saw during their second visit in 1937. In Yankee City W. Lloyd Warner and Paul S. Lunt found that "almost all of the people between seventeen and twenty-five years of age attended the movies at least once every two weeks." [36] Their study showed that movie patrons came from all social and economic levels. The richest element provides a higher proportion than its numbers warrant, and only the very poorest element provides a smaller number than its proportion in the total population. Among ethnic groups the standard is unusually even. Thus, there is much to be said for Francis Brown's contention that Hollywood Americanized the immigrant. The dimunition in movie attendance in recent years is more than made up by the growing number of television sets.

If the automobile opened up America geographically for the members of the ethnic groups, and the movies introduced them to the mansions of the American "aristocracy"—radio and television have brought America into their own homes. The last stronghold of group separation—the home—has fallen. There is no longer a walled-off ethnic island.

What economic integration, political activity, social bonds and education initiate externally, recreation completes internally. Against the former, the immigrant may still take a stand, conduct rearguard action or try to fend off their unavoidably assimilating impact; the latter he enjoys and accepts with gusto.

Intermarriage. Christine Galitzi divides the process of assimilation in the United States into three stages: (1) the economic-technological stage, which requires adjustment to new work-methods; (2) the cultural stage, which signifies the departure from old culture patterns and the adoption of new ones; (3) the ethnic stage, which includes mixed marriages.[37] The division is, on the whole, a correct one, but assimilation does not always proceed in the given order. In a non-family immigration, assimilation sometimes began with a mixed marriage, which aided economic integration and propelled cultural adaptation. Julius Drachsler, whose basic work on intermarriage, although published in 1920, still remains a classic, advances the following reasons for mixed marriages: ". . . preponderance of marriageable men or marriageable women, rise in economic status, and diminution in the intensity of the group consciousness or in the attitude of group solidarity."[38]

No single act has so disturbing an impact on group affiliation as a mixed marriage. Rarely does such a marriage leave unaltered the relations between the couple and their ethnic environment. The children who are the products of these marriages must break with the

37

ethnic group of at least one of their parents. In itself, such a marriage is an indication of a loosening of ties with the ethnic or religious group and a lowering of interest in its heritage; however, it often happens that one of the partners remains within his ethnic community and even brings the other into it too. Environment in large measure determines the post-marital group identification of the couple. If, for example, a Jew who marries a Gentile continues to live in a Jewish environment, the chances are that the family will remain Jewish. If the environment is non-Jewish, the prospects are exactly the reverse. But even in the first case, the result will be a hastening of assimilation.

If we define mixed marriages as those which move beyond the bounds of a given community, we can discern among them three categories: marriages which trespass over (1) ethnic boundaries, (2) religious boundaries, and (3) racial boundaries. To the extent that racial boundaries are understood as a function of skin pigmentation, they are not relevant to the problems under consideration—if only because children of whites and Negroes in the United States are never considered anything but Negroes. We shall therefore limit ourselves to a consideration of the first two categories.

T. J. Woofter, Jr. demonstrates, on the basis of marriage statistics in the state of New York (not including New York City) in 1929, that there is not a single religious or ethnic group in the United States which does not produce a sizable number of mixed marriages.[39]

In New York City, Drachsler found, on the basis of the 100,000 marriage certificates issued in the city between 1908 and 1912, that nearly 14 percent (13.59%) of all marriages were mixed. This was the percentage for the total number of marriages. If, however, the number is broken down into generations, a quite different picture emerges. Whereas 10.39 percent of the first generation men married outside their own group, the percentage for the second generation was 32.40. The breakdown for women showed a 10.10 percent intermarriage rate for the first generation and 30.12 for the second generation. The second generation thus revealed a 300 percent increase over the first generation in the number of mixed marriages.[40]

Edmund de S. Brunner discovered a similar situation among farmers. His study is the most thoroughgoing yet made of mixed marriages in agrarian areas. It is based on 44,643 applications for marriage certificates in the states of Nebraska, Wisconsin and New York (excluding New York City). The applicants were either immigrants, or American-born residents one of whose parents was an immigrant; only rural dwellers, chiefly farmers, were counted. This study has the special merit of taking into account two distinct periods—so that an opportunity is provided to study the situation both before and after World War I and to compare tendencies with completed processes. In Nebraska, the two periods were 1909–13 and 1921–25; in Wisconsin, 1908–12 and 1920–24; in New York, 1908–12 and 1921–25. Of the whole number of marriages, 57.5 percent were in New York; the rest were equally divided between the two other states.

Brunner grouped the marriages into three categories: (1) marriages of immigrants within their own ethnic group (he used the term "racial group") he called "in-choice"; (2) marriages between immigrants of different European groups he called "inter-choice"; (3) marriages of immigrants with native-born children of native-born parents he called "out-choice."

It is not necessary to enter into the details of the figures; the results of the studies proved that the number of mixed marriages in the agrarian part of the country was not smaller, but larger, than in the cities. Among the sons of immigrants, the tendency toward out-choice was twice as great as among their parents. In Nebraska and New York, virtually every second marriage of an immigrant's son was of this type. If we compare the situation before and after the first war, we discover a steady increase in the number of mixed marriages among immigrants' children, despite the fact that in the meantime a large number of new immigrants entered these three states and the disproportion between the number of men and women decreased. Before the war, one in every ten marriages was mixed; after the war, one in every eight. Out-choice surged upward strikingly in contrast with inter-choice. In other words, if one married outside his group, he preferred a native bride to an immigrant from another ethnic group. In comparison with the pre-war period, the number of out-choice marriages after the war increased in Nebraska three and one-half times; in Wisconsin, five times; in New York, 25 percent. Brunner concluded that, while the increase in mixed marriages was greater among West European descendants than among East European, the rise was everywhere considerable.[41]

39

Subsequent surveys demonstrate the correctness of the findings of Drachsler, Brunner, Woofter and other investigators and show the mounting rate of mixed marriages.[42]

Bessie Bloom Wessel's study of Woonsocket, R.I., made in 1926, showed that 17.8 percent of the recorded 2,876 marriages were mixed. Generationwise, they could be divided in this way: 9.6 of the marriages in the first generation were mixed; 20.9 percent in the second generation, and 40.4 percent in the third and 2/3 generations (the last category consists of native-born Americans one of whose parents was born in this country and the other in Europe). If we reckon as descendants of mixed marriages those whose two grandmothers and two grandfathers were of different origins, we find that 12.6 percent of the French-Canadian children in Woonsocket are of mixed ancestry; 36.9 of the English children; 40.9 percent of the Irish; 8.2 percent of the Slavic; 3.5 percent of the Italian; and 2.6 percent of the Jewish.[43]

Mixed marriages may be considered as one of the later phases of assimilation in that they assume major proportions after the first steps of economic and social progress have already been taken by the immigrants.

CONTINUING ETHNIC INFLUENCES

The process of ethnic levelling has gone far; but one must not assume that it has ended. Far from it. The millions of immigrants who are still alive, the more than twenty million residents who listed a non-English language as their mother tongue in 1940, the millions of members of the thousands of immigrant organizations, the hundreds of thousands of readers of the foreign-language press, the thousands of *landsmanschaften,* the great number of still extant ghettos and ethnic colonies, the ties of millions of Americans with their relatives and friends in the old countries—all these constitute a physical foundation of ethnic influence that will undoubtedly persist for quite a long time to come.

The spiritual foundation of this influence is, in a sense, even more solid because its effect is largely unconscious. It is more difficult to shake this foundation than the physical one. Thus, James Bryce, having realized that the ethnic groups would not disappear as quickly as he had predicted when his classic work on America was first published in 1888, wrote, in an introduction to a later edition of the book:

> There has never been anywhere an environment of more pervasive and compulsive power than that into which the immigrant is plunged when he lands in America. He seems to melt in it as a lump of sugar melts in a cup of tea. Yet one cannot but believe that the influence of heredity remains.[44]

The strength of this influence can be seen most clearly during those periods when Europe is drawn into a war in which America is not involved, or when some danger threatens a foreign country. According to Thomas Burgess, between forty and fifty thousand Greeks voluntarily left America at the time of the war between Greece and Turkey, in 1912, to help fight the war on the side of Greece.[45] Drachsler provides statistics which show the large number of people who returned to their homelands from America to fight for their old countries during World War I: in the space of just a few days in New York alone, some three thousand Germans and a comparable number of Frenchmen registered to return. On one day, October 12, 1915, twenty-five hundred Greeks sailed from a New Jersey port. Italians departed at an average rate of three to five thousand weekly; their total number was in the hundreds of thousands. Tens of thousands of Britons, Slavs and others also returned.[46] Practically all the returnees were immigrants, but their American-born children and grandchildren displayed open sympathy, until America itself entered the war, with the countries of their ethnic origins and rendered them every possible assistance.

A further indication of the strength of ethnic influence in the United States is the not inconsiderable success enjoyed by foreign countries in their propaganda directed at the descendants of those countries, reaching even unto the second and third generations. Such propaganda was greatly expanded after the first war, particularly by the totalitarian regimes that came to power in several European countries. The success of Fascist propaganda among Italian-Americans and of Nazi propaganda among German-Americans was largely the result of the powerful bonds which many of them had with their native countries. Other foreign countries, though they were never as successful as the totalitarian lands, also achieved significant results from their propaganda, especially among the later immigrants.

And this is only natural. The ethnic colonies of the "new" immigrants are still in existence, and their inhabitants still have intimate connections with the lands of emigration. But there is another side to the story. The first war brought national liberation for a number of oppressed European peoples. It was to be expected that this would lead to the gradual loss of the sense of national resentment felt by the immigrants who came to the United States from the liberated countries, and would hasten their integration into American society. Immediately after the war, Florian Znaniecki wrote:

> . . . the patriotic exaltation produced by Poland's oppression, by all the preparations for national struggle, by the expectation of Poland's freedom, will decrease very soon among those who decide to stay in this country; there will no longer be the feeling of duty to preserve Polish ideals intact, no feeling of guilt will be connected with Americanization.[47]

This prognosis, which is in consonance with the theses of this book, was proven correct by postwar developments. But the rise of Fascism, Nazism and Communism in Europe posed a threat to the independence of the liberated nations, and the nationalism of their descendants in the United States was correspondingly rekindled.

Communism, Fascism and Nazism also succeeded in implanting a sense of national resentment among ethnic groups that had never before felt it. Exploiting the terms of the Versailles Treaty, the Nazis constantly reminded the Germans of how much they had lost in the war, and the Fascists persistently reminded the Italians of how little they had gained. Communism reannexed to the Russian empire the Baltic lands and other countries liberated after World War I. On the other hand, the fact that England's very existence hung in the balance during the second war could not but have an impact on the one-third of America's population which is of Anglo-Saxon extraction. For the same reason, the Irish-Americans were largely isolationist.

Ethnic influences can still be signficantly felt in economic life. The tendency of ethnic groups to concentrate within specific sectors of the economy is far from exhausted, whether on the proletarian, commercial or professional levels. As a result of economic and geographical concentration, every ethnic group contains elements whose economic existence depends on the preservation of ethnic identity: religious personnel, the ethnic intelligentsia, suppliers of special foods, etc. These

42

elements are the cement that helps hold the ethnic groups together; their crucial role will really become clear when we discuss the Jews. On the other hand, discrimination against certain ethnic and religious groups is still prevalent; and, as we have seen, such discrimination always has an isolating as well as an assimilating effect.

Religio-ethnic factors can also be discerned in American political life, even though ethnic groups have never organized their own parties. Claris E. Silcox and Galen N. Fisher ask: "Is there a Catholic, Protestant or Jewish vote?" And they answer: while the existence of such a vote in normal times is doubtful, "it may nevertheless be created with the raising of certain issues." [48] Furthermore, there are among professional politicians those who have a vested interest in stimulating ethnic voting during political campaigns.

Eating habits are another factor preserving ethnic ways of life, which should not be underestimated. Greek coffeehouses are nearly as popular among Greeks in this country as in Greece itself, and they play a similar role in both countries—as clubs for the men. Italian restaurants are patronized by great numbers of Italian-Americans who have lost every other tie with the Italian colonies in this country. A variety of cheeses and smoked meats are, according to Carl Wittke, just as popular among the Dutch in this country as in Holland; and this is equally true of dozens of other groups. The consumption of Kosher food is indeed a religious injunction for orthodox Jews, but "Kosher-style" restaurants have nothing at all to do with religion; they are, rather, a product of culinary habits.

Ethnic ways of life reveal a great deal of perseverance. The study made by Niles Carpenter and Daniel Katz of Polish-Americans in Buffalo led them to conclude that assimilation in terms of economic adjustment outdistances assimilation in terms of living habits. Modes of life operate quite unconsciously, and people cannot dispense with them nearly as easily as with practices which are merely means of accommodation. That is why culture retains a hold on people long after the civilization which created it has changed. In time, of course, this influence disappears, and the speed of this process is determined by the tempo with which the changed civilization evokes a new culture. In America, the tempo is fast, despite all obstacles and the gap between culture and civilization.

AMERICANIZATION: A PROBLEM

Americanization, to the vast majority of native Americans, connoted ethnic and cultural group dissolution. This was often what Americanization meant to the children of the immigrants. As we have observed, the specific social and cultural activities of ethnic groups in the United States have been largely immigrant activities. The immigrants were seldom able to involve their American-born children in these activities, and almost never their grandchildren. In this respect, there was no difference between the "old" and the "new" immigrants. Such activities were carried over only where there were infusions of new immigrant blood; they were transferred from immigrant-contingent to immigrant-contingent, rather than from generation to generation.

American-born children of immigrants, although lacking the sense of kinship their parents have for the land of their origin, nevertheless cannot entirely free themselves from the socio-ethnic ties of the latter. This prevents the children from attaining the maximum degree of Americanization, as they understand that concept. They consequently constitute a transitional generation, one that has already departed from foreign soil but has not yet arrived in America. The children of immigrants must somehow adjust to one culture at home and to another at school, "with the result," observes Lawrence Brown, "that they do not have a world in which to live but have to vacillate between two cultures." [49] Thus a new social type emerges in the United States, one no longer old-countryish, but not yet American. William I. Thomas and Florian Znaniecki point out that the Polish immigration in the United States created a new Polish-American society, which "in structure and prevalent attitudes is neither Polish nor American but constitutes a specific new product whose raw materials have been partly drawn from Polish traditions, partly from the new conditions in which the immigrant sees and interprets them," [50] and Jerome Davis says of the Russians:

> . . . the young Russians of the second generation, in so far as they have gone to our public schools, have come in touch with some of the wholesome influences of our American life, and they respond with appreciation. They feel more American than Russian.[51]

But the ordinary child of the immigrant does not encounter only the healthy aspects of acculturation. He does not seek to translate old traditions into the terms of the new American reality, but to free himself altogether from the old way of life. While this is true of both the "old" and the "new" immigrants, the process is a more painful one among the latter because the rift between parents and children is deeper.

As a result of their higher level of education, the "old" immigrants were able to master English more quickly and thus to communicate more readily with their children. And because of the higher social status of the "old" immigrants, the disparity between the home and the street was not so fundamental. In addition, their mode of life was not so radically different from that of the indigenous population and hence less likely to attract unfavorable attention. Moreover, the "old" immigrants, except for the Irish, did not carry in their breasts a sense of national resentment, and did not, as did the "new" immigrants from oppressed lands, regard their children as deserters if the latter failed to evince interest in their ethnic activities.

The break between the parents and children of the "new" immigration was both personal tragedy and social problem. It led to the break-up of the immigrant family which, among the Slavs, Italians and other southern and eastern Europeans, was based on the woman's subordination to her husband and on strict patriarchal authority. All this was severely shaken here: the woman gained a sense of her own worth, and the children no longer obeyed unquestioningly. Among the children of ethnic groups in Yankee City Warner and Srole found that

> . . . not only does the child resent the fact that his parents do not act after the American behavioral modes; not only does he resent pressure to act after the ethnic behavioral modes; infused with the American logics, he implicitly questions the right of his father to dominate and control his behaviors.[52]

The lower the educational level of a group, the more striking was the contrast between its folkways and mores and those dictated by the tyranny of the majority and the more bitter the resultant conflict between the generations. The parents were embittered and disappointed; they felt rejected by strangers and deserted by their own; they had neither a home nor an outside world.

For their part, the children viewed the foreign customs and languages of their parents as chains that dragged them down and prevented their full integration into American life. Frequently the children were ashamed of their immigrant parents and showed them open contempt. They struggled to throw off their chains; and the harder the struggle, the greater was their rebellion against the legacy of the parents. It would be natural for a transitional generation, uprooted from old traditions and not yet anchored in the new, to have produced a large number of socially unstabilized and emotionally disturbed elements.

Anti-immigration forces exploited the statistics showing the high incidence of delinquency and crime among the "new" immigrants, refusing to recognize that it was not a racial, or religious, or nationality phenomenon, but a socio-economic problem that would have the same effect on any group subjected to similar social frustrations. The immigrants paid dearly for the transitional generation, but the responsibility belonged to American society which, in the frenetic pace of its technological upsurge, forced upon them the kind of Americanization which deprived them of great values and impoverished America as well.

Even when Americanization did not lead to obviously anti-social results, it still erected barriers between the parents and children. Second-generation Italians in New York, reported the Federal Writers' Project, frequently have forgotten the names of the regions where their parents were born. Warner and Srole found the same situation to exist in Yankee City:

> . . . Between the parent and the child . . . there is this fundamental breach. The parent uses English only in those relations that demand it, and then hesitantly. The child, in turn, uses the ethnic language only in those relations that demand it, namely, with his parents.[53]

The children are dissatisfied. A French-Canadian in Yankee City bewails the fact that the children do not even want to talk French at home. And a Jewish boy adds that Jewish women embarrass him when they speak Yiddish in public. Sometimes parents and children simply do not communicate because of language difficulties. A Russian father complains that he can never get his son to hear him out; and the son in turn complains that he cannot understand what his father is saying.

In 1921, Thaddeus Slezynski, a communal leader in Erie, Pennsylvania, suggested a five-part division of the second ethnic generation. Even though these five categories are based on a limited framework and are more than a third of a century old, they remain generally correct and are worth quoting. Of the five groups the first "largely conforms to the dominant tendencies of the foreign colony and remains a part of it." The second "entirely loses its contact with the foreign colony." The third group, "though in no way participating in the life of the colony, is claimed [by it] because of unusual achievements." The fourth, although absorbed by the larger community, still "plays an important part in the organized life of the foreign community." The fifth group appreciates the problems of the foreign colony and would like to see some of its values preserved; "at the same time it is making a conscious effort to remove the barriers that separate the immigrant colony from the larger community." [54]

The first group, in Slezynski's estimation, is still not American, although its members are American-born. The members of the second group hate the ethnic colony. The most constructive, though the smallest, is the third group. This group is the link to the third generation, which is achieving full acculturation.

We shall have occasion to refer to the third generation in the later chapters of this work; here we merely want to point out that the third generation attains the emotional stability and socio-economic rootedness absent in the second generation. That is why the relations between the third and the immigrant generations are not nearly as strained as between the latter and the second generation. The third generation feels far more secure, considers itself fully American, and is generally accepted as such. It does not suffer from the sense of uprootedness characteristic of the immigrant or from the second generation's feeling of inferiority. For this reason, the third generation often reveals greater tolerance and understanding of the otherness of the immigrant grandparents, an otherness from which the third generation itself is nearly wholly emancipated.

Among students of ethnic problems in the United States there is virtually no difference of opinion concerning the complete acculturation of the third generation. If the second generation still lives in two cultures, and sometimes in a cultural void, the third generation has both feet on American cultural soil. Even with the second generation the new land occcupies first place, shoving the native land of the parents into the background. American-born children of immigrants in

47

Yankee City finally achieve "a balance between the conflicting elements of their personality by orienting themselves principally to the American social system while still maintaining a limited number of formal relations in the ethnic community." [55] In the third generation, the last vestiges of these formal relations disappear as conscious acts, although not as psychological effects. The late great anthropologist, Franz Boas, declared:

> . . . our experience with Americans born in New York whose grandparents immigrated into this country is, on the whole, that most social traces of their descent have disappeared, and that many do not even know to what nationalities their grandparents belonged.[56]

H. G. Duncan analyzed several hundred letters from American students of the second and third generations and concluded that the correspondents of the third generation revealed not the slightest consciously active kinship with the ethnic group of their descent.[57] No friend of immigrants, Richmond Mayo-Smith was forced as early as 1890 to concede that the immigrants' children and grandchildren come in time to adjust so well to America that "they become fully identified with our customs, manner of living and habits of thought, and are thoroughly Americanized." [58]

Even among those groups which, for internal or external reasons, are assimilated with the greatest difficulty, ethnic cohesion is considerably shaken by the third generation. "Whatever may separate the Italian-American from the rest of the fellow citizens," observe the authors of the Federal Writers' study, "disappears in the third generation." [59] Carl Wittke points out that among the Dutch residents in Michigan, the forces of Americanization make deep inroads on the third generation which have a shattering impact on their group solidarity. The Irish too are unable to withstand the pressures on their third generation. The experience in Yankee City is typical in this respect for the country as a whole. Samuel Koenig predicts, "that in spite of his high ideal to preserve his culture and language intact, the French-Canadian may become amalgamated into the great American people." [60]

The picture is the same for every group, with the exception of the Jews and the colored communities. On the levels of language, general behavior and nationality, it is virtually impossible to distinguish among the third-generation descendants of the various ethnic groups. And if a small difference is still discernible at that stage, it disappears completely in subsequent generations. Anthropological studies demonstrate that the physical structure of American-born descendants of immigrants is approaching a certain norm, which reflects the prevailing geographical, climatic, social and economic conditions in the country.

This does not mean, of course, that the process of ethnic dissolution is wholly completed with the third generation. There is much truth in Koenig's contention that not only the second, but "even the third generation still faces the problems of adjustment to the dominant American society." [61] But the inevitable outcome of the process remains the same. The third generation clearly points to the disappearance of the ethnic group even when not all its members have fully integrated with the environment or shaken off the remnants of a feeling of greater comfort within their own ethnic atmosphere. Some members of the third generation still retain a token of ethnic identity, but their number is small. If we were to divide the assimilation process into its two natural stages, we should find that in the first stage members of an ethnic group seek to leave their own nationality group; in the second stage, they strive to integrate with the nationality group into which they desire to assimilate. In terms of the concrete problem with which we are dealing here, this means that whereas the second generation struggles to cast off the yoke that holds it to its parents' ethnic group, the problem of the third generation is to become organically interwoven with the prevailing American environment. However the process is conceptualized, in the third generation the cement that binds every ethnic group is almost entirely diluted.

THEORY OF CULTURAL PLURALISM

Ruthless Americanization eventually provoked protest from two directions: from social workers who could not watch with equanimity the personal tragedies caused by Americanization, and from social thinkers who believed that one of history's great opportunities to bridge the gap between culture and civilization and to create a new, multicolored culture was being sacrificed to the tyranny of the majority.

Social workers like Jacob Riis, Jane Addams, Lillian Wald, Grace Abbott and others built settlement houses where the immigrant could at least encounter friendliness rather than contempt. In the settlement houses, the immigrant was taught to understand America, and his children were taught to understand him. The immigrant was encouraged not to fear America, and his children, not to be ashamed of him. But the main function of the settlement houses was Americanization. Although this form of Americanization sought to help the immigrant adjust to his new circumstances with a minimum of pain, its objective was nonetheless assimilation.

Even in those more progressive settlement houses where the immigrants and their children were encouraged to develop their own culture, art, handicrafts and forms of entertainment, the end in view was a more orderly dissolution of the ethnic groups within the prevailing social environment. Americanization in the settlement houses, consequently, while it concerned itself greatly with the emotions and experiences of the immigrant, remained essentially unilateral. Certainly a humane attitude was no small matter, when the general tendency was to ignore completely the desires and feelings of the immigrant, and to demand immediate and unconditional surrender; but this attitude never went beyond toleration. And toleration is the relationship of the stronger to the weaker; the latter has only as many rights as the former allows him.

That the immigrant came here capable of giving as well as of taking was the revolutionary conception introduced by a small group of thinkers who, realizing not only the tragedy of the ethnic groups but also the catastrophic effects of "Americanization" upon American culture, rejected assimilation as an end. They questioned the right of the American dominant majority to spiritual preëminence and rebelled against its cultural tyranny. Against unity through conformity, they raised the banner of unity through diversity.

In 1916, when ethnic minority groups were being pilloried as hyphenated Americans, John Dewey insisted on the international character of America:

> . . . such terms as Irish-American or Hebrew-American or German-American are false terms because they seem to assume something which is already in existence called America, to which the other factors may be

externally hitched on. The fact is the genuine American, the typical American, is himself a hyphenated character. This does not mean that he is part American and that some foreign ingredient is then added. It means . . . that he is international and interracial in his make up. He is not American plus Pole or German. But the American is himself Pole-German-English-French-Spanish-Italian-Greek-Irish-Scandinavian-Bohemian-Jew-and so on. . . . The hyphen connects instead of separates.[62]

Horace M. Kallen, the father of the theory of cultural pluralism, goes even farther than Dewey. The base of American democracy, says Kallen, is diversity. American culture is founded "upon variation of racial groups and individual character . . . spontaneous differences of social heritage, institutional habit, mental attitude and emotional tone." [63] He conceives of the spiritual formation of the American nation and the creation of American democracy as a never-ending process. It is a symphony that comes to life anew with the playing of each orchestra. The ethnic groups are the instruments of the orchestra; and though each plays its own part, they all contribute to a harmonious whole. This is not the wholeness of totalitarian *gleichschaltung* but of varied tones, each of which contributes something unique to the symphony.

The variations, Kallen continues, do not disappear in the course of time. Of course, a certain common way of reacting to experience develops among the various ethnic groups that constitute the American people. But even when they react to stimuli in the same way, they do not thereby cease to be different. On the contrary, the impulse to eliminate otherness is a reflection of immaturity. When groups become stabilized and attain maturity, they tend to diversity. The inclination to dissolve the variegated ethnic groups consequently represents moral deterioration for America, a weakening of the country's true spirit or, as Kallen prefers to call it, the American idea. He is not at all apologetic about these ethnic ties; quite the reverse: "hyphenation as such is a fact which permeates all levels of life. A man is at once a son and a husband, a brother and a friend, a man of affairs and a student, a citizen of a state and a member of a church, one in an ethnic and social group and the citizen of a nation." [64]

Under the influence of Dewey, Kallen, Kilpatrick, MacIver, Cole and others, an intercultural school system has been established to inject into American education a recognition of the contribution which the non-Anglo-Saxon groups have made to American culture. But a sober appraisal of the facts heretofore discussed does not allow of an optimistic outlook. As fruitful as the intercultural approach to education may be, as correct and justified as it may be—it is today, to the extent that it possesses ethnicizing objectives and steps out of interracial confines, without a real foundation. Cultural pluralism simply came too late. Objective conditions are no longer suitable for it, and the subjective forces necessary to change the conditions are absent. Not only is the generation with the will and interest to preserve ethnic identity in the United States dying out; the generations that follow lack that interest and will. And the results are inevitable: all the evidence indicates that assimilation will proceed at a faster rate in the future than in the past.

Nor may it be expected that the processes of dissolution and assimilation will, as occasionally in the past, halt for short periods. The objective reasons have already been sufficiently detailed; the subjective reasons can be summed up in a few words: the tyranny of the majority has triumphed; the will of the ethnic groups to perpetuate their collective existence is expiring, if it has not already been wholly stifled. Growth into the new civilization causes them to abandon their old culture. It is worth noting at this point that, as a result of World War II, the attitude toward minorities has also radically changed in Europe. Every nation is now striving for homogeneity and is attempting by various means—such as transfers of population or elimination of the minority status—to rid itself of its minority groups. It is inconceivable that at the very time when Europe is seeking to liquidate its minority problems, America should begin to display a greater tolerance or understanding of ethnic minorities at home.

In sum, the last vestiges of the raw material from which a workable cultural pluralism could be shaped are disappearing. And the theory of cultural pluralism itself contains a defect which makes it unrealistic, in that it does not provide for the social area into which the cultural activity of the various ethnic groups could be fitted within the larger framework of American culture. The theory has been unable to suggest the organized form through which the ethnic groups could make their conscious contribution to the mainstream of American spiritual creativity. The exponents of cultural pluralism are too realistic to call for the use of a language other than English in the cultural activities of the ethnic groups, yet they fail to see the role of the ethnic language in holding a group together. Without the ethnic language, ethnic solidarity cannot pass from one generation to another. If the role of every ethnic group in American culture is to be comparable to that of an instrument in an orchestra, it must be the group's language that transforms the instrument into a creative force.

In order for cultural pluralism to possess the force of dynamic creativity, it must be based on the conscious efforts of the ethnic groups to perpetuate themselves in a collective way so as to bring out their spiritual potentialities. For without the element of conscious effort, the difference between the cultural orchestra and the melting pot is very small indeed. In the melting pot, the various ingredients also do not disappear without a trace; they are simply cooked together so as to produce a new dish, which is a synthesis of all the separate parts. But cultural pluralism asks for something more: it wants the separate parts to remain intact—and they cannot remain intact if they have no cultural means of maintaining themselves.

The Church understood this and so built the first parochial schools on a language basis. But when the Church ultimately had to decide between the language principle and influence on youth, it chose the latter. It sacrificed ethnic cohesion to the interests of religious expansion. And what a mighty, institutionalized Church was unable to achieve, a secular culturism with no real grounding can hardly hope to attain.

Thus, even social scientists sympathetic to cultural pluralism are forced to conclude that the fate of ethnic groups in the United States is sealed. Warren Thompson arrived at this conclusion on the basis of his demographic studies. And he is by no means alone. The National Resources Committee, at several points in its 1938 report, emphasized its sympathy for the idea of cultural pluralism, but conceded that the idea came too late:

> There is a natural tendency toward the assimilation of diverse cultures in the same communities. It is quite likely that this process has actually been forced too rapidly in the United States, with results that have often been personally and socially injurious.

At an earlier point the report stated:

> . . . the importance of diverse cultural heritages as such is rapidly waning, except where these are tied up with racial distinctions or present economic, religious, or other powerful and persistent interests.[65]

We have seen that economic interests operate, with few exceptions, in the opposite direction. The report notes that, as a result of altered technological and cultural conditions, a portion of the immigrant mass no longer has to begin its upward social climb from the lowest rung of the ladder. And we have already learned that this inevitably hastens assimilation.

Maurice R. Davie has analyzed the centripetal forces that seek to maintain minority communities in America and the centrifugal forces that operate to disintegrate groups and to dissolve them into the larger American community, and has come to the conclusion that "the latter forces are stronger. There appears to be an irresistible pressure toward assimilation, which may eventually result in complete cultural integration." [66] When this has happened, Davie says, cultural pluralism will also disappear, but not without having fulfilled an important function. Long years of research have convinced Warner and Srole that "the future of American ethnic groups seems to be limited; it is likely that they will be quickly absorbed." [67]

How quickly? This depends on the closeness of a particular group to the majority-type in the United States. Warner and Srole place the ethnic groups in various categories and suggest that, though they will all disappear in time, the rate of dissolution will vary with each group. It will take some one generation, others—six generations, even longer with still others. Unless the entire American social order changes, Warner and Srole predict, only the colored racial groups will remain as distinct groups, reduced to the virtual status of castes. We shall return to this thesis in a later chapter, for it allows of the possibility of a caste status for the Jews in America.

Is America therefore a melting pot? If that concept is taken to mean that all the specific cultural and spiritual characteristics of the ethnic groups are dissolved without leaving a trace and that only the flavor of the Anglo-Saxon ingredient remains in the American pot—then the answer is: a categorical "No." But if the concept is taken to mean the creation of a nation, the core of which is indeed the Anglo-Saxon contribution, but which also bears the imprint of other influences—even though the groups which brought these influences to bear have disappeared—then the answer is: a categorical "Yes." Perhaps Warner's and Srole's definition is the correct one:

> The American social system is not, strictly speaking, a "melting pot" which fuses its diverse ethnic elements into a new amalgam, as was once popularly believed, but is rather a system which performs the transmutation of diverse ethnic elements into elements almost homogeneous with its own.[68]

In this sense, one may certainly say that the tones remain, even after the instruments that sounded them have disappeared. Is this possible? Perhaps America will be able to construct a synthesis of varied tones which the various ethnic groups have introduced into its national life, and so further create a continuing symphony of American democracy. But the ethnic groups themselves will no longer remain. Only one of them displays the strength to maintain itself without the instrument of its own language: the Jews.

3 Jewish Immigrants in America

If there is a white ethnic group in the United States that possesses all the characteristic features of a minority—it is the Jews. In that very fact is to be found the first indication of their exceptionalism. While all other minority groups are minorities only in certain of their relations and otherwise belong to the majority, the Jews are a minority in all significant social relations.

The Irish are a religious minority, but linguistically they belong to the majority. The Germans are a linguistic minority but belong to the religious majority. There are groups whose culture is different from that of the majority, and others where the difference is in social development. The Jews diverge from the majority in religion and culture, in historical experience and social formation.

Other minorities were able to become—and actually did become—majorities in certain times, regions or situations. Catholics of several different ethnic groups, for example, together constituted a majority in several cities and in at least two states. Mormons became a majority in Utah. The Jews, however, never became a majority in any stable residential region or city. Only in a few suburbs, a small number of resorts which live off tourism, such as Miami Beach, towns in the Catskill Mountains of New York, and several points along the northeastern and southern coasts, were Jews able for a time to become a majority. And

57

if there were other groups which could not expect at any time or in any region to become a majority, such as Moslems or Buddhists, they had come from countries where they were in the majority. Jews had been a minority in all the lands of their emigration also.

A number of ethnic groups came here, as we have seen, with a sense of national resentment. This resentment was directed against a particular people that kept them in national bondage. Among Jews, this resentment was directed against virtually the entire world, because they were everywhere, if not persecuted, at least discriminated against. Precisely for this reason, the Jews, more than any other group, were ideologically motivated. With very few exceptions, individual Jews bore within them a sense of responsibility for the entire Jewish community; and to that extent, one can say that every Jew was influenced by one or another social philosophy.

In America, the Jews suffered the same disabilities and discriminations as the other immigrant groups and, in addition, felt some of the pressures directed against underprivileged native groups, like the Negroes, for example. Moreover, from the day when the Jewish settlement was first established in this country, it resisted, in a number of important ways, the tyranny of the majority. Resistance both evoked the mistrust of the majority and tightened the internal cohesion of the Jewish community. It was the old conflict between assimilating and isolating forces. Every ethnic group constituted a battleground of this conflict, and in this particular the Jews have been no exception. But they were an exception in the intensity of the conflict in their midst. We shall discover, at a later point, that the clash between external pressure and internal resistance was sharper among Jews than among others. And the Jews were also an exception in terms of the outcome of the conflict: they are the only white ethnic group in whom the factors of cohesion have so far turned out to be stronger than the factors of disintegration.

Does this mean, then, that the Jews are generally an exception in the United States? And if so—why? We shall be able to answer these questions only after having analyzed American Jewish history in terms of the processes which shaped the development of the dominant community and the other minority groups. Such an analysis will bring into focus the extent to which Jewish history here has been comparable to that of the other groups, and wherein and how the Jewish group departed from the general norms of development discussed in the preceding chapters.

THE THREE WAVES OF IMMIGRATION

The same needs that gave rise to the migrations of other ethnic groups drove the Jews to America from other parts of the world; but for the Jews, these needs were more acute. It was not only poverty from which they suffered in the old countries; more than other ethnic groups, they were subjected to discriminations, restrictions and boycotts. It was the deliberate and brutally executed policy of the governments of some of their former homelands to ruin the Jews economically and to force them into exile.

The religious persecutions from which the Jews had to flee were incomparably more severe. Some of the other groups, as we have noted, also suffered religious intolerance in their native lands, but they did not have to face the mortal dangers that threatened the Jews. Others came here to seek religious freedom; Jews came here to find physical security as well.

Furthermore, the political status of the Jews in the lands of their emigration was intolerable. The Spanish-Portuguese Jews, who came mostly from Holland and partly also from England, had still not shaken off the effects of the Inquisition. The German Jews came to America at a time when, in Germany, they had barely approached the outer rim of emancipation; it was only after the mass immigration of Germans into the United States had virtually stopped that the Jews inside Germany were given full political rights. As for the East European Jews, they fled from pogroms in Russia, from deprivation of rights in Rumania, and from political oppression in other countries.

The difference between the Jewish and the non-Jewish immigrants can be defined in the following general way: whereas the others, in the main, sought to improve their lot, the Jews frequently looked simply for a refuge. The element of compulsion was more pronounced in the emigrations of Jews than in those of others. And as in many a social phenomenon, quantity in this case was transformed into quality. In a number of significant respects, Jewish immigration into the United

59

States constituted a special situation, quite unlike the one created by all the other groups. A comparison of the number of immigrants who returned home, among the Jews and among the others, offers the first indication of this special situation. Others could, if they so chose, go back to their old countries; for Jews there was generally no way back.

Jews came here to stay. When they left their old countries, they burned all their bridges behind them; and at every opportunity they brought their families with them. Not only did women and children constitute a higher proportion among Jewish immigrants than among others of the "new" immigration—which included, as noted, a large number of birds of passage; the percentage of women and children was also higher among Jews than among others even in the "old" immigration—which was generally a family immigration. "A comparison of the proportion of females and children in the 'old' and the 'new' immigration," writes Samuel Joseph, "with that in the Jewish shows that the Jewish immigration has proportionately almost twice as many females as the 'new' immigration (Jews excepted), and surpasses even the 'old' immigration in this regard. Of children under fourteen the Jewish movement has proportionately more than two and one-half times as many as the 'new' immigration (Jews excepted), and nearly twice as many as the 'old' immigration." [1]

Joseph's study covered immigration up to 1910. Statistics produced by Liebman Hersch, in the Yiddish Encyclopedia, show that the situation did not change after World War I. These figures are based, as is Joseph's study, on United States Government statistics:

Table 1.—Number of immigrants of a given age among Jews and in general in each 100 immigrants: [2]

| YEAR | Under 14 | | 14–44 | | 45 and older | |
	GENERAL	JEWS	GENERAL	JEWS	GENERAL	JEWS
1921–'24	18.5	29.6	72.3	57.7	9.1	12.7
1925–'27	16.0	22.7	74.6	54.1	9.3	23.2
1935–'36	19.4	18.0	64.5	65.3	16.2	16.7

The figures show that the family nature of the immigrants grew substantially in the second quarter of the present century, demonstrating that after World War I the immigration was a permanent one among

60

all groups. The "Birds of Passage" type virtually disappeared. The tiny role which this type played in Jewish immigration can be seen from the following table, in which Hersch registered the extent of re-emigration from the United States:

Table 2.—General and Jewish re-emigration for each 100 immigrants [3]

YEAR	GENERAL	JEWS
1908–1914	30.8	7.1
1915–1920	56.6	4.3
1921–1924	25.8	0.7
1925–1937	40.0	3.8
1908–1937	34.6	5.0

From 1908 to 1937, general reverse migration from the United States was never less than one-quarter of the immigration; among Jews, it was never greater than 7 percent. Between 1915 and 1920, reverse migration, under the impact of World War I (during which great numbers of immigrants returned to help their old homelands win the fight), amounted to more than one-half of the immigration; Jewish reverse migration during this period amounted to only slightly more than 4 percent. The Jews felt far more obligated to the United States during the war than to their old countries. During the period, 1925–37, which included the depression years in the United States, the general reverse migration was over two-fifths of the immigration. Nowhere else could Jews hope to find better economic conditions; their reverse migration was barely 4 percent.

As for the "old" immigration, Joseph's figures show that for every 100 immigrants, there were one and one-half times as many returnees among other immigrant groups than among the Jews. His assertion that "the Jewish immigration must thus be accorded the place of distinction in American immigration for permanence of settlement" [4] was correct in 1914, when he made it, and it remains true to this day.

But this distinction was far from being the fundamental factor that differentiated the Jews from the other immigrants. The most important difference was that, whereas members of other ethnic groups all came

61

from one country—or, as in the case of the Poles, from one territory which was governed by three separate political entities—the Jews came from a variety of lands. The differences among these lands were not only geographical but, more importantly, also political, economic, social and cultural. Between Catholic, feudal Spain and Portugal from which the Sephardic Jews stemmed, and the Protestant, capitalist German provinces from which most of the German Jews came, there was a political chasm of centuries. No less a chasm separated the constitutional monarchy of Germany and the Tsarist despotism of Russia. The three waves of Jewish immigration—the Spanish-Portuguese, the German, and the East European—reflected, in the first instance, the political situations of the countries of emigration. And it must be borne in mind that each of the major waves was actually made up of a number of smaller waves emanating from different countries.

Other ethnic groups also came here in waves, but there was continuity in those waves; and they all flowed from one place. Each of the three waves of Jewish immigration, on the other hand, was an independent stream that had practically no relation with the other streams. Just as there was no political similarity between one wave of Jewish immigration and another, so were they also disparate in time. The Sephardim came here during the colonial period; they belonged to the category of settlers and participated in the creation of the American republic. The German Jews arrived during the Civil War epoch and contributed their share to the unification of the American nation. The East European Jews came here during the "Gilded Age" and contributed to the expansion of the American industrial empire. These divisions marked the categories and the levels of prestige within the Jewish community in America.

The sharp social differences among these waves were molded by the following three factors: (1) the economic conditions that prevailed in the lands of emigration; (2) the economic conditions that prevailed in the United States during the periods when each of the waves of immigration arrived; (3) the forms which the economic integration of the immigrants assumed in each of the waves.

The Sephardim—the Spanish-Portuguese-Jews—came from countries which possessed colonies on several continents. They brought with them an experience of mercantilistic operations on a world-wide scale.

62

They settled in several of the larger port cities and engaged largely in import and export, transoceanic and intercolonial trade, and other forms of commerce. These functions were readily adapted to the central economic task of the colonies, the main objective of which was the development of their domestic economy and the finding of a place of their own on the world market. The Sephardic Jews, after achieving adjustment, belonged almost without exception to the possessing classes.

The first German Jews came to America from small towns, and they were very poor. Arriving during the period when the westward expansion of the frontier was in full swing, great numbers of them shouldered packs and followed the routes of the covered wagons. We have already referred to Turner's definition of the frontier as the point where civilization and savagery met in the United States; the appearance of a German-Jewish peddler at a frontier point made it easier for civilization to triumph over savagery. Because of the enormous and hectic mobility within the country at the time when the German-Jewish immigration reached its peak, this wave displayed a much greater tendency than either the first or the third waves to spread out geographically; thus, dozens of Jewish communities throughout the United States owe their establishment to the German Jews. When they first came here, these Jews belonged to the lowest levels of the petty bourgeoisie. Aside from peddlers, there were also a great variety of small traders, white-collar and wage workers.

The Jews of eastern Europe came from countries where capitalism was just beginning to take its first steps, and in this country they encountered a capitalism that was soon to be more advanced than any in the world. By that time, the geographical boundaries of the United States were permanently fixed, and free land was exhausted. The East European Jews concentrated in the larger industrial centers and became a huge proletariat.

The cultural differences among the three waves were even more pronounced than the economic and political ones. The Sephardic Jews, upon their arrival, spoke Spanish or Portuguese; the German Jews, German; the East European Jews, Yiddish. But the cultural differences were not only linguistic. The Sephardic Jews possessed a considerable measure of general education, but little Jewish culture. They com-

63

bined a strict pietism in religious affairs and a broad worldliness in secular matters. As a group, the German Jews were not as homogeneous internally. Germany itself was still divided into scores of provinces and principalities, which were far from being on the same level of development. Attitudes toward the Jews were not identical in all the provinces, and the cultural status of the former varied accordingly. In general, however, the German Jews lived within a broadly European atmosphere, which eased their adaptation to America. The great mass of East European immigrants brought with them a good deal of Jewish learning but little general education. They came from countries with a high percentage of illiteracy.

In sum, Jewish immigration to America is almost as old as America itself. It proceeded in three waves, none of which had much relation to the other, and each of which was in turn subdivided into smaller wavelets with few points of contact.

SOCIAL DIFFERENCES AMONG THE IMMIGRANTS

Other ethnic groups, as we have pointed out, had, in the early years of their immigration, a more or less homogeneous social structure; the process of social differentiation among them began only after they had been here for a time. It was an entirely different matter with the Jews. For a long time—and to a certain extent even today—social differentiation among Jews was not only based on their economic evolution in this country, but bore the imprint of the variations in their background abroad. Gunnar Myrdal's observation that social stratification in America has to some extent been shaped by racial and ethnic factors is also in large measure relevant to the American Jewish community: its economic structure in part reflects the waves of its immigration. Each of the waves was larger than the preceding one, and began after the earlier wave had subsided and after the Jews of that earlier wave had attained a considerable degree of economic and social stability. The Spanish-Portuguese Jews had already joined the wealthier classes when the immigrants from Germany were still sunk in poverty; and the latter were already well established economically when the East European Jewish immigrants brought an even more desperate poverty. For

64

a while, the relation between German and East European Jews was that of employers and employees.

The Sephardim considered themselves the aristocracy of the Jewish community and viewed the Ashkenazim (Jews from Germany and eastern Europe) with contempt. They would not marry Ashkenazim if they could help it, nor could they bring themselves to be buried in the same cemetery. As late as the mid-nineteenth century—when the aristocratic Sephardic families were in process of disappearing and Sephardic youth was forced increasingly to marry Ashkenazim or face the prospect of intermarriage with Gentiles—the Sephardic community of New York still considered itself enough of an elite to avoid, insofar as possible, any contact with the "plebs" from Germany and Poland. In his outstanding monograph on the history of the New York Jewish community from 1654 to 1860, Hyman B. Grinstein notes that between 1830 and 1850 the Sephardic Jews, virtually all of whom were American-born, constituted "an exclusive coterie whose members mingled only among themselves and married within their own group. They had their own charitable societies, their own educational system, their own mode of worship. This group was said to be 'genteel,' refined, and cultured; it had its own social parties and celebrations, rarely going out as a unit to participate in the activities of the general Jewish community." [5] The barrier between the Spanish-Portuguese and German Jews has been described laconically but clearly by Anita Libman Lebeson: It consisted of "money, land and origins." [6]

The superior attitude of the Sephardim to the German Jews was displayed by the latter, in turn, to the Jews from eastern Europe. As Lee J. Levinger puts it, the German Jews had to suffer "prejudice on the part of the proud Spaniards, and, though so recently out of the ghetto themselves, they passed on the same prejudice to the Jews from Poland and Galicia." [7]

One of the reasons for which the eighteenth-century Portuguese Jews in Georgia refused to have any dealings with the German Jews there was that the latter were poor and, unlike the Sephardim, had not been able to cover the expenses of their trip to America. In the nineteenth century the German Jews accused the Russian Jews of being *schnorrers* (beggars) and charged them with failing to undertake their share of the finanical burdens of the Jewish community. And just as the Spanish-Portuguese Jews sought to isolate themselves from the German Jews, the latter sought to isolate themselves from the East European Jews. The German Jews, writes Louis Wirth, "did not wish to have these [Russian] Jews too close to them. These Russians were all right—of that they were quite certain—but, like the Southern Negro, they had to keep their place." [8] Rudolph Glanz quotes from a letter, written by an American Jewish correspondent, that appeared during the 1840's in the Berlin *Allgemeine Zeitung dem Judentum*: "The Polish Jew is the dirtiest of all creatures, and thanks to him the word, 'Jew,' is here too coming to be used as an insult." [9]

Forty years later, a B'nai B'rith lodge in Chicago explained that it declined to accept Polish and Russian Jews as members because, as Polish and Russian Jews, they were not yet civilized, were inclined to Orthodoxy and not fit to belong to a respectable organization of American Jews.[10]

In Rochester, N.Y., the German Jews and the Jews from eastern Europe constituted two distinct communities at the end of the nineteenth century. While the former, states Stuart E. Rosenberg, "were prepared to defend their Russian co-religionists publicly, privately they had come to regard them as a threat to their own secure position in America." Immigrants from eastern Europe, declared the United Jewish Charities of Rochester in 1889, "are a bane to the country and a curse to the Jews." [11]

These instances adequately describe the nature of the relations among the various Jewish groups until the beginning of the twentieth century. The changes that were introduced into these relations will be described at a later point. But it is immediately necessary to avoid two errors that are often made in analyzing the rise of the Jewish community in the United States. In the first place, it must not be thought that no Ashkenazim entered the country during the Sephardic period, or that no East European Jews entered during the German period. According to the most recent data, it is evident that the Sephardic Jews constituted a majority of the American Jewish population only in the seventeenth century. In the eighteenth century, they had already become a minority, although the leadership of the community rested firmly in their hands. In the nineteenth century they lost the leadership too. Polish Jews were among the oldest members of Sephardic synagogs. When Isaac Mayer Wise came to New York in 1846, he found that "the Portuguese congregation was the oldest, and the oldest Portuguese was a Polish Jew." [12]

That the number of East European immigrants was by no means small during the German period can be seen in the fact that the former established a considerable number of synagogs in the middle of the nineteenth century and that Russians Jews were to be found among the leaders of Reform temples. Even in as "aristocratic" a Jewish community as Charleston, S.C., which had attracted no substantial Jewish immigration since the beginning of the nineteenth century, Polish Jews were sufficiently numerous by 1857 to found their own synagog.

No matter how stand-offish the various Jewish groups may have been, they could not, nevertheless, wholly avoid contact with each other either on the communal level or in social relations. This fact should be remembered.

A second error that should be avoided in tracing the history of the Jewish community in America is the belief that social stratification among the three waves of immigrants was always rigid and unilinear. In the first place, there was a certain amount of intermingling among them. Secondly, we have already drawn attention to the fact that each separate wave was broken down into smaller wavelets, which means that the immigrants in each wave were not socially homogeneous. In the mid-nineteenth century, for example, there was in New York a substantial group of Jews who had come from England and who, because they came from an Anglo-Saxon country and knew English, regarded themselves as socially superior. Among the German Jews, there was a great difference between the strictly Orthodox poor immigrants who came from the backward German provinces, and the more cultured and worldly immigrants of 1848 and after. Even among the East European Jews, there were more and less "aristocratic" elements. Grinstein, speaking of the mid-nineteenth-century New York Jews, writes: "The Polish Jews, particularly those from Posen, set up social distinctions between themselves and the Russian Jews." [13] This demonstrates that from the outset the Jews in the United States were far more divided than the more inclusive view of the three waves of immigration

67

might seem to imply. They were from a social standpoint virtually the most fragmented ethnic group in the country.

DIFFERENCES IN HISTORY AND TRADITION

In order to bring into sharper focus the full social and ethnic import of the fact that Jewish immigration stemmed from many lands rather than one, it is necessary to probe more deeply into the cultural differences among the various immigration waves. The emphasis here will be on the three major waves, but the reader will have to bear in mind the two errors of generalization against which he has been warned.

The Sephardim were heirs to the traditions of the Golden Age of Spanish Jewry. The Jews of that age distinguished themselves for their steadfast loyalty to their religion, on the one hand, and for their broad worldliness in political, social and cultural affairs, on the other. They produced important works of Jewish religion and philosophy and expressed the traditional Jewish longing for the ancient homeland of Palestine in wondrous poetry, much of which was subsbequently adopted by Jews of all countries and is still chanted as prayers in every type of synagog. At the same time, they created works of general human interest and value. They were at home in everything that affected their country and the world. They sought to probe the heart of Jewish ethics and to ascend the heights of universal esthetics. Not until the rise of the American Jewish settlement did a Jewish community in the Diaspora succeed so well in establishing as harmonious a balance between their own religious culture and the general secular culture, between the responsibilities of Jews as members of a separate ethnic community and their duties as denizens of their homeland as in the Golden Age in Spain.

The harmony was shattered when the provinces of Arab Spain fell under the political and spiritual domination of Catholic Spain. The fires of the Inquisition destroyed, in the first instance, Jewish learning. Neither in Spain nor in Portugal could the Jews continue to devote themselves to Jewish studies and to observe freely the injunctions of the Jewish religion. From the Jewish point of view, they degenerated; but those who remained Jews brought with them, after the Expulsion from Spain in 1492, that same excruciating loyalty to Judaism which earlier had enabled so many of their co-religionists to accept the martyrdom of the auto-da-fes. The Sephardim carried the selfsame loyalty with them to the New World. Among them were Marranos who only in America finally found communion with the Jewish God. This was not lightly gained. The first Jews came to North America from Brazil, where the Inquisition had followed them from Portugal. It was only in the American colonies that they finally found their long-desired opportunity to live openly as Jews.

The Sephardim salvaged from their heritage the inner harmony between Jewish religiosity and worldly interests. They possessed a rather high level of secular culture, and what they lacked in Jewish learning they tried to make up for by their piety and devotion to the rediscovered faith of their ancestors. They raised no doubts as to the foundations of Jewish being: they accepted their Jewishness and all its varied social manifestations, which centered on the synagog, as an unquestioned and self-evident matter. The Sephardim were strictly Orthodox and were also, as we shall have occasion to see, intolerant of backsliders. In great measure, this intolerance was a reaction to the uncompromising rigidity of the Catholic church, under whose pressure and in whose shadow—and in many cases, in whose bosom—the Spanish-Portuguese Jews had been reared. In contrast, the German Jews lived in an atmosphere of chronic skepticism during the nineteenth century. This was the shining period of rationalism, to which religion, on the defensive, sought means of adaptation.

Capitalism opened the way to the Emancipation of the Jews of western Europe, and the Jews of Germany embarked on that road full of hope and ambition. In Spain, the Inquisition came after a long period of freedom for the Jews; in Germany, Emancipation came after centuries of ghetto life. In Spain, the Jews faced the problem of being pushed out of the positions they had long enjoyed; in Germany, the problem was to enter positions that had previously been closed to them. As a result of the Inquisition, numerous Spanish Jews sacrificed the high social status they had attained in order to remain true to their religion; as a result of the Emancipation, many German Jews sacrificed their religion in order to attain a higher social status.

Although only the first rays of Emancipation appeared in Germany itself during the period of mass German-Jewish immigration to this country, they were sufficient to cause fundamental modifications in the spiritual life of the German Jews. The latter were no longer able to take their Judaism for granted; they were beginning to raise basic doubts about its essence. Therewith, they brought the ancient debate about the nature of Judaism down from the heavenly spheres on which rabbinic literature had fixed it, and placed it on the more mundane level of terrestrial interests. The German Jews sought not a theological answer but a social one.

That Jews lived in two cultures wherever they were able to establish material or spiritual contacts with their Gentile neighbors was a familiar enough fact even before the Emancipation. Emancipation, however, made them aware of a sharp conflict between the two cultures. Previously, Jews had been "citizens" only of the ghettos; the Emancipation made them citizens of the West European countries as well— but the ghettos remained, nevertheless. The conflict between the two cultures could not be resolved so long as the Jew was not free of the ghetto itself.

The Spanish Jews also experienced a conflict, but it was only an external one; the conflict experienced by the emancipated Jews was an internal one—a conflict within their own souls. Social psychologists have described people with such conflicts as marginal persons. In Stonequist's view, marginal persons passed through three phases: in the first phase, they were not yet aware that their own personal careers were involved in the racial or nationality conflict in which their religious, racial or ethnic group was caught up; in the second phase, they grasped this fact; and in the third phase, they sought means of adapting to the situation.[14]

This classification requires amplifying. Being placed in a situation where racial or nationality conflicts affect his life does not make a person a marginal man. He becomes such only when he seeks to free himself from this situation and cannot. In this sense, the Jews of former times who accepted persecution from the outside as a natural phenomenon were not marginal men, even though they too had the problem of adjusting to an alien environment. In the same way, the first Sephardic Jews in America, though they were, as we have pointed out, worldly in matters that did not affect their Jewishness, were essentially not marginal men because they did not seek to alter the balance they had established in their relations with the non-Jewish environment. It was otherwise with those German Jews whose balance was upset by the Emancipation and who viewed their Jewishness as an obstacle to the building of a new balance. They belonged to Stonequist's second category; from this arose their internal spiritual conflict, which they tried to resolve through assimilation and even conversion. Graetz noted that in Berlin there were 1,236 cases of conversion in 1823, and that constituted one-half of the entire Jewish population of the city. In the other parts of Prussia there were 1,382 additional conversions.[15] It is likely that these figures are more accurate than the official statistics provided at the time. Uriah Zevi Engelman, in *The Rise of the Jew in the Western World,* cites the official figures and adds that between 1815 and 1840 more than 1,200 conversions were registered in Berlin. When one considers that the Jewish population of Berlin in 1840 counted no more than 6,458 souls, one realizes the scope of conversion even if the official statistics are accepted.[16] But no matter how extensive conversion was, the majority of German Jewry did seek a modus vivendi between Judaism and the outside world without totally discarding the former.

The United States in mid-nineteenth century provided an especially favorable background for such a modus vivendi. Economic opportunities were so unlimited that Jews did not find it necessary to sacrifice their Jewishness in the interests of economic integration. America had no state religion, and the tradition of religious freedom was deeply rooted in the land; conversion was therefore valueless. An article that appeared in a Baltimore newspaper on November 24, 1819, at the time the Assembly of the State of Maryland debated the question of removing a Christian qualification from the oath of those assuming public office, which barred Jews from holding appointive or elective government positions, read in part:

A Jew here may worship according to the tradition of his fathers, and be revered and respected, where government is administered by the hands of Christians—he is in almost every state other than this [Maryland], eligible to office, capable of rising to the highest dignity without renouncing the religion of his ancestors,—if he does renounce it from such a motive, he is a base and detestable hypocrite, and would make a worse Christian than a Jew.[17]

71

If the Jews here felt any pressure, it was not pressure, as in Germany, from the state, but rather a social pressure: from the tyranny of the majority. This tyranny, to be sure, did undermine the will of the minority to deviate from the course charted by the majority; but wherever this will remained adamant, American utilitarianism provided the possibility of a compromise. The vast majority of German Jews, steadfastly refusing to abandon their Jewishness, availed themselves of that possibility. This quest forced them to pose a question that had simply not existed for the Sephardim: what, actually, was the basis for Jewish group existence? The answer of the German Jews was: the Jews were not a people but a religious association.

The German Jews had left regions which had experienced a radical religious reformation, and they came to a country where the dominant religion—Protestantism—was broken up into hundreds of denominations. Judaism too could not remain forever rigid, and attempts at its reformation began to appear. Anita Lebeson placed the beginning of Jewish Reform in America in the year 1766, with Isaac Pinto's translation of the Sephardic prayer book into English. The first organized attempt to introduce reform into American Judaism was made in Charleston, S.C., in 1824.

A group of members of the Sephardic synagog, K.K. (*Kahol Kadosh*) Beth Elohim, requested the congregation's leadership to change the service so as to incorporate a number of English prayers and a sermon in English. When this request was rejected, the group founded its own synagog, which lasted only a few years. This first venture in Reform Judaism lacked two features indispensable to success: (1) a mass base and (2) a competent religious leadership. Isaac Harby, the leader of the Charleston revolt, did not possess sufficient Jewish learning to become the spiritual head of a new movement within Judaism. Both features, missing in the Charleston experiment, were subsequently provided by the German Jewish immigration, and Reform must therefore be considered its legitimate offspring. This immigration brought large numbers of Jews who were psychologically and culturally prepared for Reform; indeed, because of their actual or potential marginality, and because of an economic impulse which will be described below, they stood in need of Reform. This immigration, furthermore, provided leaders, such as Rabbis Isaac Mayer Wise, Leo

72

Merzbacher, David Lilienthal, David Einhorn, Samuel Wise and Kauffman Kohler, who combined a great amount of Jewish learning with
considerable secular culture. These founders of Reform did not pursue
ethnic objectives. On the contrary, through Reform they aspired to
liquidate the ethnic problem. But life had its own logic. Viewed his-
torically, Reform Judaism in the United States constituted the first
organized attempt to adapt Jewish ethnicity to the American frame
of reference.

The Jews of Russia, Poland, Lithuania, Rumania, etc., came from
countries where the ghetto survived as both a physical and a cultural
institution. If the first two waves of immigration were carried over
from areas where conditions had a certain similarity to the situation in
the United States at the time of the immigrations, the third wave came
from countries that bore not the slightest resemblance, materially or
spiritually, economically or politically, to America. And if the German
Jews came here after they had already lived for a short time in an atmosphere of near-emancipation, which served them as a bridge to civic
equality in the United States, the Jews from Russia and Rumania altogether lacked a transition period.

The cultural life of the Jews in mid-nineteenth-century Russia was
not far different from Jewish cultural life in western Europe at the
beginning of the eighteenth century. The rabbinic tradition was still
the dominant culture in the Jewish Pale at the time when mass Jewish
emigration to America began. But capitalist and democratic winds
from the West, which had already been felt by the Tsarist regime, also
blew secularist breezes into the ghetto, especially in the later years of
the nineteenth century, when a Jewish labor movement was coming
into being. The changes that subsequently occurred in Jewish life were
out of all proportion to the extent of the spiritual incursions from the
West. Because of political oppression and the long cultural isolation,
the East European Jews at the end of the nineteenth and beginning of
the twentieth centuries lacked the basis for gradually reforming their
mode of life in a purely evolutionary way. Any step off the beaten track
came into sharp conflict with both the internal and external environment and became a revolutionary act. This was particularly true in
matters concerning religious and cultural tradition.

East European Jews were overwhelmingly Orthodox in religion.

Those who departed from Orthodoxy moved, as a rule, in the direction not of religious reforms, but of a complete break with religion. The division within the Jewish community was consequently not between conservators and reformers, but between traditionalists and radicals. And this division was equally marked from the very beginning of the East European immigration in the United States. On the one hand, this mass immigration enormously strengthened Orthodoxy and made it the dominant religious trend of the majority of the Jewish population in this country. On the other hand, the same immigration included large numbers of Jews who, despite their irreligiosity—and, in many cases, even atheism—nevertheless considered themselves an integral part of the Jewish community. To the old question—What are the Jews?—the East European immigration came to give a new answer: a people. The seeds of a secular Jewish nationalism were sown, with the Yiddish language playing an extraordinary part in the process.

RELIGIOUS DIFFERENCES

Orthodoxy was the major trend in Jewish religion when the American Jewish population consisted of a small layer of well-to-do Sephardic Jews—and also when it consisted of a huge mass of workers and common people from eastern Europe. The dominant trend between these two periods was Reform, although it is difficult to ascertain whether it was also the religious denomination of the majority at the time. The first German-Jewish immigrants were staunchly traditionalist in their faith, although the level of their Jewish knowledge was low. According to Isaac Mayer Wise, there was no Jewish leader in New York in 1846, aside from Rabbis Lilienthal and Merzbacher, who could read unvocalized Hebrew. And he knew only three laymen who possessed any substantial Jewish learning.

The most distinguished Orthodox leader of that period was Isaac Leeser, an immigrant from Germany who lived in Philadelphia. His impact on American Jewish life has never been properly appreciated. In his memoirs, Wise disparages Leeser, recounting that the latter had confessed to him an inability to read unvocalized Hebrew. But Wise attributed too much significance to this fact; he forgot that in those days it was entirely possible to possess a great amount of Jewish erudition and still have small command of Hebrew grammar. Leeser's considerable learning is attested to by his articles and his translation of the Bible into English. However that might have been, he was not able to withstand alone the encroachments of Reform. Under Wise's leadership, the Reform movement met with increasing success during the Civil War period and immediately thereafter.

The founders, as well as the historians, of the Reform movement confirm the fact that the demand for accommodation to American circumstances was one of the impelling forces behind Reform. It goes without saying that economic considerations played a significant role in this need. Wise himself quite unconsciously testifies to this when, in his memoirs, he relates an episode connected with his founding of the first Reform temple in Albany. This temple was involved in a bitter struggle with the Orthodox synagog from which he had broken away, and Wise thus describes the reaction of the non-Jewish community:

> The non-Jewish world sympathized with us, since we alone were actuated by regard for the needs and the spirit of the age, and matters reached such a pass that merchants who were members of another congregation or of none had to deny this fact to their beautiful female customers, because these took for granted that every decent Jew had to belong to the new congregation.[18]

The economic aspects of the divisions within American Judaism will be dealt with at greater length below. Several more instances should be cited, at this point, to illustrate and clarify the religious divisions during the last quarter of the nineteenth century and the first two decades of the twentieth century.

In the course of those years, the most important Reform temples transferred their Sabbath services from Saturday to Sunday. Hebrew was virtually eliminated from their liturgy. *Kashruth* (dietary laws) and other ritualistic features of personal Jewish life ceased to have the force of religious law and were relegated to the area of free individual choice; at the same time, Reform Jews were given to understand that the quality of their Judaism would in no wise be diminished if they failed to observe these practices—and the rabbis themselves were among the first to break with them publicly. David Philipson, an early Reform rabbi, recounts an amusing but characteristic incident.

75

In 1894 he delivered a lecture at a Unitarian church in Cincinnati. His theme was: "Why I Am a Jew." When he had concluded, he was approached by a woman from the audience who said to him, "If that is Judaism, I am a Jew and did not know it." Philipson ends his recital of this incident with the remark: "I received many similar words of commendation." [19] A rabbi explains Judaism in such a way that a Unitarian considers it identical with her own faith—and the rabbi proudly views this interpretation as praise. The same attitude is evinced in the opposition of some Reform circles to the attempt to organize Orthodox religious life in New York under Rabbi Jacob Joseph, who was brought over to the United States in 1888 to serve as chief rabbi of the Orthodox community. The *Jewish Tidings*, a weekly appearing in Rochester, New York, and closely identified with the Jewish Reform group of that city, urged that Rabbi Jacob Joseph "go back to the land that gave him birth." When taken to task for this position, the editor of the weekly replied:

> Rabbi Joseph is unfamiliar with the language of this country and is there-fore unfitted to exercise authority, or influence over American Jews. The Jews of this country do not need a Grand Rabbi and one from a foreign country; one who is reared among the prejudices and bigotries of the Eastern countries will certainly prove an obstacle to the people over whom he is expected to exercise control.[20]

Philipson's memoirs confirm the fact that in form and content the more radical Reform temples resembled liberal Christian churches far more than traditional synagogs. We will yet see that the situation has changed drastically in recent years, but even today it is still difficult to recognize Reform temples which have retained the spirit of the late nineteenth century as Jewish houses of worship. Here, for instance, is what Leonard Bloom reported on the basis of his research in a city which he calls "Buna": "Protestants who visit the Temple say they recognize little difference between its services and those which they attend in their own churches." [21]

The difference between one Protestant denomination and another was certainly not as great as that between Orthodoxy and Reform dur-ing the period under discussion. In some respects, the difference be-tween Orthodoxy and Reform was greater even than that between

Protestantism and Catholicism. Two facts can be cited as measures of the distance between late nineteenth-century Reform and the traditions of Judaism: (1) The Central Conference of American Rabbis resolved, at one of its conventions, that a Gentile who desired to be converted to Judaism need not be circumcised; (2) the same convention declared that it was not necessary for a Jew to be buried in a Jewish cemetery. These decisions touched on two of the most fundamental elements in Jewish religious symbolism. Judaism without circumcision and without Jewish burial is like a wheel without an axle to the traditional Jew.

Such was indeed the visage presented by the Judaism of the radical Reform wing led by Rabbi David Einhorn, who began his career in America as spiritual leader of Temple Har Sinai in Baltimore and later removed to Temple Emanu-El in New York. A conference held in Philadelphia in 1870, under Einhorn's influence, declared that the dispersion of the Jews was an act of God designed to enable the Jews to realize "their high priestly mission, to lead the nations to the true knowledge and worship of God." It was the Messianic task of the Jews, the declaration continued, to achieve "the unity of all the children of God in the confession of the unity of God, so as to realize the unity of all rational creatures and their call to moral sanctification." [22]

This article of faith contains nothing that cannot apply equally to any other religion. On the basis of such conceptions of Judaism, the *Jewish Tidings* of Rochester was fully justified in proposing that the Jewish Sabbath be changed from Saturday to Sunday since "it matters little to a just and merciful God on what day His worshippers see fit to bow before Him." [23] It was not long before the *Tidings* proposal became a general practice in all Reform temples in the United States. Only in recent years has this practice been abandoned, as will be shown later.

Apropos of the "Priestly Mission" of the Jews, it is worth citing the remark of Adolph Krause, an important leader of the American Jewish community during the early twentieth century. For two decades, he recalled, he was president of the Reform Temple Isaiah in Chicago, but that he was a *Cohen* (a member of the traditional priestly caste) became known to his children only upon the publication of his memoirs in 1925.[24]

LANGUAGE DIFFERENCES

Parallel with the religious division there was also, in the early years, a linguistic division among the Jewish immigrants. They brought with them a babel of tongues, which only served to accentuate the fragmentation of the Jewish people in the United States. Aside from the dozens of languages spoken by Jews as individuals—in addition to Hebrew, which in one form or another was common to all the Jewish groups—there were five languages, excluding English, which Jews as organized communities used. These were Spanish, Portuguese, German, Yiddish, and Ladino.

The language current in the early years among the Sephardic Jews was Spanish-Portuguese (for our purposes, these can be considered as one). Portuguese was taught in their schools; it was also the language they used at Jewish communal gatherings. Synagogal affairs, other than the liturgy (which was exclusively in Hebrew), were conducted in Portuguese. The first sermons introduced into Sabbath and holiday services were also in that language.

But the Sephardim did not hold to their own language for very long; they soon adopted English entirely. It was otherwise with the Germans. For them, German was not only their everyday social and secular language but their religious language as well. Their prayers and the rabbis' sermons were in German. As late as the 1880's, David Philipson was invited to take the Reform pulpit in Baltimore because he included among his other qualifications a mastery of the German language.

German Jews were ardent partisans of German culture and were assiduously devoted to championing it and maintaining its vigor on these shores. Isaac Mayer Wise himself founded general German culture associations, first in Albany and later in Cincinnati. The German Jews established a Jewish press in German and gave the language much attention in the schools they maintained for their children. In 1846, Congregation Beth Ahavah in Richmond advanced, among other justifications for opening a religious school, the argument that "a number of German Israelites . . . [were] desirous that their children should obtain a grammatical knowledge of the German language, which at present they only learn by routine and without principles." [25] The early

Jews from Germany, like the rest of the Germans in their days, remained strongly attached to German culture and sought to enhance its position in this country.

We shall discuss the role of Yiddish in greater detail later. The cultural life created in the United States in the Yiddish language was truly an extraordinary achievement. It is worth recalling, in order to regain a fresh image of the widespread scope of the Yiddish language in the United States, the statistics provided by the 1940 Census. One and three-quarter million persons listed Yiddish as their mother tongue; of them, 924,440 were immigrants, 773,680 were native-born Jews, one or both of whose parents were immigrants, and 52,980 were native-born children of native-born parents.

Ladino played no significant role in Jewish life in this country. It was the language of a number of Levantine and Balkan Jews, and a weekly in Ladino still appeared in 1950. In addition to the above-mentioned languages—and the English-Jewish press, which is a subject in itself—Jewish periodicals also appeared in Hebrew, Hungarian and Polish. Each of these languages represented a separate circle in the Jewish communal structure, and each circle existed within its own unique spiritual framework. A similar cultural edifice is not to be found in any other ethnic group in the United States.

INSTITUTIONAL DISUNITY

Jewish institutionalism was one of the most important factors making for Jewish group cohesion in the United States. But general, community-wide Jewish institutionalism did not become consolidated until around the time of World War I; previously, it too reflected the fragmentation characteristic of all of Jewish collective endeavor here.

The foundation of Jewish institutionalism was, and to a considerable degree has remained, the synagog. For the Sephardim, the synagog was actually the sole center of all their Jewish social activities. Through the synagog they met all their obligations to the Jewish community and all their charitable objectives. When a number of rich Jews in Newport, R.I., founded a men's club in 1761 for purposes of entertainment, they wrote into its constitution a provision imposing a fine on members guilty of discussing synagog affairs at the club. It is only by the 1830's that we find a Sephardic communal institution in New York function-ing outside the synagog's purview.

The Sephardic Jews had displayed a contemptuous attitude toward Ashkenazic Jews even in the lands of their emigration. The Jewish population of Amsterdam, for example, was a small one, but it was nevertheless divided into two communities, each with its own synagog, rabbi, school, cemetery, etc.; and the two communities rarely came in contact with each other. The Sephardim imported this attitude into America; and although the Ashkenazim were certainly by the end of the eighteenth century a majority in the community, the Sephardim held the reins of Jewish communal leadership firmly in their own hands and effectively prevented the German and Polish Jews from a share in that leadership. This explains why all five synagogs operating in the Revolutionary period maintained the Sephardic ritual.

The Sephardim also brought with them an iron discipline in syna-gogal affairs. They were inflexible not only about traditions and cus-toms, but about communal authority as well. The leaders of the Sephardic synagogs ruled in a dictatorial manner. They imposed the strictest fines for the least infringement of the regulations they estab-lished. The constitution of K.K. Beth Elohim, in Charleston, S. C., imposed severe penalties and sanctions on newly-arrived Jews who failed to join the synagog within a specified time; moreover, it made the following provision for members of the synagog who were aware of such derelictions and failed to report them to the synagog author-ities:

. . . And if any person under the jurisdiction of this Congregation be guilty of such an atrocious offense, as either to be concerned, aid, or assist as aforesaid, he shall on sufficient proof thereof before the Private Adjunta [appointed by the President], forfeit all his rights and privileges in this Congregation, and be subject to a fine not exceeding two hundred dollars; and such offender or offenders shall never be reinstated into his or their rights and privileges, and moreover be deprived of the right of burial inside of the Beth Haim [cemetery] until he or they by themselves, executors, or administrators, relations, or friends, pay up and settle the fine that may be inflicted. And any person or persons placing themselves into such a predicament, shall incur the penalty, inasmuch as the same, either in joy or in sorrow, shall extend to the whole family under his or their control or jurisdiction.[26]

Barnett Elzas was of the opinion that this type of stringency, so much at odds with American democracy, was responsible for the revolt in that congregation, led by Isaac Harby in 1824, that subsequently resulted in the founding of the first Reform congregation in the United States. In this I believe Elzas was mistaken, for the process of synagogal regrouping was in any event inevitable. The Ashkenazim were bound to revolt as they did. In 1825, a group of Ashkenazic Jews split off from Congregation Shearith Israel in New York—the oldest synagog in America and still clinging to the Sephardic ritual—and founded Congregation B'nai Jeshurun. Later the founders of B'nai Jeshurun began to deal just as highhandedly with Jews of less prestige and lower socio-economic status as the Sephardim had dealt with them and thus brought in further cleavages.

Even the most democratic conduct on the part of synagog leadership would not have averted splits—first, because of the growth of the Jewish population, and second, because of the radical changes that came to be introduced into the liturgies. Until the second quarter of the nineteenth century, the largest Jewish community in the United States was not so populous as to require more than one synagog. Later, the German Jews, like the Sephardim, were guided in the establishment of synagogs more by the land of their origin than by their birthplaces. The East European Jews introduced something new into congregational organization: they established *schulen* on the *landsmanschaft* principle, leading to extreme synagogal fragmentation in the United States. Every institution that was founded in or around the *landsmanschaft* synagog became an independent principality, as it were.

While a great variety and number of synagogs would in any case have come about, the duplication of charitable institutions was the direct result of the social barriers dividing one Jewish group from another. Until 1825, the whole of American Jewish philanthropic work was under the leadership of the Sephardim. They themselves were in no need of charity, and the little amount required for disbursal in Europe, Palestine or for the needy in this country could easily be collected within their synagogs. Later, however, they were forced to expand this activity; in 1822, they founded the Hebrew Benevolent Society in New York and distributed through it the help that was not channeled through Congregation Shearith Israel. One may presume that the Society's clients were needy Ashkenazim who must certainly have felt uncomfortable under its wings.

For the poor Ashkenazim, most of whom came from rural German areas, the problem of charity was considerably more serious, one with which the synagog alone could no longer cope. Several years after the B'nai Jeshurun group broke off from Shearith Israel, Anshe Chesed split from the former, and later Shaarey HaShomayim broke off from Anshe Chesed, etc. As a result, it was inevitable that the number of philanthropic societies should greatly increase. The scope of the Hebrew Benevolent Society was too small, its leadership was too tightly knit, and its spirit too narrow; so the German Jews of New York founded the German Hebrew Benevolent Society in 1844.

The Sephardim responded by isolating themselves even further. Thus, until far into the nineteenth century, Shearith Israel refused its cemetery for the burial of poor Jews who did not belong to the synagog. In this, the Congregation followed the same principle it applied to charity for the living: Jews must concern themselves for the needy of their own circle and not apply for help to Jews who belonged to other groups. The very name of the German Hebrew Benevolent Society signifies that the German Jews adopted the same principle for their own charitable enterprises. The constitutions of a number of the charitable organizations they founded initially forbade help to Jews from eastern Europe. A special concern of the German Jews was that their charitable activities should not serve as a spur to East European Jewish immigration to the United States. In fact, they utilized every means, not always soberly considered, to discourage this immigration. In 1874, the Board of Delegates of American Israelites boasted that it had succeeded in stemming the tide of Jewish immigration from eastern Europe. This illusion was soon enough dispelled, and it must be said that, when confronted with a truly formidable challenge, the German Jews abandoned their philanthropic isolationism and provided every possible aid to the Jews from Russia, Poland, and other East European countries. But this relates to a later chapter and does not vitiate the historical fact of segregation in the field of early Jewish institutionalism.

The East European Jews did not wait long to build their own institutions. Because of their vast numbers and the many lands and innumerable towns and regions from which they came, they carried the *landsmanschaft* principle to its logical conclusion and shattered Jewish institutional life into countless subdivisions. It was only during World War I that a unified network of charitable, cultural and social service institutions began to arise out of these subdivisions.

The fragmented institutions did not develop as parts of any general plan. Almost all of them were improvised to meet specific needs and, as a result, virtual chaos reigned, further exacerbating the strained relations among the various Jewish groups.

4 Jewish Accommodation to Life in America: General Considerations

Everything we have learned thus far about the origins of the Jewish community in the United States leads to the inescapable conclusion that it must have been very poorly prepared to cope with the onslaught of American assimilation.

The fateful nature of Jewish wandering, its family character, and the impossibility of return to the old country combined to confront Jewish immigrants from the outset, more than any others, with the problem of integration into American life. This in itself could only strengthen the influence of assimilatory factors upon them. Utilitarianism should certainly have accelerated the tendency toward adaptation in such a group and should have resulted in the consequences of adaptation as they affected other ethnic groups. The Jews should also have displayed less resistance to the tyranny of the majority. And when a group is as divided on every level of social and ethnic life as the Jews were, it should have been an easy matter for the American melting pot to have completely absorbed it. If social differentiation, as has been noted, led to the disintegration of other ethnic groups, then it might have been expected that disintegration would proceed more quickly among Jews, who were socially fragmented when they first came here. But what has actually happened? Before we can answer this question, we must probe the economic aspects of Jewish adjustment in America.

IMMIGRANT OCCUPATIONS

Jewish immigration, especially in its vast East European phase, stemmed from countries whose governmental policy toward the Jews was based on oppression and discrimination. This policy was often openly directed toward the economic ruination and pauperization of the Jews, with the ultimate aim of forcing them to emigrate. The huge proportions of the mass immigration from eastern Europe, especially from Tsarist Russia, testify to the fact that these policies were in considerable measure successful. Immigration to America moved like a mighty torrent, sweeping away all barriers before it; Jews came first by the thousands, later by the tens of thousands, then by the hundreds of thousands. Some two million Jewish immigrants entered the United States from eastern Europe between 1879 and 1924, over one million of them in the one decade 1904–1914. Many public documents have described the dire poverty they left behind them. In this connection, it is revealing to examine the occupations cited by the Jewish immigrants when they arrived here, and those from which they derived their livelihood in the first years of their sojourn in this country.

Jewish immigration provided a high percentage of skilled workers. This was true both of the "old" immigration, in which Jews provided one and one-half times as many skilled workers as non-Jews, and of the "new" immigration, in which the proportion of skilled workers among Jews was four times that of non-Jews. But this should not be taken to mean that the living standards of the Jewish immigrants were higher than those of their non-Jewish neighbors. In the first place, American immigration statistics included artisans within the category of skilled labor. Under the conditions that prevailed in the East European countries, a handicraftsman would often toil harder and earn less than a wage worker. Then, too, there are grounds for believing that the number of skilled workers among the Jewish immigrants was considerably exaggerated: Jews without any particular occupation frequently referred to themselves as skilled workmen. Furthermore, nearly two-thirds of the Jewish immigrants who registered as skilled laborers were concentrated in the production of clothing which, during the last quarter of the nineteenth century and the first years of the twentieth in Tsarist Russia, was far from being among the best-paying industries.

Since nearly 40 percent of all Jewish artisans in the Russian Pale at the end of the nineteenth century worked in the clothing industry, it is no wonder that so many of them took to the needle trades upon arrival in this country. The low wages they earned here at the beginning of this century are revealed in a table constructed by the Congressional Commission on Immigration, which from 1908–1912 investigated the wages of male workers, eighteen years of age and older who were resident in the country less than five years and were employed in the clothing industry.

Table 3.—Percentage distribution of foreign-born adult male clothing workers, 18 years of age and over, residing in the United States less than five years, by race and weekly earnings.[1]

RACE	UNDER $10	$10 TO $15	$15 AND OVER
Hebrew (not Russian)	33.9	42.2	23.9
Hebrew (Russian)	39.1	39.9	21.0
Russian	35.3	46.8	17.9
Lithuanian	40.2	49.8	10.0
Italian, North	45.3	45.3	9.4
German	40.0	51.4	8.6
Italian, South	57.6	33.9	8.5
Polish	37.4	54.1	8.5
Bohemian and Moravian	35.5	57.0	7.5

Despite the higher purchasing power of the dollar at that time, the fact that from one-third to two-fifths of the foreign-born Jewish tailors earned less than ten dollars a week during the early years, and that between 75 and 80 percent of them earned less than fifteen dollars a week, provides a clear picture of the poverty that characterized the life even of those immigrants who had a trade.

The number of Jewish immigrants who had no trade or specific occupation was quite high. It was, as a matter of fact, one and one-half times greater than among the non-Jewish members of the "old" immigration and nearly twice as great as among non-Jewish immigrants who entered the country in the period, 1899–1909.[2] Of necessity many Jews became peddlers after they arrived here. It is interesting to note that, in this particular, there was little difference between the German-Jewish immigrants of the mid-nineteenth century and the East European Jewish immigrants of the late nineteenth and early twentieth centuries. Grinstein estimated that perhaps 30 percent of the Jewish immigrants in New York around 1850 were peddlers. And he added this comment: "If these men had known any craft, they would at least have attempted to follow their vocations. Since they did not do so, we may assume that they had had no training in any craft whatever." [3] Rabbi Joshua Trachtenberg presented the following figures on the proportion of peddlers in the Jewish community of Easton, Pa., during the "old" immigration: in 1840, they constituted 46 percent of the Jewish breadwinners; in 1845, 70 percent; in 1850, 50 percent; in 1855, 59 percent. From that point on, the number of peddlers declined sharply, until by 1880 they constituted no more than 3 percent of the Jewish gainfully employed in the city.[4]

There are no statistics on peddling among the "new" immigrants, but the vast literature that has arisen about this aspect of economic adjustment attests to the very large number of Jews engaged in this occupation.

INITIAL RESPONSE TO PROCESSES OF INTEGRATION

Two clear tendencies can be discerned in the acculturation of the American Jews: (1) in some respects it assumes forms similar to the processes of integration that mark the acculturation of other ethnic groups, but proceeds at a more rapid tempo; (2) in other respects it diverges from these processes and takes on unique forms. An analysis of both tendencies is indispensable to an understanding of the development of the Jewish community in the United States; and such an analysis must proceed from certain demographic facts.

It is impossible to ascertain the precise number of Jews in the United States. Harry S. Linfield's figures, which for a quarter of a century were accepted as a basis for estimating the size of the Jewish population, and according to which there should be some six million Jews in the United States today, have proved to be without substance and have been discarded by all students of Jewish demography in the United States. On the basis of all available surveys of American Jewish communities Ben B. Seligman and Harvey Swados placed the Jewish population at 4,500,000 in 1948.[5] The compilers and others have subsequently revised the figures upward. Alvin Chenkin, using as his source a survey of 740 communities and data derived from a study of the population in New York City conducted by the Health Insurance Plan (HIP) in 1952, estimated that there were about 5,000,000 Jews in the United States in 1955.[6] Examining the same HIP figures, Henry Cohen, in a study prepared for the Federation of Jewish Philanthropies of New York, arrived at the conclusion that there were 2,050,000 Jews in New York City in 1955.[7] This figure is confirmed by a subsequent survey carried out under the auspices of the same agency, which placed the Jewish population of New York at 2,114,000 (2,579,000 if Nassau, Suffolk, and Westchester counties are included).[8] Since New York City is estimated to have 40 percent of American Jewry, this would make the total Jewish population in the United States 5,285,000. According to a survey conducted by the magazine *Catholic Digest* of St. Paul, Minn., there were 3,500,000 Jews 18 years old and over in 1952, indicating a total Jewish population in the country at the time of 5,000,000.[9]

We also have the sample survey of the religious identification of the American civilian population taken by the U.S. Bureau of Census in March, 1957, on the basis of which there were at the time 3,900,000 Jews in the country 14 years old and over.[10] Allowing for accretion from abroad and natural growth in the last few years, we would be safe in placing the American Jewish population at between 5,250,000 and 5,500,000 at the beginning of 1960.

The Jewish population grew by leaps and bounds until World War I and resumed its growth in the early 1920's. The increase slowed down substantially, if it did not altogther cease, in the 1930's and early 1940's. This was the result of two factors: (1) Jewish immigration was drastically cut, and (2) the natural increase fell sharply, so much so that, had the situation continued, America Jewry would have entered a period of rapid decline. However, the trend has been reversed since World War II.

Reflecting general conditions in the United States, the Jewish family has been rising in size since the mid-1940's. Even so, the Jewish family is still smaller than the non-Jewish, and the birth rate among Jews is still lower than among the general population. In addition, the Jewish population is aging at a faster pace than the American population as a whole. The HIP study shows that the proportion of Jews in the age group of 45 and over was higher in New York City than the proportion of non-Jewish whites in the same category, while the proportion of children was lower among Jews than among the general white population. The median Jewish age was 35.5 years compared with 33.5 years for the non-Jewish white population, with the average Jewish household consisting of 3.1 persons as against 3.2 persons for the average non-Jewish white household. The size of the Jewish family in the country as a whole was probably somewhat lower than in New York, while the average family in the total population consisted of 3.5 persons in 1950.

That the birth rate among Jews continues to lag behind that of the general population is shown in the following table compiled by Ben B. Seligman:

Table 4.—Fertility ratio of Jewish and general white populations (1950 Census) of selected cities [11]

	Children under 5 per 1000 females age 20–44		Children under 5 per 1000 persons 20–54	
	JEWISH	GENERAL	JEWISH	GENERAL
Los Angeles	450.0	408.0	160.0	159.0
Newark (city)	—	406.0	134.1	159.0
Newark (suburbs)	—	428.4	189.1	164.2
Miami	380.0	391.0	147.4	152.2
Passaic	362.6	391.0	139.5	153.0
Atlanta	—	407.0	120.8	166.0
New Orleans	496.5	447.6	186.0	199.0
Trenton	412.8	419.0	158.2	163.0

	Children under 5 per 1000 females age 20–44		Children under 5 per 1000 persons 20–54	
	JEWISH	GENERAL	JEWISH	GENERAL
Portland	387.7	461.0	139.3	179.0
Camden	354.6	468.0	138.0	196.0
Indianapolis	399.8	484.0	147.9	192.0
Utica	395.3	462.0	142.1	181.0
Gary	575.9	501.0	202.2	193.0
Port Chester	435.0	452.0	163.2	179.0

The Jewish population is becoming more and more native in the United States. The ratio between American-born and foreign-born Jews in the cities studied before World War II is given in Table 5.

Table 5.—Percentage of American-born and foreign-born Jews in 10 cities studied before World War II

CITY	BORN IN THE U.S.	FOREIGN-BORN
Buffalo	64.1	35.9
Chicago	55.0	45.0
Cincinnati	62.0	38.0
Minneapolis	60.1	39.9
New London	64.3	35.7
Norwich	64.0	36.0
Passaic	62.0	38.0
Pittsburgh	61.8	38.2
San Francisco	56.2	43.8
Trenton	65.7	43.3

For the communities that were studied since World War II we have the following figures: Los Angeles—68 percent of the Jewish population native-born; Newark (city)—69 percent; Newark (suburbs)—78 percent; Passaic—70 percent; New Orleans—83 percent; Port Chester—74.6 percent. We may safely assume that the native-born sector comprises at least 75 percent of the total number of Jews in the United States, with the percentage somewhat lower in New York City and higher in the rest of the country.

The proportion of American citizens among foreign-born Jews is also very high; higher, in fact, than among most immigrants who arrived since the turn of the century. However, the difference between Jews and non-Jews in this regard is not as wide as it would seem. All immigrant groups tend toward increasing nativization and naturalization, and the tempo among Jews is not much faster than among others.

URBANIZATION

Urbanization as a process has affected both Jews and non-Jews, although in considerably differing degrees. There has always been a steady march from farm to city in the United States. In 1880, when the massive East European Jewish immigration began, only 29.5 percent of the population lived in cities; 70.5 percent lived in rural areas (places with a population below 2,500). In 1940, 56.5 percent lived in cities and only 43.5 percent in rural areas; in 1950, nearly 65 percent of the total white population lived in urban areas. We have already seen that the vast majority of the ethnic groups settled in the large cities. Some statistics should be cited in order to compare the degree of urbanization of Jews and that of other immigrants and their native-born children. Unfortunately, we only possess figures for two generations; but since the bulk of the Jewish immigration has been here only three generations, a comparison is possible.

In 1950, there were 33,750,653 persons in the foreign stock category of the United States Census, which includes immigrants, native-born children of immigrants, native-born Americans with one parent born here and the other an immigrant. Five out of six foreign-born whites lived in urban centers at the time, compared with three out of four in 1920. The figures for the the native-born children of foreign or mixed native-foreign parentage were not much different, according to the 1950 census. In 1920, 69 percent of all the persons in this category lived in the urban centers; in 1950 the percentage rose to 80.[12] With the exception of the Norwegians, there is not a single group in the foreign stock sector that is less than two-thirds urbanized. But even the Norwegians are moving toward greater urban concentration. Thus the foreign-born among them were divided 47.2 to 52.8 percent between urban and rural areas in 1920, whereas in 1950 the percentage stood

67.4 in the urban centers and 32.6 in the rural areas. The native-born in this group who were only 34.6 urbanized in 1920, showed an urbanization degree of 57.7 percent in 1950.

It is significant that in respect to urbanization it makes hardly any difference what part of Europe the groups stem from. The process affects them all, as it does the entire American population, Yankees as well as ethnic minority groups, natives as well as immigrants. In general, it can be stated that the farther removed a group is from the majority-type, in the ethnic and/or religious sense, the greater its urbanization.

Jews are the most urbanized group in the country, a natural and understandable phenomenon for a group that came here with a highly urban background in the first place. However, they are no exception so far as the general trend is concerned; and even with 98 percent of them in the cities, the disparity in the tempo of their urbanization is not very great when compared with other specific ethnic groups.

The same can be said of Jewish concentration in a small number of large cities. In 1955, some 40 percent of the entire American Jewish population lived in the city of New York; 75 percent lived in 14 communities. But here too we are dealing with a difference in the tempo of the process of urbanization, rather than in the process itself. When we compare Jewish concentration in several large cities with the general population distribution, the difference is overwhelming. But if we compare it with that of a number of other ethnic groups, the difference, though still very great, may not be nearly so one-sided. The 1940 Census shows that in the cities of New York and Chicago, where one-half of the American Jewish population lived, there were also to be found 15 percent of the Germans of foreign stock, 29 percent of all Italians, 25 percent of all the Irish (from the south of Ireland), 26 percent of all the Poles (the rubric, "Poles," presumably included a great number of Jews). About one-fifth of the entire Greek immigrant population in the country lived in New York City. And this was more or less true for group after group: a tendency toward concentration in a small number of great cities was revealed among them all, especially among the "new" immigrants. Nearly 70 percent of the over ten million foreign-born persons counted in the 1950 Census lived in the large cities of California, Illinois, Massachusetts, Michigan, New

York, Ohio and Pennsylvania, seven states that accounted for the overwhelming majority of America's Jews.

Jews have joined the march toward the suburbs which has assumed mass proportions since the end of World War II. No conclusive statistics are available, but all indications point to a degree of concentration among the Jews in the new areas, which is greater than among non-Jewish suburbanities, confirming the thesis that where Jews move in the direction of the country as a whole, they usually move at a faster pace.

Naturally, the quantitative difference is sufficiently great to arouse qualitative repercussions which are still to be discussed. But it is important to bear in mind that Jews are moving in the same direction as the population at large. This fact becomes particularly clear when we consider the economic dynamics of the American Jewish settlement: at no time did the latter swim against the current.

Like others, the vast majority of Jews began the social climb at the bottom of the ladder, although they were able to ascend more quickly and even skip some rungs occasionally. Other groups were transformed into an urban element only in the United States; the Jews, as noted, were already an urban element when they arrived. They were consequently able to save time, and they displayed a greater capacity to adapt themselves speedily to economic fields which lay on the main line of material progress in their new country. Nathan Reich puts it this way:

> American Jews in search of employment obviously needed to congregate in those areas of economic enterprise which were expanding most rapidly. . . . The fortunate circumstance that American economy was ready to receive what the Jew had to offer, in the way of skill and services, was responsible, in no small measure, for the solid achievements of the Jewish immigrants in their new American home.[13]

As we have seen, economic expansion in America has always been bound up with increasing urbanization. This provided an opportunity for the Jews sometimes to be the first to penetrate new economic areas making for the growth of the country. This was true of the Sephardic Jews, who transported here the commercial relations they had already established in their old countries and were thus able to contribute substantially to the mercantile expansion of the colonies. It was also true of the German Jews, who took to trade and peddling. Peddling

94

has often been viewed with disdain and contempt; but viewed from the proper historical perspective, its true importance in mid-nineteenth century American expansion becomes more apparent. Thousands of frontiersmen and pioneers would have had to return to their original homes embittered failures had it not been for the peddlers, and later, the shopkeepers supplying necessary merchandise not available at the new points of settlement.

The East European Jews built an enormous needle trades industry at a time when the country required it. Today, when the general tendency is increasingly toward the professions and white-collar occupations, the Jews fall in line and are not infrequently in the vanguard of the procession.

5 The Jew and the Dynamics of American Society

ECONOMIC TENDENCIES

Broadly speaking, the economic life of the Jews in the United States can be considered under two headings: (1) meeting the needs of the Jewish population itself, and (2) participation in the country's general economic activity. It is clear that both aspects are intimately bound up with the general trends in America's economic development: the Jews would not have attained the economic status they now enjoy had they not entered fully into the mainstream of American economic dynamics.

As with all the other ethnic groups, the geographical concentration of the Jews proceeded concurrently with their economic concentration, but at a faster pace. Although the second wave of Jewish immigration, that of the German Jews, was geographically decentralized, the situation was different with the much larger third wave of immigration. Had it not been for their unusual concentration within the larger cities, especially New York, the massive proletarianization of the East European Jewish immigrants would not have been possible. The selfsame concentration, as we shall yet see, stimulated their drift away from the class of industrial workers. And just as their

97

proletarianization occurred during a period when the number of industrial workers multiplied enormously, so their de-proletarianization took place when the number of industrial workers either remained steady or was beginning to fall in proportion to the total number of gainfully employed persons. As a result of their urban character, the Jews were often able to discern the direction of economic tendencies at an early stage and swiftly adjust to them.

Mass immigration from eastern Europe may be divided into two periods. In the first period, which extended from 1870 to 1900, the immigrants were mostly artisans, unskilled laborers and economically déclassé elements. The second period witnessed the arrival of large numbers of skilled workers. Seventy percent of all breadwinners among the Jewish immigrants during the first quarter of the twentieth century were skilled workers, whereas the proportion of such workers in the general immigration of the period was only 20 percent.[1] Nevertheless, it is only up to the time of World War I that one may speak of increasing Jewish proletarianization in terms of growing numbers of industrial workers. Thereafter, a drift away from the shops began, leading at first to a relative decrease in the number of Jewish industrial workers, and later to an absolute decrease, in relation to the Jewish population as a whole. Nathan Goldberg has pointed out that in 1900, 59.6 percent of Jewish gainfully employed were in industry, but by 1930 the percentage was only 13.7. One-fifth of all Jewish earners were engaged in trade in 1900; by the 1930's, more than one-half were in trade. Of the gainfully employed Jews, there were nearly 3 percent in 1900 in the professions and 13 percent in the 1930's; the clerical occupations employed 6.7 percent in 1900 and 9.3 percent in the 1930's.[2] Although these classifications are not always exact, and though Goldberg based his estimates for 1900 mainly on the Russian Jews, his figures nevertheless do give a fair picture of the economic transformations in American Jewry during the first four decades of the twentieth century. On the basis of several studies in 72 cities, Goldberg constructed a table which gave an economic portrait of the American Jewish community at the time of World War II. The table covering 66 cities with a total of 913,276 Jewish breadwinners, included: (a) the 5 cities of New York, Detroit, Stamford, Worcester and New Orleans; (b) 61 other cities of varying sizes.

98

*Table 6.—Percentage distribution of gainfully employed Jews in 66
cities in the 1930's* [3]

OCCUPATIONS	61 COMMUNITIES OF VARYING SIZES	NEW YORK, DE-TROIT, STAMFORD, WORCESTER, NEW ORLEANS
Manufacturing	12.4	34.8
Trade	47.3	33.3
Professions	11.9	11.3
Clerical	15.7	—
Domestic & Personal	6.8	12.4
Public Service	2.9	2.6
Transportation, Communication	1.9	3.7
Other and Unknown	1.1	1.9
TOTAL	100.0	100.0

On the basis of virtually the same material, Lestchinsky prepared a
table which compared the occupational distribution of Jews and non-
Jews:

*Table 7.—Occupational distribution in percentages of Jewish and
general gainfully employed in 1940* [4]

OCCUPATION	% JEWS	% GENERAL
Trade	50.0	20.8 *
Industry	28.0	32.0
Professions	10.0	6.8
Domestic and Personal Services	6.0	10.3
Transportation and Communication	2.5	9.2
Agriculture	2.0	18.0
Public Service	1.5	2.9
TOTAL	100.0	100.0

* includes about two-thirds of the clerks.

The reader must be cautioned that while the figures for the general population are accurate, based as they are on the Census, the figures for the Jews are no more than estimates; however, these estimates have sufficient grounding in statistical material and careful personal observations to be regarded as a reflection of the real economic distribution of the Jewish community in the mid-1940's.

Surveys conducted since then all seem to confirm the pre-war conclusions that the economic mobility of the Jews follows the general trend at a more accelerated rate. Table 8 compares the occupational distribution of the Jews in the 15 cities studied after World War II with that of the non-Jewish population in the same cities, which had a total experienced labor force of 2,242,023 in 1950 and a Jewish civilian labor force of 187,699.

Table 8.—Occupational distribution of experienced civilian labor force in 15 cities [5]

OCCUPATION	General Population Except Jews, 1950		Jews (including Newark Suburbs)	
	NUMBER	%	NUMBER	%
Professional, Technical and Kindred Workers	198,064	9.6	30,584	16.3
Managers, Officials and Proprietors, except farm	172,481	8.4	62,355	33.2
Clerical, Sales, and Kindred Workers	480,494	23.3	55,760	29.7
Draftsmen, Foremen, and Kindred Workers	298,345	14.5	16,599	8.8
Operatives and Kindred Workers	421,849	20.4	11,026	5.9
Private Household and Service Workers	296,046	14.3	5,571	3.0
Laborers, except farm and mine	141,460	6.9	2,642	1.4
Others	13,220	0.6	581	0.3
Occupations not reported	42,068	2.0	2,581	1.4
TOTAL	2,064,027	100.0	187,699	100.0

According to the HIP survey, more than half of the Jews 15 years or over, 40 percent of the total Jewish population in the metropolis, were in the labor force in New York City in 1952. In the age group of 14–24 a smaller proportion of Jewish males was employed than non-Jews; but a higher proportion of Jewish males over 25 years old was employed than non-Jews in the same age level. The proportion of females employed was lower among Jews than among non-Jews. Over two-thirds of the employed Jews were in non-manual occupations compared with one-half of the non-Jewish white employed. "The Jews," Henry Cohen concludes, "are heavily represented in the professions, proprietor, managerial, sales and clerical categories. They are low in the craftsmen, operative and service categories." [6] Unlike the Jewish population of other cities, the Jews of New York retained a substantial number of skilled and unskilled manual workers. This category, representing 28 percent of the Jewish labor force, was second among the occupations in which New York Jews were engaged in 1952.

Impressive as the cited figures are, they still do not in themselves mirror all the changes that have been taking place in Jewish economic life since World War II. These changes are marked by a rise in the proportion of professionals and governmental employees among the Jewish breadwinners and a decline in the proportion of small tradesmen and lower white-collar workers such as clerks and salesmen. A comparison between ten communities surveyed during 1935–45 and fourteen communities surveyed during the period 1948–53 shows that the proportion of professionals has risen from 11 to 15 percent of the gainfully employed Jews in the course of a decade while the proportion of lower white-collar workers has dropped by ten percent.[7]

The proportion of non-manual occupations was more than twice as high among the Jewish gainfully employed in the 1935–45 group of communities than among the non-Jewish. Considering that the same ratio would probably obtain for the country as a whole, it becomes quite evident that we are dealing with a phenomenon of American Jewish economic life that represents a sharp *quantitative* divergence from the economic pattern of the population at large. But our problem is to discover whether this phenomenon is *qualitatively* in line with the country's general economic processes or is in conflict with them.

A bird's-eye view of the economic development of the United States during the years 1870–1940, as given in a table constructed by H. Dewey Anderson and Percy Davidson, will supply the answer insofar as the pre-World War II period is concerned.[8]

Table 9.—Number and percentage distribution of all gainful workers, male and female, by occupational categories—1870–1940

CATEGORY	1870	1900	1920	1930	1940	1940 OVER 1870
Agriculture	5,919,987	10,248,935	10,665,812	10,471,998	9,271,998	3,352,011
	47.3%	35.3%	25.6%	21.4%	17.5%	56.6%
Forestry and Fishing	53,196	177,035	270,214	250,469	270,469	217,273
	.4%	.6%	.6%	.5%	.5%	408.4%
Extraction of minerals	169,499	581,417	1,084,751	980,199	1,140,199	970,700
	1.4%	2.0%	2.6%	2.0%	2.2%	572.7%
Manufacture & Mechanical Industries	3,463,781	9,054,982	12,457,631	13,620,875	13,864,875	10,401,004
	27.7%	31.1%	29.9%	27.9%	26.3%	300.3%
Transportation & Communication	403,274	1,456,732	3,053,783	3,998,206	4,874,206	4,470,932
	3.2%	5.0%	7.3%	8.2%	9.2%	1,108.7%
Trade	573,574	2,232,771	4,418,751	6,277,574	7,277,574	6,704,000
	4.6%	7.7%	10.6%	12.9%	13.8%	1,168.8%
Public Service	70,367	260,392	897,024	1,218,257	1,518,257	1,447,890
	.6%	.9%	2.2%	2.5%	2.9%	2,057.6%
Professional Service	332,179	1,148,155	1,999,168	2,927,322	3,583,322	3,251,143
	2.7%	3.9%	4.8%	6.0%	6.8%	978.7%
Domestic & Personal Service	1,208,142	2,777,610	3,534,604	5,255,803	5,412,803	4,204,661
	9.9%	9.5%	8.5%	10.8%	10.3%	348.0%
Clerical Occupations	311,889	1,135,204	2,950,769	3,829,217	5,521,297	5,209,408
	2.5%	3.9%	7.1%	7.8%	10.5%	1,670.0%
TOTALS	12,505,923	29,073,233	41,614,248	48,829,920	52,735,000	40,229,077
	100.1%	99.9%	99.9%	100.0%	100.0%	321.7%

Anderson and Davidson arrive at this general conclusion: in 1870, three-quarters of all workers were engaged in the production of physical goods in agriculture, mines, factories, work-camps and the building industries. Only one-quarter of the workers were engaged in the professions, distribution, commerce, service, etc. By 1930, only one-half of the workers were employed in production; the other half were engaged in distribution, the service industries, the professions, white-collar occupations, etc.

In order to point up the significance of Table 9 in terms of American Jewish economic dynamics, we must consider several of the occupations separately.

1. The number of people engaged in agriculture, in which there are practically no Jews, is steadily decreasing. While the whole population tripled in size between 1870 and 1940, the absolute number of people engaged in agriculture increased by only 60 percent. But the proportion of such engaged people fell from nearly one-half of all gainfully employed in 1870 to less than one-sixth in 1940.

2. In absolute numbers the labor force in industrial enterprises increased 300 percent during this period, but in relative terms the proportion decreased from 27.7 percent of all gainfully employed in 1870 to 26.3 percent in 1940. Since a great number of Jews were engaged in small industry (and in a narrow sector of middle-sized industry), it is necessary to take a closer look at this category. The late Lewis Corey analyzed the colossal shifts that have occurred in the ranks of American breadwinners and pointed up the impact of this shifting process on the middle classes. On the basis of Census figures, he established that the number of industrial entrepreneurs (manufacturing, building and mining) was:

In 1870	47,500
" 1910	424,327
" 1930	390,924
" 1940	257,000 [9]

Between 1910 and 1940, the number of entrepreneurs decreased by more than one-third. Since industrial production has grown enormously during those thirty years, the figures testify to a vast development of trusts, which has crowded the small and medium

entrepreneur off the stage. This is of especial significance in an evaluation of the impact of this process on the industrial enterprises com-
monly identified with the Jewish population. The number of Jews
affected is quite small, since the clothing industry, in which Jewish
owners are heavily represented, has not thus far become a monopoly.
This industry still belongs to the category of small and medium-sized
capital, but for this very reason it is still far from stabilized. The
mortality rate of garment shops is very high. According to Joel
Seidman's estimates, the average life of a men's clothing firm by 1935
was seven years. Seidman conceded, however, that many of the
changes in the needle trades industries were not liquidations, but re-
organizations.[10]

Thousands of people formerly employed in the garment industries
—workers, contractors, jobbers and even employers—have entirely
abandoned the field; and despite the great expansion of these industries, they have attracted few Jews from other economic sectors.
This has resulted in the gradual diminution of the number of Jewish
owners in the needle industries, just as it has led to a drastic decline
in the number of Jewish workers in the needle trades.

The fact that growth of trusts has pushed only a relatively small
number of Jews out of industry should not be taken to mean that
it has had no effect on the economic status of Jews in America. Such
a conclusion would be false. In the first place, the number of Jewish
entrepreneurs displaced from industry is small only in the production
of wearing apparel. But American Jews were also involved in other
industries; and, as small and middle-sized entrepreneurs, they too
were affected by the concentration of capital. (We refer here only to
production and not to distribution.) In the second place, when an
enterprise has been absorbed by a trust, the former Jewish owner
rarely has found a place in it. At a later point, we shall learn that the
greater the concentration of capital, the smaller is the role of the
Jews in it.

3. The Marxian prediction that the middle classes would be wiped
out in the struggle between large capital and the proletariat has failed
of realization in certain sectors of the economy, just as it has proved
true in others. The Anderson and Davidson table shows that the
economic and social significance of trade has grown greatly in the
course of the last three-quarters of a century. In 1870, those engaged

in direct trade constituted 4.6 percent of all gainfully employed; by 1940, they were 13.8 percent. In other words: while the absolute increase between 1870 and 1940 was 60 percent in agriculture and 300 percent in industry—it was over 1,100 percent in trade. The number of people engaged in trade increased over 18 times more than the number in agriculture and nearly four times more than that in industry.

It is important to remember that the industrialization of the Jewish immigrants assumed mass proportions in the early twentieth century. However, that industrialization was not an automatic transplanting of old world economic functions. Jews did not, upon their arrival here, always take to the occupations they had pursued in their native lands, notwithstanding the great number of skilled workers included in the Jewish immigration. This can be seen, as noted earlier, in the great number of Jews who came here without specific occupations. This fact is also confirmed by comparing the economic structure of the Jewish population in Russia and in the United States at the beginning of the twentieth century. Goldberg has made just such a comparison.

In 1897, 30.9 percent of all Jewish breadwinners in Russia were engaged in trade; in 1900, in the United States, only 20.6 percent were so engaged. Nearly twice as many women wage earners were in trade in Russia as in the United States. Thirty-seven percent of all Jewish persons gainfully employed in the United States were engaged in the production of men's and women's clothing, shoes, caps and hats— while in Russia these occupations, augmented by textile work and the production of artificial flowers and similar articles, employed only 17.2 percent. In Russia, 16.1 percent were engaged in domestic and personal services; in the United States, exactly one-half this number.[11] Describing the background of the immigrants who became workers here, Hertz Burgin, the first historian of the Jewish labor movement in America, observed: "In the old country, these immigrants had belonged to various classes of the population. . . . Necessity levelled all of them [here], and the shop more or less infused them with a proletarian psychology." [12]

It is clear, therefore, that the contemporary widespread American Jewish involvement in trade, the professions and white-collar work arose in the United States. The substantial mercantile experience of the

Jews throughout the world, and their urban background, helped to prepare the Jewish immigrants for this development, which, it should be emphasized once more, coincided with the economic direction of the United States.

4. According to Anderson and Davidson, the category of professional and white-collar occupations has shown the greatest increase since 1870, both relatively and absolutely. In 1870, there were 332,179 persons—2.7 percent of all gainfully employed—engaged in professional services; in 1940, there were 3,583,322—6.8 percent of all gainfully employed—so engaged: an increase of nearly 1,000 percent. In 1870, there were 70,367 persons—0.6 percent of all breadwinners engaged in the public services; in 1940, the number rose to 1,518,257 or 2.9 percent: an increase of over 2,000 percent. In 1870, there were 311,889 persons—2.5 percent of the total labor force—in the clerical occupations; in 1940, there were 5,521,297—10.5 percent: an increase of nearly 1,700 percent. Corey cites even more striking changes in the status of professional and white-collar occupations, and he compares them with the shifts the working classes had experienced during the same period.

If the working class is taken to include industrial workers and farm laborers as well as workers in the home and personal services, its number grew from 6,035,000 in 1870 to 29,518,000 in 1940—so that relative to the total number of gainfully employed in the country, the working class has remained virtually stationary: it represented 53 percent of the total labor force in 1870, and 57 percent in 1940. But if we reckon only the industrial proletariat, a wholly different picture emerges. Although industrial workers represented 55 percent of the working class in both 1870 and 1940, this similarity provides no conception of the dynamics of industrial evolution. To gain an adequate conception, this seventy-year period must be subdivided into shorter periods. According to Corey's calculations, industrial workers represented—

55	percent	of	all	workers	in	1870
66	"	"	"	"	"	1910
67	"	"	"	"	"	1920
62	"	"	"	"	"	1930
55	"	"	"	"	"	1940

The import of these figures is clear: the relative weight of the industrial proletariat within the American working class rose until 1920 and fell in subsequent years. Corey sums it all up in the following words:

> This relative shrinkage in the proletariat appears clearly from another angle: as a proportion of all gainfully occupied persons the industrial workers rose from around 30 per cent in 1870 to 37 per cent in 1910 and 1920, falling to 34 per cent in 1930 and 31 per cent in 1940.[13]

What was happening meanwhile with the middle classes? While the working class multiplied sixfold between 1870 and 1940, the middle class (entrepreneurs, self-employed, white-collar and salaried employees) multiplied eightfold. And if we reckon only what Corey called the "new middle class"—professionals and salaried white-collar employees—the middle class multiplied sixteen times over.

What is the make-up of the new middle class, as Corey sees it? There are four general categories: (1) technicians, whose number increased forty times between 1870 and 1940 and stood at around 700,000 at the end of that period; (2) managers and supervisors, whose number grew from 121,380 in 1870 to 1,707,576 in 1940; (3) salaried professionals, who increased numerically from 204,305 in 1870 to 2,660,843 in 1940; (4) white-collar workers, whose number grew from 374,433 in 1870 to 7,606,522 in 1940. We shall soon see that each of the groups within the new middle class, and each of the sectors in the white-collar category, attracted masses of Jews.

How can we explain the vast professionalization and expansion of the white-collar occupations in the United States (and, incidentally, in all other industrially advanced countries)? Corey cites five factors: (1) the increasingly technical-scientific character of industry; (2) the increasing complexity of production and distribution, and the separation of ownership and administrative control; (3) the growing role of regulation, planning and supervision in industry; (4) the multiplication of goods, including the expanded production of luxuries and articles of convenience, and the need to provide greater amounts of leisure time; (5) the growth of the functions of government and public organizations and services. Anderson and Davidson provide, by way of statistical illustration, a simple explanation for the enormous growth in the number of clerks occupied in trade—an occupation which plays a considerable role in Jewish economic life: in 1870, only 5 out of every 100 workers were needed to dispose of manufactured goods and provide the necessary services for the business community; by 1940, 12 of every 100 workers were needed to fulfill this function.[14]

The trend that became so marked in 1940 continued after World War II as the following table clearly shows:

Table 10.—Experienced civilian labor force, U.S. 1950[15]

OCCUPATION	NUMBER	PERCENT
Professional, technical and kindred workers	4,988,963	8.5
Farmers and farm managers	4,322,809	7.3
Managers, officials, and proprietors, except farm	5,076,848	8.6
Clerical and kindred workers	7,071,283	12.0
Sales workers	4,044,251	6.9
Craftsmen, foremen and kindred workers	8,162,499	13.8
Operatives and kindred workers	11,708,022	19.8
Private household workers	1,488,388	2.5
Service workers, except private household	4,511,677	7.6
Farm laborers and foremen	2,514,843	4.3
Laborers, except farm and home	3,765,394	6.4
Occupation not reported	1,360,487	2.3
TOTAL	59,015,464	100.0

In 1940 there were 4,384,274 employed clerical and kindred workers in the United States; their numbers grew to 6,894,374 in 1950 for an increase of 57.3 percent, more than twice the percentage increase of the total number employed during the same decade. This group constituted 9.8 percent of all employed persons in 1940, and 12.3 percent in 1950. The number of employed sales workers also grew faster than the total number of employed, jumping from 3,075,086 in 1940 to 3,926,510 in 1950.[16]

In 1956, according to government statistics, the number of service workers for the first time surpassed that of the producing workers in this country. The number of gainfully employed persons increased by 7,300,000 since the war; of these almost 90 percent were in the "non-goods" area. The number of goods-producers has risen by only 825,000, a little over 3 percent, although production has increased by nearly 50 percent during the period. Factory workers now comprise only about a fourth of the gainfully employed people.[17]

These developments stem from the intensified urbanization and greater intellectual requirements of the American economy; the Jews were well situated to take advantage of both these factors.

JEWISH YOUTH AND EDUCATION

We have seen that all ethnic groups—even those that arrived here last and brought with them only a minimum of education—tended to move from less to more intellectualized occupations, that this tendency was a direct consequence of the acculturation of the immigrants and, more particularly, of their children and grandchildren. With the educational level of the general American population steadily rising, with the acquisition of higher education directly related to closeness to the larger cities, and with Jews carried by general processes at a faster pace than others, the proportionately greater attendance of Jews at high schools and colleges should come as no surprise to us. A few statistics will demonstrate that this is not an accidental, local or temporary phenomenon. As early as 1907, an investigation in New York City elicited facts which led the researcher to the conclusion that "when we come to a consideration of the secondary schools, we are struck with the large percentage of Jewish scholars and their relatively high rank, particularly in examination tests." [18] Similar studies conducted in Chicago and Philadelphia showed that the situation was the same in those cities. Thirty years later, Nettie McGill and Ellen Matthews, in their study of New York's youth, established that the children of Jewish foreign-born attended higher classes of school in greater numbers than non-Jewish children.[19]

Of great interest are the figures assembled for the period beginning with the mid-1930's. A survey made of the Jewish community in New Orleans, La., in 1953 affords a basis for comparing the educational level of Jewish youth 16 to 25 years old with that of the total white population of the same age range, showing that the standard of the former is considerably higher.

Table 11.—Level of educational achievement, Jewish and total white population, New Orleans, La., 1953 [20]

	Jewish 1953		Total White 1950	
	16–20 YEARS	21–25 YEARS	16–20 YEARS	21–24 YEARS
No formal Education	—	0.7	0.5	0.4
Elementary	—	0.7	20.6	18.5
High School	53.8	15.8	65.3	53.9
College	46.8	82.8	12.2	25.5
No answer			1.4	1.7

In Dallas, around 25 percent of the Jews whose period of schooling was at an end had completed college. In Pittsburgh, about 20 percent of the Jews who, at the time of the investigation, were under the age of thirty and had at one time or another attended an American school, had either attended or completed college, and 60 percent had completed high school. In Cincinnati, 14 percent of the Jews over the age of fourteen had completed college and 40 percent, high school. The surveys upon which these figures are based were made in the late 1930's and early 1940's. In the mid-1950's the same relation obtained. According to the HIP study, Jews had an educational median attainment of 10.3 school years in 1952 compared with a median 9.6 for non-Jewish whites. About 26 percent of the Jewish male population 25 years old and over attended college at one time or another compared with 16 percent of non-Jewish white males in the same age range. The corresponding figures for females was over 15 percent among Jews and 11 percent among white non-Jews.

A survey conducted in 1956 shows that in Washington, D.C., Jews had a higher level of education than the general population whose educational standard was also unusually advanced. For the country as a whole, we have reliable figures, compiled by the Vocational Service of B'nai B'rith, which show that in 1935, and again in 1947—when the Jewish community numbered little over 3 percent of the population in the country—Jewish students constituted some 9 percent of the total enrollment in the colleges and universities, a proportion nearly three times as great as that of the non-Jewish population.

Interestingly enough, a comparison between Jewish and all other students in respect to the professions for which they prepare themselves at schools demonstrates that in this area, too, Jews follow the general trend. Table 12 lists the main professions American students take up and shows that the pattern is the same among Jews and non-Jews.

Table 12.—Distribution of all students and Jewish students by major fields of study [21]

PROFESSION	PERCENTAGE DISTRIBUTION ALL STUDENTS			PERCENTAGE DISTRIBUTION JEWISH STUDENTS		
	1955	1946	1935	1955	1946	1935
Business Administration	16.5	20.1	11.7	23.6 *	30.3	21.9
Dentistry	1.2	1.0	2.0	1.8	2.5	5.8
Education	28.0	26.3	46.1	18.9	17.4	16.1
Engineering	19.8	22.7	11.7	17.6	16.9	8.9
Fine Arts	2.3	2.4	0.7	1.9	2.8	1.2
Law	3.3	4.3	7.9	8.2	6.1	22.3
Medicine	3.4	3.0	6.8	7.6	5.3	12.2
Pharmacy	1.7	1.9	1.7	5.2	3.2	4.5

* incomplete data, probably about 30 percent.

We see from this table that the professions registering gains among all students also scored gains among Jewish students. Business administration and engineering are in this category. On the other hand, we find such professions as dentistry, law and medicine losing ground in both columns in relation to the total number of students. In pharmacy there is hardly any change in the twenty-year period, and only in education does the trend diverge, with this profession proving much less attractive to the student body as a whole but slightly more attractive to the Jewish student. It may well be that as the non-Jewish student moves to other professions, he opens up new opportunities for the Jew in education, where discrimination, as we shall see, was formerly marked.

The latest study conducted by the same B'nai B'rith body discloses that the proportion of Jewish students in the colleges of the United States and Canada dropped from 9 percent in 1945 to 7.5 percent in 1955. The drop does not signify a decline in Jewish interest in higher education; it indicates, as the study points out, "that the Jewish college population may have reached its near saturation-point a decade or more ago," while the general population, being behind the Jewish, moved up at a faster rate during the past ten years. It is also possible that the Jewish population of college age did not score the same rate of increase as the general population. Be that as it may, the fact remains, as the latest study clearly demonstrates, that, in proportion to their numbers, Jews have at least more than twice as many students in the colleges as non-Jews. With 2.5 million out of a total non-Jewish population of 9.4 million in the college age group (18–21) enrolled in colleges compared with 200,000 Jewish students out of an estimated population of 325,000 in the same age group, we find that 62 out of every 100 Jews of college age are actually enrolled as against 27 out of every 100 non-Jews.[22]

Frank Lorimer and Frederick Osborn examined the educational achievements and capacities of the various ethnic groups from the point of view of the general cultural level in the United States and came to the conclusion that Jewish children displayed a higher degree of intelligence, and approached, in regard to educational attainment, the accomplishments of the "old stock groups." [23] This statement, made in 1934 and still retaining its validity, confirms the thesis that on the cultural ladder, too, the Jews skipped a number of steps. They are consequently not to be found on the rungs now occupied by other groups of the "new immigration" but rather close to the ones held by the so-called American "aristocracy."

Such a cultural status naturally has economic and social implications. Only very rarely will descendants of the "old stock" engage in hard physical occupations. They are the social leaders, the residents of Hill Street in Yankee City, viewed enviously by the residents of the "lower" City's streets. There is a Hill Street in every city, and everywhere it is populated by the selfsame social group—the so-called Nordics, especially the Anglo-Saxon elements. On the basis of a study conducted in the state of Connecticut, Koenig makes the following observation which applies to other states as well: Although the British-Americans "are decidedly a minority, they nevertheless still occupy first place in wealth, prestige and influence. They have greater opportunities for education and leadership; they are generally the element which sets the pace and is being emulated by others." [24]

In our introductory survey, we observed that the Anglo-Saxon elements are economically and socially the privileged group in the United States, and that all ethnic minority groups aspire to attain or approximate the status of the privileged group. In this endeavor, they rarely succeed. Although all ethnic groups tend to move to ever "higher" occupations, the Yankees themselves do not remain stationary, and so it is difficult to overtake them. The investigators of Yankee City sought to determine the rate of occupational mobility of the various ethnic groups there. Their conclusions are worth reproducing here because the conditions they describe are more or less comparable to those in other cities.

These are the occupational categories established by Warner, Srole and their associates:

Ia—unskilled labor
Ib—skilled factory
Ic—skilled craft
IIa—management-aid
IIb—management
III—professions [25]

On the basis of this division, the investigators worked out an index which represents the occupational composite of the various groups in Yankee City. The index for the Yankees in 1933 was 2.56, the over-all index for all the ethnic groups—the Irish, French-Canadians, Jews, Italians, Armenians, Greeks, Poles, Russians—was 2.42. The Jews had an index of 3.32 in 1933, as compared with 3.10 in 1913; this means that it took them 20 years to rise 22 steps on the occupational ladder. It took the Irish fully 43 years to make comparable progress—from 1850, when their index was 1.62, to 1893, when they attained an index of 1.84. The study arrives at this conclusion: "in the first decade year the Jews reach a much higher occupational status than do either the Irish or the French Canadians and are more mobile, occupationally, on the average, than are the latter groups." [26] These latter groups, it is worth recalling, are the Italians, Armenians, Greeks, Poles and Russians—groups with less of an urban background and a lower educational level than the Jews. The Jews initially began with a higher index, which again confirms the fact of their greater qualifications immediately upon their arrival in this country. We shall yet see that although the Jews have the highest occupational status in Yankee City —higher even than the Yankees—their social status is much lower than their economic position would appear to warrant. This very disproportion will serve as one of the keys to an understanding of the unique aspects of Jewish evolution in the United States. Meanwhile, we must examine further the similarity of the Jewish and general processes of development; the faster pace of Jewish development, to which we have already drawn attention, proceeds with the greatest acceleration in the professions and white-collar occupations.

OCCUPATIONAL MOBILITY

The American-born Jewish generations are displaying a greater tendency toward the more "intellectual" occupations than to trade.

The word "trade" gives a distorted view of the Jewish role in American commercial life. The term does not tell of the many little candy and delicatessen stores, the groceries and bakeries, the lunch counters and rooming houses, the newspaper stands and cigar stores where thousands of Jewish "business men" put in twelve to eighteen hours day in and day out, with no Sabbath or holiday the year round, and where they often earn no more, and sometimes less, than well-paid wage workers or salaried employees. In comparison with peddling, a lunch counter was considered progress before World War I and even later, and a restaurant represented economic advance over a soda stand. These little shops and stores, so very much a part of Jewish trade, did not fall victim to the general process of concentration of capital because they were subject to their own peculiar economic laws, on the basis of which no modern business enterprise could have survived. The Jewish delicatessen proprietor, butcher or candy storekeeper did not take into account his own time,

114

or figure that his wife and children should be paid for helping out in the store, or know of a normal working day, and often saved on rent by living behind his store. This kind of "economics" had nothing to fear from the trusts, particularly when the merchant dealt in kosher products. But times have changed and the old business ventures have lost much of their lure.

The Jewish immigrant's path moved from the peddler's bundle to petty trade. But his son and daughter reveal small inclination to tread that path. This trend is summarized by Nathan Goldberg in the following words: "Generally speaking, American-born Jews do not want to be grocers or proprietors of candy, cigar or other retail stores." [27] Goldberg arrives at this conclusion on the basis of an analysis of Jewish economic dynamics since 1900, and his view is substantiated by every study that has been made in the last two decades. Koenig, for instance, shows that in 1938, 575 Jewish immigrant breadwinners in Stamford, Conn., included as many self-employed as 859 native-born breadwinners.[28] Bessie Bloom Wessel, in another study made in Connecticut, notes that while 54.5 percent of the 326 Jewish earners in New London were self-employed in 1938, in nearby Norwich, with a greater immigrant population, 64.0 percent of the 315 Jews in business were self-employed.[29]

In Trenton, N.J., Sophia Robison found in 1937 that "the foreign-born Jews tended to concentrate in trade to a much greater extent than the native group." [30] At about the same time, Lena Meyers studied the occupational tendencies of a group of 2,272 foreign-born Jews and another group of 2,313 native-born Jews in New London, Stamford and Staten Island. The former included twice as many persons engaged in industry as the latter, and the latter included three times as many persons in the professions as the former. It is interesting to note that 62.2 percent of the foreign-born were in trade, as against only 53.0 percent among the native-born.[31]

This process has continued at an accelerated rate during and since World War II. Not only have Jews of the second and third generations manifested a greater predilection than their parents for the professions and white-collar occupations than for small trade, but they have also increasingly preferred wage earning in mechanical crafts to self-employment in struggling business enterprises. The 1953 survey of the Jewish population in New Orleans showed 60 percent of the foreign-born Jewish labor force to be engaged in wholesale-retail trade compared with 48 percent of the native-born. In the professional services the proportion was 10 percent for the foreign-born and 19 percent for the native-born.[32]

In sum, the Jews of the United States are in a particularly advantageous position to move with the current of general economic development in the country, which accounts for their moving with greater intensity and impetus than other ethnic groups. They did not create the general current and could not change its course even if they so desired, but they were better prepared than others to navigate it. Thus we must conclude that in economic status, as in other areas, the difference between the Jews and others lies not in the processes through which they have passed but in their capacity to inject themselves into the processes. In this sense, it can be demonstrated that the Jews have accommodated themselves more quickly than others to the vicissitudes of American life.

6 *Uniqueness of the American Jewish Community*

All the factors of Jewish accommodation in the United States have been such that, when operative among other ethnic groups, they have had a disintegrating effect. These factors should have had the same effect for the Jews, had their development been governed by the same "laws" as shaped the history of the other ethnic groups in this country. For one thing, their greater capacity for merging with the general economic stream and for swifter upward social mobility should have evoked a decidedly stronger urge to dissolve their group within the larger American society. At the same time, the extreme social, cultural and religious fragmentation of the Jewish community should have weakened its resistance to the pressure of disintegrating forces. Had the Jews followed the same lines of development as the other white ethnic groups in the United States, their assimilation should have been speedier and more complete.

Has this been the case? Have they indeed become assimilated faster than other groups? Are they becoming assimilated at least to the same extent as others? Is the Jewish group tending, in the course of time, to disappear entirely? The answer to all these questions is—No. And therein lies the uniqueness of the Jews in America. This makes the

Jewish community a singular phenomenon, unlike every other white ethnic group in the country. If this uniqueness persists, the Jews will prove to be the only ethnic group not to have lost its distinctive collective identity within the American melting pot.

Utilitarianism, the quick accommodation of the Jews to this country, their entry into business, their speedy absorption of American cultural patterns and the resultant high proportion of their share in "intellectual" occupations, their swift adoption of significant aspects of American mores and their acceptance of American forms of entertainment, their nearly uninterrupted economic progress—all of these factors that hastened the assimilation of all other ethnic groups, did they have no impact at all on Jewish group cohesiveness?

They did indeed, and a very great one at that. Many individual Jews dropped out of the community. It is impossible to determine their number, but there can be no doubt that it was quite large. Whole families defected from the Jewish camp. This can be seen from the great number of Jewish names borne by non-Jewish families. Most of the families that stemmed from the Spanish period and from the early German period are no longer in the Jewish community. There has at all times been a steady trickle of Jews who left the Jewish fold and disappeared without a trace. Because of this trickle, Grinstein thinks it possible that, had immigration been halted at the beginning of the nineteenth century, there would be no Jews in New York today. And if Grinstein has some doubts about New York, Julian Feibelman is quite certain about New Orleans. He writes:

> This much is certain, if the original Jewish community had had no increment of German and later, eastern European additions, there would be today no Jewish community in New Orleans.[1]

Some one hundred years ago, Isaac Mayer Wise, in a communication to Rabbi Leeser in Philadelphia, bemoaned the fact that Jews were leaving the House of Israel. "Of all the Jews who had emigrated to these shores," he wrote, "between 1620 and 1829, there were not two hundred families left that belonged to congregations, while the great majority had disappeared among the masses." [2] And this, he added, during a period when thousands of Jews came to America from Holland, England, Germany and Poland. An appeal for aid in building a synagog, addressed by a group of Cincinnati Jews to the Jewish community of Charleston in 1825, complained:

> We are well assured that many Jews are lost in this country from not being in the neighborhood of a congregation. They often marry with Christians, and their posterity lose the true worship of God forever.[3]

This transpired at a time when the American Jewish community was very small. But the trickle of defection was evident even later, when the community numbered in the millions. The number of mixed marriages, though it is still not large among Jews, has been steadily growing.

The Yiddish language, which in America produced a rich literature and a very significant culture, is steadily dwindling in importance. All the Yiddish daily newspapers and weekly periodicals outside New York have closed down; and in New York only two Yiddish weeklies and three dailies (including the insignificant Communist organ appearing in Yiddish) have survived. Not only are the remaining publications steadily losing circulation, but they are losing it at a faster rate than publications in other foreign languages do. For the two-year period of 1955–56 the Yiddish dailies had a combined circulation of 295,569 which represented 68.6 percent of the total Yiddish daily circulation in 1947–48 (430,906). During the same period the Polish dailies came down to 97.2 percent of their 1947–48 circulation, the Italian to 88.0 percent, and the New York *Staatszeitung und Herald* to 75.5 percent.[4]

The market for Yiddish books has virtually disappeared. The schools in which Yiddish was at the center of the curriculum are finding it more and more difficult to maintain their position in recent years. A number of them closed down chiefly because they were unable to attract enough students to warrant their continued existence—although, paradoxically enough, they were in better shape financially than at the time of their founding. Another reason for their liquidation has been the growing shortage of teachers. The element attending gatherings conducted in Yiddish has been steadily becoming older and less numerous. Of the score of Yiddish theaters that existed in this country at one time—and that was only two short decades ago—hardly one has remained. In the past third of a century, not a dozen Jewish writers in Yiddish have been produced by the younger generation of American

Jews—and this, despite the fact that one and three-quarter million persons listed Yiddish as their mother tongue in 1940. All these have indeed been heavy losses to Jewish ethnic life.

And yet, when we view these and other losses in the perspective of the previously analyzed distintegrating factors, we marvel not that the losses were so great but that they have been so few. As an ethnic community, the Jews of America have never before been so consolidated and enterprising. We have seen that among other ethnic groups communal activity within an ethnic framework was almost entirely immigrant activity, rarely second-generation and never third-generation activity. In the American Jewish community, on the other hand, the bulk of the leadership has passed into the hands of the second generation, with a third generation coming into its own and asserting itself. Even the fourth generation is beginning to play a not-insignificant role in Jewish leadership. One can still find communally active scions of families that settled here in the eighteenth century.

In 1936, the editors of *Fortune* asked: "Can this universal stranger be absorbed in the country which has absorbed every other European stock? Does he wish to be absorbed? Can he live happily and in peace if he is not absorbed? The answers must be guesses." [5] The very fact that the editors felt it was impossible to make a definite prognosis about the future of the Jews in the United States indicates that they had no doubts about the *present* status of the Jewish community. And no wonder: social scientists and scholars as well as practical communal leaders, Jewish and non-Jewish alike, are unanimous in observing that the Jews have revealed a stauncher sense of group identity and have thus far put up a more successful resistance to the external forces of assimilation than any other white ethnic group in the country's history. Varying interpretations and explanations of the fact may be given, but about the fact itself there are no differences of opinion among students of the subject. Jews are maintaining their ethnic identity—this is a reality. As for the future, there is general agreement that if the Jewish group ever disappears at all, it will take a very long time indeed.

Warner and Srole, on the basis of their classification of ethnic groups in the United States, attempt to estimate the amount of time it will take for the various groups to disappear. According to this classification, Jews are grouped into three categories: (a) those who stem from

England, (b) "light-skinned" European Jews, and (c) "dark-skinned" Jews from Europe and the Near East. If it can be expected that the first two groups will perhaps disappear in six or more generations, it is, in Warner's and Srole's opinion, even hypothetically impossible to predict how long it will take for the third category to disappear. Stonequist, citing the reasons for the remarkable vitality of the Jewish group, concludes that "it would be foolish to predict an early end to their group identity." [6] There are also social scientists who believe, correctly in my opinion, that in the light of existent social conditions in the United States and the present status of the Jews throughout the world, it is quite impossible for the Jews as a group to dissolve in this country.

If the Jews do remain the only identifiable white ethnic group, it is not impossible that they will become a kind of caste within the American social structure. As a matter of fact, there are those who hold that the Jews already resemble a caste. The status of the Jews, in Raymond Kennedy's view, is significantly different, on the one hand, from that of every other white ethnic group and, on the other hand, from that of racial caste groups such as the Negroes or Orientals. The "social location" of the Jews, Kennedy asserts, is "somewhere between that of the European immigrant groups, which we may designate as 'foreign ethnic classes,' and that of the racial groups, notably the Negroes, which are clearly castes." [7] Though he uses the concepts of "caste" and "class" in a very loose way, he does define correctly the social geography of the American Jewish community. From the standpoint of this geography, H. G. Wells had some ground to designate the Jewish districts of New York as a state within a state. But Horace Kallen is much closer to the truth when, partly agreeing with Wells, he adds that although the Jewish districts "are far more in tune with Americanism than other quarters, [they are] also more autonomous in spirit and self-conscious in culture." [8]

Kallen here penetrates to the very core of Jewish uniqueness in America. Jews retain their ethnic identity in the United States not because they cannot adjust to the country; on the contrary, they retain their identity in spite—Kallen would say precisely *because*—of their accommodation to American conditions of life. The Jews attain through accommodation and adaptation a degree of adjustment to and absorption in the life of the country which other ethnic groups achieve only through assimilation. Another way of putting it is this: for other groups, assimilation and isolation are alternatives, for the Jews they are concomitants.

This duality is the basis of Jewish acculturation and development in the United States. Our first task must therefore be to ascertain the sources of this duality and its concrete manifestations. Thereafter, we must clarify the way in which this duality is affected by the tendency toward integration of ethnic groups within the American social structure.

THE DUALITY OF JEWISH CULTURE

"The captivity of the Jews presents the spectacle of a whole people being transported bodily to a strange country and yet not only retaining but even purifying their religion because their prophets, priests and Levites had gone with them into exile; because they remained a separate entity even in captivity." In these words Roman Catholic Bishop Gerald Shaughnessy characterized the peregrinations of the Jewish people.[9] He failed to note that the Jewish people has, in the course of its history, been transported not just to one land but to many, and that the Jews were never allowed to remain in one place even as captives, but were continually forced to seek new homes. America became one of these homes.

When other groups emigrated, they were like leaves which social winds scattered to a foreign land; the tree from which they were blown remained rooted in the old territory. When Jews emigrated, it was not just leaves that were wind-blown, nor even branches, but whole segments of the tree. For from the time the Jews lost their national independence till the establishment of the State of Israel, the Jewish tree itself was uprooted. Immigrants of other nationalities sought new homes for themselves as individuals; Jewish immigrants were part of a people which was itself homeless. Others first became minorities in America; the Jews had for ages been a minority everywhere. For others, minority status was the exception; for Jews, the rule. The need to adjust to conditions of life in a strange country first became a problem for other groups only in America; for Jews, it was a problem they had

had to face uninterruptedly for many centuries. Others came to their new country with one culture; the Jews came with two, and frequently more than two, cultures. One culture—their own—they carried deep *within* themselves, within their spiritual and psychic being. The other they bore *upon* themselves, like an outer garment. Each time they trod new ground, they changed their outer garment, but always they succeeded in retaining at least in part their inner culture.

Thus the Jews were the only ethnic group which arrived in America with a past experience of being a minority; they were consequently able to skip that whole period of accustoming themselves to minority status which, as we have seen, demanded so much energy and caused so many physical and spiritual tribulations for other groups. I believe it was to this fact that Robert Park alluded in his introduction to Everett Stonequist's study of the marginal man. The marginal man, said Park, forced to live in two worlds and two cultures, absorbed much greater experience of life and displayed a more flexible and greater capacity for adjustment than the man who lived under normal conditions. Therefore, Park continued:

> The marginal man is always relatively the more civilized human being. He occupies the position which has been, historically, that of the Jew in the Diaspora. The Jew, particularly the Jew who has emerged from the provincialism of the ghetto, has everywhere and always been the most civilized of human creatures.[10]

Bearing in mind the definitions we have accepted of culture—as the sum total of man's spiritual values—and of civilization—as the sum total of his material acquisitions—we may say that the Jews were in a position to use their outer culture as a bridge to the civilization of others. The Jews were able to integrate themselves into the conditions of life of the countries in which they were a minority only through the language, social forms, and political processes of the majorities among whom they lived. This was of course also true of other ethnic groups who occupied a minority status—but with one great difference: in order to adjust to new circumstances, other groups had to give up their national cultures; the Jews only had to exchange one foreign culture for another.

As a result, the Jews were able, in their own life, to narrow the distance between culture and civilization. We should recall, at this

123

point, how this distance was created in America. Among the Yankees, it arose from the fact that the settlers built a new civilization upon the foundations of an old culture. Among the other ethnic groups, it arose from the fact that they had to surrender their old cultures in order to adjust to the new civilization, thus finding themselves in a cultural void until such time as they were able to grow into the American culture. The Jews were spared this temporary cultural emptiness by their possession of an outer culture. In addition, the inner Jewish culture, in its deeper essentials, had much in common with the spirit of American democracy. There was a considerable kinship between the social visions of the Hebrew prophets and the principles enunciated in the Declaration of Independence, sufficient to make the Jews feel far more at home here than in any of the other countries of their dispersion. This kinship was, in a negative way, sensed, if not clearly understood, by Waldo Frank who wrote:

> He [the Jew] responded the more easily to pioneer demands in an hour when his old mystical equipment seemed particularly futile. In this mystical equipment resided the culture of the Jew. As he dropped the first, the other fell away. Unlike the Latin and the Slav, he had in consequence no painful cultural assimilation to submit to. Like the Puritans, his old cultural habits were already weak at his coming: his power to face new worlds to that extent enhanced.[11]

Frank implied that the Jews arrived here with their Judaism already shaken, and that this made it easier for them to adjust to new circumstances. There is in this view indeed a kernel of truth. But Frank, on the one hand, did not understand the dual nature of Jewish culture and, on the other hand, exaggerated the extent of Jewish assimilation in the United States. In any case, the Jews had had considerable experience in "meeting new worlds." A man, said William James, had as many personalities as the number of social environments to which he was forced to adjust. The same is true of a people. Jews have had to adjust to many environments; what makes them unique is that, despite this experience, they have managed to preserve their own personality.

The bicultural nature of Jewish spiritual life has found its clearest expression in the role played by language in Jewish history. We have seen that language was the bond holding all ethnic groups together as communities. The moment they ceased speaking their own language, their group identity began to dissolve. The reverse was the case with the Jews. The Spanish-Portuguese Jews came here without a language of their own, as did most of the German Jews. Both groups spoke the languages of the countries of their origin. The East European Jews did indeed come with their own language, but their ceasing to use it has not been marked by the degree of assimilation engendered by the comparable experience of other ethnic groups. Among the others, the transition to English bespoke departure from the ethnic group; the remarkable feature of Jewish development in this country is that it was only through the agency of the English language that the previously fragmented, separate Jewish colonies were crystallized into a consolidated Jewish community. Among all other ethnic groups, language was the very heart of their ethnic culture; in Jewish culture language never occupied so important a position. This is why it has been possible for the Jews to be the only group in this country to create its own ethnic culture in English. A study conducted by the Common Council for American Unity in 1956 listed 228 periodicals —ranging from weeklies to quarterlies and publications of irregular frequency, not counting mimeographed leaflets and bulletins— published by or for ethnic groups in English. Fully 128 of these were put out by and for Jews, which means that the Jews alone had a larger press in English than all other ethnic groups combined. Of the 75 ethnic weeklies appearing in English, Jews had 50.[12]

The Jewish personality is always split because the Jews of the Diaspora always live in two or more cultures, because they are constantly confronted with the problem of adjusting to conditions created by non-Jews and of adapting themselves to processes set in motion by non-Jews. They must always struggle for elementary existence and forever prove their right to survival as a group. No wonder so many sociologists and psychologists present the Jew as the classic example of the marginal man.

Other marginal groups seek to liquidate their marginality in one of two ways: either (1) by becoming the dominant group in a certain social sphere, or (2) by complete assimilation within the dominant group. Ideologies reflecting both of these solutions are indeed making themselves felt within the Jewish community; but the

Jews have for so long been in a marginal state that large numbers of them come to accept their marginality as a normal, indeed, desirable, state of affairs. Among those who share this view are many who do not want the Jews to become a majority anywhere; neither do they want the Jews to disappear. In Jewish marginality they see a providential design and the fulfillment of Jewish destiny. At one time, perhaps the majority of German Jews in this country adhered to this notion, although it was not restricted to them. Nor are anti-Zionists alone in seeking to eradicate the tragic complications of marginality by perpetuating it as the Jewish way of life. Mordecai M. Kaplan and other Zionists have for years been extolling the virtue of the Jew's living in two civilizations.

With the formula that the Jews were a religious group rather than a people, classical Reform tried to interpret Jewish collectivity in terms of criteria applicable to faiths which cut across national boundaries and were shared by a variety of ethnic groups. But Jewish group existence rested on quite different foundations. The very fact that Judaism was the faith of only one group in the whole world placed religion itself at the very heart of Jewish ethnic identity. Protestantism, Catholicism, Islam—all transcended nationality divisions; but Judaism created a kind of ghetto even in the heavenly spheres. It is not necessary for us to enter into the old debate as to whether the Jews became an ethnic unit because they possessed an exclusive religion, or whether they developed an exclusive religion because this was the surest way to secure their ethnic integrity: after so many centuries, cause and effect have become so intertwined that it is no longer possible to determine where one left off and the other began. What is significant is that no other ethnic group displayed any desire to break the Jewish monopoly on Judaism and that the Jews themselves did not extend themselves to seek proselytes.

In their early days in America, the Jews tried to impede the entry of converts into the Jewish community. Until the nineteenth century, Congregation Shearith Israel refused membership to Jews who had married Christians, even if the latter had been converted. At the beginning of the nineteenth century, the congregation had become somewhat more liberal; but in 1836 it reinstituted a by-law which read in part: "Any person marrying contrary to our religious law or renouncing Judaism shall not be considered as an Elector or member of this congregation." [13] While under this regulation a Jew married to a Christian could still rent a seat for prayer in the synagog, this privilege was rescinded in 1847. Such a Jew was not even permitted to buy a plot for himself in the congregation's cemetery. Comparable regulations prevailed in the other synagogs as well. These rules applied, it should be remembered, to the Jew who was a partner in a mixed marriage. Until the middle of the nineteenth century there was no place for the non-Jewish spouse in the synagog or in its cemetery. Even the liberal Temple Emanu-El of New York, which in its early years granted the Jew of a mixed marriage full membership rights, denied his partner a place in the synagog and cemetery.[14] It was only around 1860 that proselytes began to be included in the Jewish community. But by then the number of converts to Judaism was certainly smaller than the number of Jewish converts to Christianity.

Another defect of the theory that the Jews were only a religious sect is the failure to take into account the non-religious Jews. Among the latter a different version of the view that the Jews were not a people was also widespread. A consideration of this group and its approach to Jewish life must wait upon a closer analysis, in a subsequent chapter, of the Jewish labor movement in this country.

ACCULTURATION OF THE THIRD GENERATION

Jews, as has been noted, attain through accommodation what other groups achieve through assimilation. A point is reached, however, when further accommodation is impossible without assimilation, and this accounts for the trickle of defection mentioned earlier. Nor is direct defection the only or the most important evidence of the inroads which assimilation is making into Jewish life. As the acculturation of the American Jew deepens, the tyranny of the majority becomes a stronger factor in shaping his attitudes toward society at large. This is especially true of the third generation, which, before long, will constitute the majority of the Jewish population.

The first generation resided in America but largely lived, emotionally, psychologically and culturally, in the lands from which it had migrated. The second generation, like the second generation of all ethnic groups, was a marginal, in-between generation, one that was torn out of the texture of the immigrant past and not yet woven into the fabric of the native present. The third generation is thoroughly acculturated.

Acculturation on the part of a minority means adjustment to a way of life which the majority population has evolved. It means acceptance of standards set up by the majority. It means, in other words, a desire on the part of the minority to restrict the area of disagreement with the majority and extend the area of agreement. Jews, the great dissenters in human history, are increasingly losing their ability and capacity to dissent in America. Religious differences, of course, remain; but, as a result of the growing acculturation, Jews display an inclination to reduce these differences to details. The tables are turned: it is they who carry the banner of non-sectarianism, and it is the non-Jew who dissents. If the latter ever joins in interfaith demonstrations, it is on his own terms, expecting the Jews to make all the compromises; and for the most part, they gladly oblige.

The non-religious Jew among the immigrants and the second generation transferred his dissent from the sphere of faith to the field of social action. The Jewish neighborhoods of twenty-five and fifty years ago seethed with social protest. Many a Jew, to be sure, had gone astray and fallen prey to false prophets; but there is no gainsaying that the motivation, at least in part, had its roots in the Jewish tradition of opposing injustice.

Today there is not much social dissent left in the Jewish environment; the heaven-storming of yesteryear has given way to middle-class respectability. Jews are, true enough, still among the most liberal groups in American political life. But their radicalism, if any there be, hardly goes beyond voting with greater consistency for the candidates of the Democratic party. The third generation is avoiding the ideological mistakes made by many of the second generation, but it also lacks the social passion with which the latter approached human problems. In proportion as Jews stop dissenting, they acquire the habit of conformity. The third generation is a living demonstration of this evolution.

Surveys conducted in a number of universities all show that

Jewish students are losing the distinctiveness that characterized the Jew on the campuses in former years. In an earlier chapter we have shown how closely Jewish students are following general patterns in planning for a career. The same tendency is to be discerned in other areas. In clothing, physical appearance, choice of subjects, reaction to social events, and forms of recreation, Jewish students are coming to resemble their non-Jewish colleagues. The growing conformity is altering even those forms of living which throughout the ages have been directly tied up with Jewish religious and social values.

Reports from Jewish and government welfare agencies indicate a substantial rise in this country in the number of broken Jewish homes and abandoned children. There is still a wide difference here between the Jewish population and the country at large, but we are concerned with the dynamics of the situation rather than with present conditions. What is significant, in terms of the future, is the fact that the gap between Jew and non-Jew is narrowing in this area, and that a basic traditional value is losing its hold.

The same can be said of the drinking habits of the American Jews. Although Jews have never been total abstainers, drunkenness has been a rare occurrence among them from time immemorial. Recent studies show that this tradition, too, although still strong among American Jews, is yielding to the pressure of the prevailing general behavior, with the difference between Jew and non-Jew smallest in areas where both meet in the same social setting. Thus we find relatively heavy drinking among Jews in the armed forces and on the campuses where the Jew wants to demonstrate that he can hold his liquor with the best of them. To be sure, he may cut down on his drinking after he leaves these institutions, but this is more than made up by the increasing consumption of intoxicants among American Jews generally.[15]

Another area bound up with traditional Jewish values is juvenile delinquency. Sophia M. Robison analyzed the cases dealt with in the Juvenile Court in New York in 1952 and found that in only 3 percent of them were Jewish youngsters involved. Considering that Jews constituted some 27 percent of the total population in that city, Jews may congratulate themselves on the fact that their share in juvenile delinquency was nine times smaller than their proportion in the population as a whole. However, there is a fly in the ointment. Dr. Robison also conducted a study in 1930, when she found that "Jewish children accounted for almost 20 percent of all cases called to the attention of the court." We thus see a tremendous drop in the proportion of juvenile delinquents between 1930 and 1952—due, no doubt, to improved economic conditions and greater social stability. But there is also to be observed an impressive "shift in the category of offenses." The leading offense in 1930 was peddling or begging without a license. In 1952 the leading offense was the wrongful appropriation of property which included burglary, robbery, theft and stealing automobiles. Considering this shift, we cannot help agreeing with Dr. Robison's conclusion that "the Jewish child who was brought to the court in 1952 came because his behavior was more similar to that of the non-Jewish delinquent than was true two decades earlier."[16]

As the attachment to Jewish values becomes weaker, the similarity between Jew and non-Jew becomes stronger; and the hold of tradition gets lesser as the Jew moves away from his orthodox moorings. That the trend is away from orthodoxy is clear. A recent survey of the membership of Orthodox congregations in Milwaukee, conducted by Howard W. Polsky, discloses that only 30 percent of the married sons of the members regard themselves as Orthodox; 37 percent join the Conservative or Reform temples, and 33 percent remain unaffiliated. The same study gives an insight into the practices of the Jews belonging to Orthodox synagogs. Here we have a case history of three generations comprising the members themselves, their fathers, and their married sons, and what do we find? While 67 percent of the fathers observe the Sabbath, no more than 12 percent of the members and only 2 percent of their married sons do so. Eighty-six percent of the fathers observe *kashruth* outside their own homes against 34 percent of the members and 2 percent of the sons. Inside their home, 94 percent of the fathers observe *kashruth*, 62 percent of the members do so, and only 19 percent of the sons.[17] A country-wide study of the religious practices of the leaders of the Conservative synagogs reveals an even greater disparity between profession and performance regarding observances that should go with membership in a Conservative congregation.[18]

Not even Jews can adjust to American conditions solely on the basis of exchanging outer cultures. Those whose inner culture is weakened gradually begin to divest themselves of it altogether so as to make their way more easily into the general environment. When Gustave Poznanski of Charleston, S.C., proclaimed in 1841 that "America is our Zion and Washington our Jerusalem," he hit at the very heart of inner Jewish culture, not merely at its outer raiment. But when we find, a century later, that only an insignificant number of Jews transformed this declaration into a program, and we also find that the same college students who make so light of their Jewish loyalties at school become members of synagogs, builders of community centers and organizers of Jewish schools when they move into the suburbs and enter upon their business or professional career, we must conclude that the assimilation of the Jews has encountered obstacles not present in the experience of any other white ethnic group. If we will here recall our earlier definition of a minority as a subgroup within a culture which, in the process of its integration into the life of the larger community, encounters resistance from the dominant group, we shall have to seek an explanation for the relatively small degree of Jewish assimilation not only in Jewish inner forces of resistance, but in external obstacles—the "isolating" factors, as we have called them—as well. The economic development of the Jews in America bears re-examination from this perspective.

Economic integration, it has been established, is the most significant factor in assimilation. The quicker and more basic the integration, the speedier the assimilation. That is why assimilatory tendencies appear more clearly among the richer segments of ethnic groups. They are everywhere the first to break away from their ethnic environment.

The Jews had a larger proportion of these elements than others. The Sephardic Jews were a wealthy group; the German Jews embarked on the road of economic advancement soon after their arrival, likewise the East European Jews, though not so quickly or in so great a proportion. Why, then, was there less, rather than more, assimilation among well-to-do Jews than among the wealthier sections of the other ethnic groups? The German Jewish immigration provides the best material for an answer to this question, for it produced Jews who attained the highest level of material success ever achieved by

Jews in the United States. What will be said of the German Jews applies more or less to other Jewish groups, regardless of their place of origin, who belong to the upper and middle middle class. In other words, what we can establish about the relation between economic integration and ethnic consolidation as regards the German Jews can be taken as representative of the laws of development which regulate the processes of accommodation of all wealthier Jews in the United States. The formulation "German Jews" will thus be used symbolically as well as literally.

What, in brief, are the factors which, in the normal course of ethnic group development, should have hastened the assimilation of the German Jews? Though they were deeply devoted to German culture, they nevertheless quickly exchanged it for American culture. Within the span of just a few decades, English became the exclusive language of all their religious, cultural and communal activities. Moreover, when they came to this country, their inner culture had already been substantially undermined, and it was even further disrupted here—so much so that Reform Judaism more closely resembled some of the liberal wings of Protestantism than Orthodox Judaism. Once in this country, they dispersed over a very broad geographical area, and outside of New York City they did not constitute large communities. Their material integration was quick, and they soon struck roots in commerce which made them all the more dependent on non-Jewish elements. They lorded it over the East European Jews and sought to avoid physical and spiritual contact with them. They submitted quickly enough to the tyranny of the majority in that they adopted the outer forms of life imposed by the "aristocracy" and the leisure forms dictated by the environment. It required a considerably less potent combination of assimilatory factors to lead other ethnic groups to a state of disintegration. The German Jews reversed the trend, though the trickle of defection flowed with greater impetus from among them than from the other Jewish groups.

REVERSAL OF ASSIMILATORY TRENDS: GROWTH OF JEWISH RELIGIOUS AND SECULAR INSTITUTIONS

A reversal of the trend toward assimilation may be seen by examining the growth of Jewish religious and secular institutions—both in number and in scope. Here we see positions of ethnic strength developing concurrently with upward economic mobility. At the time of the Revolution, a Jewish population of some 3,000 maintained 5 synagogs—an average of 1 synagog for every 600 Jews. By 1848, the number of synagogs had grown to 77, in a population of about 50,000—an average of 1 synagog for every 650 Jews. And by 1877, a Jewish population of 250,000 supported 277 synagogs—1 synagog per 900 Jews.[19] This growth was chiefly the result of the German immigration. The higher average of 1877 as compared with 30 years earlier was the result partly of the organizational ability of the German Jews and partly of their great geographical expansion. As early as the 1840's, one could find German synagogs in such midwestern cities as Cincinnati, Louisville, and Chicago, and as far west as San Francisco. And if we bear in mind that the numbers cited above included communities which sometimes barely possessed a quorum for prayer (ten male adults), we can infer from the enormous achievement of maintaining so many synagogs that assimilation did not keep pace with the extent of German-Jewish acculturation.

Evidence of even greater weight can be seen in the rise and unexampled expansion of Jewish communal institutionalism outside the synagog. This is not the place to refer again to the factors that gave birth to this phenomenon or to describe in detail the role it played in solidifying Jewish ethnic identity. Suffice it to note that by the middle of the nineteenth century, the Jewish community throughout the United States was covered by a network of Jewish hospitals, orphanages, homes for the aged, schools, cultural organizations, social service agencies, mutual aid societies, etc.

These institutions did not develop on the basis of any plan: they were improvised to meet the growth of the Jewish population and the number of its needy. They were initially established independently by individual Jewish groups, each seeking to maintain its own cohesiveness; however, the barriers separating the institutions have gradually broken down and have now virtually disappeared.

All the external and internal factors which eventuated in the consolidation of the Jewish community and in the transformation of parochial agencies into general Jewish communal institutions are already to be seen in the amalgamation, in 1860, of the Hebrew Benevolent Society, founded in New York by the Spanish-Portuguese

Jews, and the German Hebrew Benevolent Society. If the separate existence of these two societies originally reflected the social distance between the Sephardim and the Ashkenazim, the merger reflected a *rapprochement* induced by time. This *rapprochement* resulted not merely from the fact that, by mid-nineteenth century, the Sephardic community had become insignificantly small and could no longer remain in isolation, but also by the fact that, by that time, the material status of the German Jews had altered appreciably. They were no longer so financially backward in relation to the Sephardim and were in fact on the way to socio-economic equality with the Jewish "elite." German Jews had begun to produce presidents of synagogs and temples, founders of important secular organizations like B'nai B'rith (1843), and of philanthropic institutions that became exemplars throughout the country. Concomitantly, German Jews assumed more important positions in the country's economic and cultural life. In sum, they ceased being takers and became instead givers—givers, indeed, on a vaster scale than the Sephardim.

The various groups within the Jewish community could afford the luxury of segregation so long as their number was very small and each group was able to provide for its own needy. With the growth of the community and the substantial increase in the number of needy Jews, prestige boundaries came into conflict with a Jewish tradition which has placed its ineradicable stamp upon the entire course of Jewish history and has been among the most important factors in the survival of the Jewish people in dispersion. This is the tradition of mutual responsibility—of the responsibility of one Jew for the other, of the individual Jew for the Jewish collectivity, of the Jewish community for the single Jew in distress, of the better-situated Jew for the underprivileged one. When Peter Stuyvesant demanded of the first Jews in New Amsterdam that they provide for their needy brethren and prevent the latters' becoming public charges of the general community, he was breaking down an open door. True, the Jews who debarked from the *St. Charles* in 1654 were so poor that at first they had to seek outside help; but later, neither they nor those who came after them would have entertained for a minute the idea of transferring to non-Jewish society the responsibility for the Jewish poor. Some Jews might indeed introduce limitations about the sort of Jews for whom they would assume responsibility, but in practice such limitations fell by the wayside if they ran contrary to Jewish communal obligations. The various Jewish groups were perhaps guilty of planlessness and of abetting separatism, but in the end, they could only bow to the force of Jewish tradition.

The following figures, cited by Maurice Karpf, testify to the great and steady increase in the number of Jews in need of communal assistance: Around 1853, the Hebrew Benevolent Society (Sephardic) alone supported some 1,200 applicants a year. By around 1856, the number had risen to 1,900, for whom the Society expended some five thousand dollars a year—no small sum, considering that the whole community in New York totalled only between fifteen and twenty thousand persons. Of this number 10 to 20 percent, a huge proportion, needed aid, which was supplied by other groups as well as by the Hebrew Benevolent Society.[20] The amounts of money spent during that period were a mere drop in the bucket, not only in comparison with the enormous sums being raised today, but even compared with the sums expended during the last quarter of the nineteenth century, when the third wave of immigration was at its height. Just as the Sephardic Jews, despite their regulations, had to extend help to the German Jews, so the latter, despite their reluctance, had to help, in incomparably greater measure, the East European Jews. I use the word "had" advisedly, so as to underscore the fact that this was a process that contradicted the initial articulated positions of the various Jewish groups. But as always in Jewish history, the welfare of the group as a whole overrode sectional ideologies at the decisive moment.

Some sociologists and historians view this phenomenon merely as the result of negative pressures. That is to say, they hold that the mutual dependence of the Jews was strengthened solely as a result of the persecution and discrimination to which the Jews were subjected by the outside world. From this they infer that Jewish national existence has no positive foundation, that in the absence of persecution and discrimination Jewish ethnic identity would in time disappear.

This theory has more in common with metaphysical hairsplitting than with social science. There is no social process in which an effect does not in time become a cause. What might have happened—had the Jews been allowed to remain peacefully in one place, had they not been driven from land to land, had they not suffered the tribulations which were in fact their lot—whether such an eventuality would have led to their dissolution it is impossible to say. Jewish history was what it was, and during its course there was hammered out a will to collective life which has no parallel in any other people. Whatever the original source of this will, it is one of the great positive factors in Jewish existence and the molding of the Jewish fate. Religion and group responsibility are the two most significant sources of the Jewish will to live. This is clearly demonstrated in the experience of the German Jews in the United States—and once again I draw attention to the fact that I use the term "German Jews" to include symbolically all Jews of well-to-do status.

Despite the extreme forms which Reform Judaism assumed, it did not attract other ethnic groups to itself, nor was it seized by any particular desire to do so. It remained exclusively within the Jewish community and could expect reinforcement only from there. It will therefore come as no surprise when we discover later that instead of moving further in the direction of narrowing the distance between itself and Christianity, Reform Judaism actually backtracked toward a greater acceptance of Jewish tradition. And it should be even less surprising to discover that communal institutionalism, which, at its establishment, reflected the differentiation and fragmentation of the American Jewish community, became one of the main pillars of Jewish ethnic solidarity. Jewish institutions developed quite differently from those of other ethnic groups. Among the other groups, these institutions were initially established as narrow ethno-denominational positions; only later did they become broadly religious agencies. Jewish communal institutions were originally founded on the basis of religious impulses, though outside the synagog; only later did they become ethnic strongholds.

It must of course not be assumed that positive factors alone contributed to this development. They were abetted by a number of negative factors, which should be examined before we proceed with our analysis.

7 Isolating Factors in the Experience of the American Jews

Jews have moved upward on the social ladder at a faster pace than others. But the higher they have moved the greater has been the resistance they encountered, until a point was reached beyond which it was impossible to go. Further advance was blocked for them. That is, they were able to advance in wealth but not in economic weight or in social status. Between them and the country's "aristocracy" there remained a barrier which they were never able to hurdle. Thus, the faster tempo of Jewish upward mobility applied only to their movement from the lower to the middle rungs of the social ladder; from that point on, their tempo slowed down until it came to an almost complete halt. The previously mentioned occupational index of the Jews in Yankee City revealed that in their first 20 years there their index rose by 22 points—a jump which the Irish were able to match only in twice that time-span. But this speedy advance of the Jews is apparent only if we compare the first 43 years, 1850–93, of Irish residence in Yankee City with the first 20 years, 1913–33, of Jewish residence there. An altogether different picture emerges from a consideration of the subsequent years. In 1913, when the Jewish community got its start in Yankee City, the Irish had an

137

index of 2.14; the Jews began with 3.10. Twenty years later, the Jewish index had risen to 3.32, and the Irish to 2.52. This means that in the course of those two decades, the Irish improved their occupational status nearly twice as fast as the Jews.[1] The Yankee City investigators thought that this was due to a greater proportion of Jews than of other groups leaving the city. There may be some truth in this, but the whole story is explainable only by the fact that Jews moved upward at a faster tempo from the bottom to the middle level, but at a slower pace than others from the middle to the top.

Economic Barriers. For Jews, religious or otherwise, and irrespective of wealth and particular denominational affiliation, certain economic fields are closed. In general, the following principle can be laid down: the more financial and political power a given economic area represents, the fewer Jews will be found in it. For example, the Jews brought with them to this country a rich background in banking. They once played a distinguished role in this field in the United States too, but only during the period when the banks were small or independent. When the unprecedented concentration of finance capital got under way, Jewish participation in the management of the banking institutions diminished. The study of the Jews carried out by *Fortune* Magazine in 1936 found no more than 30 Jews among 420 directors of the 19 banks which belonged to the New York Clearing House in 1933. One-half of the Jewish directors were in two banks in which Jews had large investments, and the other half were dispersed among 17 banks.[2] The proportion of Jews in banking leadership has further declined since 1936. This being the situation in New York, it is not hard to imagine what it is in other parts of the country.

In 1954 the Chicago Bureau on Jewish Employment Problems found only 2 percent Jews among the 15,000 persons holding administrative positions in 24 insurance companies operating in the Chicago area. Further information on the employment of Jews in administrative positions in the insurance field is provided in a survey made by the Anti-Defamation League of B'nai B'rith in 1959. Based on an examination of the executive rosters of seven major national life insurance companies who in 1957 employed 6,100 executives at an annual salary of $10,000 or more, the survey discloses the following facts:

1. Of the 6,066 employees whose religious identification was definitely ascertained 327, or 5.4 percent, were Jews. A direct relationship was established between the number of Jews employed and the proximity of the employing company to a large Jewish insurance market. One company did not have a single Jewish executive. The percentage of Jewish executives in the 5 companies operating out of the New York metropolitan area—"an area covered by enforceable fair employment laws"—ran from 2.7 percent to 6.4 percent of the total employed.

2. A different picture emerges when the rosters are broken up between executives in the home offices and those in the district sales offices. The proportion of Jews in the latter (6.4 percent) is almost twice as high as in the former (3.6 percent). "Of the 327 Jewish executives employed throughout the nation by all the companies 200, or 60 percent, are employed in the Greater New York area, primarily in the non-home office sales branches." Seventy-seven percent of all Jewish executives were found in four states: New York, New Jersey, Pennsylvania, and Illinois.

3. Nearly two-thirds of the 73 Jewish executives working in the home offices of the six companies having Jewish executives were employed as actuaries, physicians, lawyers and accountants.

Evaluating the findings, the Anti-Defamation League draws two main conclusions: (1) The conspicuous absence of Jews in the insurance industry, noted by *Fortune* magazine in 1936, no longer obtains in life insurance companies; (2) Although Jews have been employed increasingly in executive positions, discrimination against Jews continues throughout the insurance industry.[3]

We have noted the unusually high proportion of Jews in trade. But to speak of trade in general can produce misleading conclusions and a distorted picture; for the term "trade" includes Macy's and Gimbels'—and it also includes the corner candy store. What is characteristic, however, is that the *Fortune* study found that only 5 percent of the chain stores were in Jewish hands. No statistics are available for the more than two decades elapsing since *Fortune* published the results of its survey; it is the impression of this writer that the proportion of Jews in the supermarkets has since increased.

As for the role of the Jews in industry, *Fortune* states, "If the Jews have a subordinate place in finance, which they are often said to control, they have an even more inconspicuous place in heavy industry." [4] In the industries which control the country's technological life very few Jews are to be found. They do put in an appearance in light industry, especially in those of its branches where, as *Fortune* puts it, producer and merchant meet. Ismar Elbogen sums it all up very well: "In these fields, which were elsewhere regarded as the special domains of the Jew, the Jews of the United States never reached the front ranks." [5]

Jews do occupy leading positions in real estate, department stores, radio and television and in a few more new industries. They have forged ahead since World War II to top positions in a number of very large enterprises—in some cases as a result of stock fights. At this writing (May, 1960), Jews for the first time hold the office of president in two major railroad systems—the New York Central and the New York, New Haven and Hartford—but it will be noticed that both systems operate in the red, and the presidents of both are merely the functioning executives, not the controlling heads. The total picture so far as dominating positions are concerned has only slightly changed since the *Fortune* study, although occupational discrimination against Jews has generally receded in recent years under the impact of technological changes on the one hand and the enactment of fair employment practice laws on the other hand.

This phenomenon is not so puzzling if one takes into account that, after they had gone as high as they could go, the Jews encountered a resistance to their further mobility which they could under no circumstances overcome. This resistance was no longer that of ordinary business competition in which the abler and more competent man won out. At this point they have had to deal with discrimination which inhered in their very position as a minority. Precisely because they were so unlike the stereotype of the "real American" which the tyranny of the majority has created in the popular imagination, it was that much easier to evoke against them the mistrust which the country normally displayed toward the stranger. So it was that economic competition was intertwined with religious, "racial" and national prejudices. No matter how long a Jewish family resided in this country, its members remained "foreigners" in the minds of those who were swayed by these prejudices—whereas in relation to other ethnic groups, the notion of "foreigner" was applied only to immigrants, but not to their children and grandchildren. Jews, according to Stonequist, are both helped and handicapped in confronting business rivalry:

> Their background of urban experience, their intense group consciousness, and their developed organizations enable them to make rapid progress in adjustment to American conditions. Thus they offer keen competition to the older inhabitants and arouse their hostility.[6]

The hostility does not derive from the economic functions performed by Jews in the United States and in all other countries but from the fact that it is they, the *Jews*, that perform them. The very functions which are considered perfectly respectable economic activities when others engage in them somehow become suspect when Jews enter them. Methods normally used by others in business by some alchemy turn into conspiracies when Jews employ them. "Nothing succeeds like success"—and a successful merchant, if he is not a Jew, elicits not only respect but awe, especially if he began with nothing and rose to the top by his own abilities. And what success means in America can be seen from its huge pulp literature, which is the largest in the world. There is not a single novel in this literature, not a single film or television play which describes the hero's attainments in terms of his remaining a factory worker or small farmer. Invariably the story is of a poor boy from the small town or farm who ventures quite alone into the great world, encounters heartbreaking difficulties and setbacks, only to overcome them all in the end, and reap the prize for his integrity, courage, hard work and enterprise by becoming a great merchant, banker, industrialist or professional. The very fact that a man has raised himself to the heights by his own bootstraps wins him the plaudits of the people even if, in the process, he has employed dubious practices. For the average American, determination, initiative, aggressiveness, skill in exploiting opportunities and outwitting competitors, are all virtues that carry their own reward. But these virtues become vices when possessed by Jews: the same qualities that elicit applause for a non-Jew provoke prejudice against a Jew. This ambivalence is aptly characterized by Raymond Kennedy:

> The self-made man and the "log cabin to White House" president are type heroes of our national folklore. We idealize our open-class society—but only so far as caste lines allow. The success of the Jews in business or the professions is not generally praised; rather is it regarded as a threat. They are not said to have "made a success of" the clothing business and the cinema industry; they have "got control" of them.[7]

We shall discuss the question of anti-Semitism in a subsequent chapter; here we are merely concerned with the double standards to be observed in the evaluation placed by American society on economic pursuits. One is applicable to the country as a whole, the other to the Jewish community. "The economic stereotype of the Jew as a businessman is more relevant to modern anti-Semitism," writes John Higham, since "the impression of Jews as aggressive businessmen had always been widespread in America, even in an age of biblical piety when most people had never seen a Jew."[8]

The most insuperable obstacles encountered by the wealthier elements among the Jews have been social. The authors of a study of interreligious relations, conducted by the Institute of Religious and Social Research, found that the attitude of non-Jews toward Reform Jews was friendlier than toward the Orthodox and offered the following explanation: "Wherever Reform Judaism has been comparatively strong, as compared with Orthodox Judaism, the antipathy of Gentiles towards Jews appears to have been distinctly modified."[9]

This puts the cart before the horse. The modification derives not from modernization of religious forms, but from the fact that where Reform is stronger than Orthodoxy, the Jews are generally wealthier, of longer residence in the United States, on a higher educational plane, and bear a greater similarity to the general population in their clothing, behavior and leisure habits. Whatsoever Jewish element might have achieved this status, the attitude of non-Jews toward them would have been the same. No doubt Reform Jews seek, more than do Orthodox Jews, the acquaintance of their non-Jewish neighbors; but our concern here is to discover whether the non-Jewish neighbors are willing to accept them on a level of social equality. All the objective and subjective signs point to a negative answer.

The same answer must also be given to the question: do the prejudice against Jews and the tendency to ascribe grasping motives to them operate only against immigrants and Jews of a particular religious wing? On the contrary, there are prejudices, especially of a socio-economic nature, whose weight is in direct proportion to the success that the Jews, employing accepted American methods, achieve. The number of people who believe that the Jews have too much economic and political power grew until recent years, according to a number of research studies. One, directed by Elmo Roper for *Fortune* Magazine in 1947, provides the following information:

Thirty-six percent of the American people believed the Jews had too much economic power in the United States. Only 2 percent believed it of the Protestants and only 12 percent, of the Catholics. Twenty-one percent thought Jews had too much political power, as against 4 percent who believed it of Protestants and 15 percent, of Catholics.

On the other hand, the same study showed that there was only a minute difference between the answers regarding Jews and non-Jews to the question: which group deserved better treatment in the United States? Seven percent wanted a better deal for Catholics, 8 percent wanted it for Protestants, and around 10 percent would have liked to see the Jews faring better.[10]

Later polls indicate a considerable decline in the number of those believing that Jews have too much economic power; but even at the reduced figures, the proportion so believing is quite substantial.

We have seen how unwarranted this belief actually is; however, prejudice against Jews is based not on facts but on self-delusions. It must of course be said that the unique appearance of the Jewish economic structure makes it easy to maintain and spread such delusions. Though this uniqueness is one of degree rather than of substance, it nevertheless smooths the path for those who play upon anti-Jewish feelings. The editors of *Fortune* characterize this uniqueness thus: "What is remarkable about the Jews in America . . . is not their industrial power but their curious industrial distribution, their tendency to crowd together in particular squares of the checkerboard." [11] This tendency, while far from giving Jews a monopoly on American industry, has nevertheless enabled them to make "fair progress toward monopolizing those sub-divisions of industry in which they have established themselves." [12]

This conclusion is not so surprising if one remembers that the Jews must restrict themselves to particular economic levels from which external pressures prevent their breaking out. If there is anything remarkable about this phenomenon, it is the extraordinary disproportion between the economic status of the Jews and their social prestige.

Social Barriers. Social barriers are for all ethnic groups the most difficult ones to break down; for Jews they are sometimes impregnable. The Yankee City study provides illuminating corroboration of this point. The authors of the study divided the population of Yankee City into six classes: (1) Upper upper, (2) Lower upper, (3) Upper middle, (4) Lower middle, (5) Upper lower, (6) Lower lower. Financial income naturally plays an important, but by no means the sole, or even the most decisive, role in determining class affiliation. The lower groupings may contain individuals with a higher income than the upper groupings. For example, the Lower upper, as a group, has a greater per capita income than the Upper upper. The relevant figures are: an annual per capita income of $2,652.61 for the Lower upper, $2,133.61 for the Upper upper.[13] From the perspective of the ethnic composition of the six classes, it appears that the higher the class, the smaller the ethnic component that enters into it. Class One is 100 percent Yankee. Yankees comprise 94 percent of Class Two, 81.2 percent of Class Three, and 58.2 percent of Class Four. The Irish, resident in Yankee City for a century, constitute barely 6 percent of the Lower upper class. It is no wonder, then, that the Jews, who, as was noted, have the highest occupational index in Yankee City, are not to be found at all in the first two classes, and in only insignificant numbers in the third class. They are concentrated in Classes Four and Five—52 percent in the former, nearly 40 percent in the latter.[14]

The situation in Yankee City is characteristic of the entire country. According to Donald Young, European immigrants, in crossing the social line that separates minority groups from the higher classes of the majority, encounter no greater difficulties than those which confront the "native farm-boy of pioneer ancestry who makes good." It is different for the Jew: *he* "has had to create his own social classes, although many individuals mingle freely with Gentiles on all levels." [15] Even the intercourse between individuals is truly free only so long as it remains on a personal level or inside organizations of a mixed character; this intercourse, too, stops at the doors of the exclusive institutions which remain permanently closed to Jews. It was so in the colonial period, and it is so today.

It remained for the wealthier Jews, who were able to afford membership in the clubs and recreational centers of the "aristocracy," to discover that ordinary standards of admission did not apply to them. They were thus forced to establish parallel institutions with an exclusively Jewish membership. It was probably for this reason that, in 1761, the Jews of Newport established their previously mentioned club for entertainment purposes. It was certainly for this reason that the German Jews had to create their own golf and country clubs and their own sport and amusement centers.

After the Civil War, the Jewish elite in Rochester, N.Y., consisting of affluent Jews of German origin, was "firmly entrenched in the community," relates Stuart E. Rosenberg. "They were entering civic life, assuming their share of responsibilities, and gaining the admiration of their non-Jewish friends." Nevertheless, "the Jews still found it necessary to organize a social club of their own." [16] Albert I. Gordon tells the story of a Minneapolis Jewish family of German origin which produced three native-born generations in this country. The grandfather, born in Albany in 1862, moved to Minneapolis in 1883. His "family associated exclusively with Jewish families," for although as an attorney he had some non-Jewish clients and friends, "excepting for business relations [he] never saw very much of [his] non-Jewish neighbors."

The son's story is a simple one: on his own evidence he "was never interested in Jewish life or Jewish organizations." If his "daughter were to marry out of her faith," he would not have "seriously" objected, and he was even a member of a Christian Science church "for about six or seven months." And yet, when he applied for membership in the Minneapolis Athletic Club, he was told "that they don't want any Jews" there. When "the same thing happened in the Automobile

Club," he was "very much upset about it," but he still did "not think that there ought to be Jewish clubs."

The granddaughter had "no awareness of . . . Jewishness." She "never resented the fact that there was a quota system at the school" and "always had friends among Jews and Christians," predominantly among the latter until her days at the university. At the time she related her story, she found that her real friends were "in the Jewish group." [17]

Three generations with the same experience: in social relations they are fully accepted only by Jews. Only in case of the granddaughter does exclusion from without stimulate desire to make more meaningful her Jewish identification from within, something to remember when we discuss the effect of discrimination upon Jewish life.

It does not take long for wealthy Jews to find out that it is no simple matter for them to register at famous hotels or to spend their vacations at exclusive resorts. Joseph Seligman was by 1877 one of the richest men in the country and had little to do with the Jewish community; nevertheless, he was not permitted to stay at the Grand Hotel in Saratoga Springs—only because he was a Jew. And if this incident evoked a storm of protest at the time, this type of exclusion later became such a natural matter that it ceased to cause attention. To quote from Young again: "Probably no other white minority group which has sufficient money and cultural polish to fit into the accepted standards of vacation life is absolutely barred from the ordinary summer resort." [18]

On April 28, 1957, the Anti-Defamation League of B'nai B'rith released the results of a survey it had conducted to ascertain the degree of religious discrimination prevalent among hotels on the North American continent. The survey included 2,731 resorts and hotels situated within the United States. Adequate information was received for 933 of them, or 34 percent. Of these 214, or 23 percent, were found to discriminate in their admission policies against Jews. Of the 1,798 resorts and hotels about which no current information was received, 505 were known to have carried on discriminatory practices in the past. Even among the 77 percent of the establishments that declared a non-discriminatory policy, 11 percent gave cause for misgiving as to the purity of their record. The Anti-Defamation League was therefore convinced that its overall finding that one in every four hotels in the United States discriminated against Jews in its admission practices was probably an understatement. It should be added that discrimination was not evenly divided. There was more of it in some parts of the country than in others; and the general picture would have been even worse, had there been no laws in some states barring discrimination because of race or religion.[19]

At the time of their first study of Middletown, in the 1920's, the Lynds found that "Jewish merchants mingle freely with other businessmen in the smaller civic clubs, but there are no Jews in Rotary; Jews are accepted socially with just enough qualification to make them aware that they do not entirely 'belong.' "[20] When they returned, seven years later, the situation was in many respects worse. The average Middletowner believed that "individual Jews may be all right but that as a race one doesn't care to mix too much with them."[21] The same attitudes were found to prevail in Yankee City, and in Buna, the pseudonymous town somewhere in the "American industrial midwest," studied by Leonard Bloom.[22] The phenomenon of Jewish social segregation has been found in every community, including suburbia. It is partly voluntary, partly imposed from the outside.

On the other hand, there is nothing voluntary at all about the residential segregation forced upon some sections of the wealthier Jewish group. They would much prefer not to be cut off in this manner, but the matter is entirely out of their hands. Social segregation explains why the proportion of mixed marriages involving rich Jews is relatively so small, as contrasted with the much higher percentage among persons of similar economic status in other ethnic groups. The reason is obvious: for others, marriage to a member of the "aristocracy" or of a group close to it is a card of admission to a higher social plane; a mixed marriage involving a Jew has the very opposite consequences. The Jew who marries a non-Jew of a higher social level does not thereby enhance his social position; the non-Jew, concomitantly, loses prestige. This is how Young sees it:

. . . the nordic is continuing to intermarry quite freely and without social ostracism with all white stocks except the Jewish. When the Jewish and

147

the colored groups are involved, but with the exception of the Indian, caste is lost by intermarriage, and the offspring are denied majority membership.[23]

A striking illustration of the loss in social prestige suffered by a non-Jew who marries a Jew was provided by an incident in Washington in 1948. A non-Jewish woman purchased a home in a certain "aristocratic" section of town, where a restrictive covenant against Jews and Negroes was in effect. As soon as the neighbors discovered that she had a Jewish husband, they filed suit in court to force the family out of the neighborhood. The suit was dropped only because of the strong protest which the incident evoked, but the neighbors pledged themselves to find other means of getting rid of the unwanted family.

A paradoxical situation emerges: it was precisely the richer elements, possessed of a greater interest in leaving their ethnic environment than any other segment of the Jewish community, who were the first to sense that there was a boundary which a Jew could not cross. Hence they were the first to come to a halt at the barricaded rung of the social ladder. They, who viewed themselves as members of a religious rather than ethnic group, made the painful discovery that even for them only the Jewish street was fully open. And so to their synagogs were added their own exclusively Jewish communal and charitable institutions, their own clubs, recreational centers and means of entertainment. Their social circles were chiefly Jewish, they met more Jews at the resorts, their homes had to be in a Jewish neighborhood. If one word were needed to describe this entire situation, it is—*ghetto*.

FORCES OF COHESION WITHIN THE JEWISH COMMUNITY

There was one fundamental difference between the Jewish ghetto and that of all the other ethnic groups in the United States: for the others, the ghetto was a passing phenomenon; for the Jews, it became a permanent institution.

The other groups created ghettos for the first time only in America; the Jews brought the ghetto here with them. During the course of long centuries, the ghetto was the closest thing to a national territory that the Jews possessed. There were times and places where the ghetto walls were solidly built and carefully guarded from the outside; and there were times and places where the walls were invisible and unsupported. America belongs to the latter category. Here the ghetto boundaries were purely symbolic, and theoretically the Jews could readily cross them. Formally, their departure from the ghetto would have had the law on its side, especially where the law was informed with the spirit of the Declaration of Independence. But the Jews had to reckon with unwritten, and therefore more potent, laws: the law of their own ethnic requirements and the law of unfriendly majority social attitudes. The totality of religious customs, communal needs and cultural requirements, which the Jews have always had to conserve in order to maintain their collective existence, they were able to carry on only within their own environment. This was the source of the psychic impetus which supported the ghetto walls from within. On the other hand, those Jews in whom this impetus had greatly diminished, if not altogether disappeared, quickly sensed that the ghetto walls were also shored up by pressures from the outside. It is clear that the ghetto was not simply imposed upon the Jews from the outside; it was also held together by an inward Jewish force. In his study of the Jewish community of Stamford, Koenig comments aptly on the dual nature of the ghetto:

> There is, on the one hand, the strong urge on the part of Jews to preserve their cultural heritage and group life, and hence to live a life of their own, and, on the other, the unwillingness of the Gentiles to admit them into their society on equal terms. The Jews have, therefore, been forced to create a social structure that would fill the needs of their own making, so to speak, as well as those brought about by outside forces.[24]

Like all other immigrants, the Jews, and especially their native-born children, tend to depart from the ghettos just as soon as they can afford to settle in better neighborhoods. But while for the others the ghetto episode ends after they have left the immigrant areas of settlement behind them, the Jews can only exchange an old ghetto for a new one—traditional Jews, because they do not *want* to leave a Jewish environment; assimilated Jews, because they *cannot*.

Orthodox Jews must live near a synagog and in an atmosphere which enables them to satisfy their socio-religious needs. The shifting addresses of Congregation Shearith Israel, since its establishment three centuries ago, graphically describe the route Jews followed since they formed the first ghetto in New York. It was not a straight route, for it branched off into numerous byways which corresponded to the geographical and social integration of the Jewish population in the city. The sites of the ghettos constitute the map of Jewish mobility in the United States.

The old ghettos never remained empty as long as immigration continued, for new immigrants always took the place of older residents who were moving out to better neighborhoods. Since the immigrant ghettos were invariably in the poorest and most neglected sections of town, those who departed from them made their homes either in better established sections, where more prosperous non-Jews had previously lived, or in altogether new sections. Physical barriers were thus frequently created between the various Jewish ghettos in the larger cities in the form of Jewish islands in the midst of non-Jewish settlements. These physical barriers, reinforcing the social divisions of status and material prosperity, reflected the stratification of American Jewish life.

However dissimilar the new Jewish neighborhoods might have been in esthetic and cultural ways from the old, they had one thing in common—non-Jews shied away from them. The assimilated Jews of West European origin who thought they had more in common with non-Jewish Americans than with the immigrants from eastern Europe realized, when they moved into new sections, that they might leave the ghetto but could not liberate themselves from it. As Louis Wirth puts it, "In their attempt to flee from the ghetto, the partially assimilated group have found that the ghetto has followed them to their new quarters." [25]

This was written in the late twenties. Thirty years later the situation has remained the same, although the Jews have since moved not only from the immigrant colonies, but from the areas of second settlement as well. There is a vast difference between the Jews who inhabited the areas of first settlement in the large cities and the Jews residing in the areas of the third settlement, but the tendency toward Jewish concentration, as a result of both internal desire and external avoidance, persists. Nor has the trend toward the suburbs changed the situation substantially. The lines between Jew and non-Jew in social contact are, if anything, even more sharply drawn in suburbia than in the urban centers. To be sure, there is more civic and cultural cooperation in the suburbs, especially in school work and adult education, but in personal relations, it is the old story: Jews keep to their own and non-Jews keep to their own. Geographically, Jews and non-Jews live in closer proximity, but this is in itself a somewhat separating factor. "Not only," writes William H. Whyte, Jr., "does suburbia tend to attract Jews who are less 'different'; it speeds up the process in which anyone—Jewish or non-Jewish—becomes even less 'different.' At the same time, however, there has been a revival among Jews of religious and cultural practices which intensify one's sense of Jewishness." [26]

Park Forest, writes Herbert J. Gans in his thorough study of that community, "is not an ordinary suburb but rather a partially planned garden city." Part of the planning, from inception in 1948, was the promotion of good neighborliness among the inhabitants and the breakdown of racial or religious segregation. As a result, there has been closer cooperation there than is usually the case among Jews and non-Jews. During the day women of the various religious groupings would "visit with" each other, play bridge, join sewing clubs and maintain relationship in which "ethnic distinctions were minimized." In the evening, however, Jewish couples would turn "primarily to other Jews." Gans quotes a Jewish housewife as sizing up the situation in the following words: "My real close friends are Jewish, my after-dark friends in general are Jewish, but my daytime friends are Gentile." [27]

Gans made his original study in the fall of 1949. By that time the residents of Park Forest had constituted an informal community which "came together only once," at a village dance. The experience of that dance is illuminating: "As both Jews and non-Jews later reported, the Jews at this affair congregated in one section of the hall." Gans explains the situation thus:

> Since sociability is primarily a leisure activity, and in a suburban community one of the major forms of relaxation and self-expression, the belief that there is likely to be less tension in social relationships with other Jews becomes all-important.[28]

The possibility that close relations with members of different faiths would lead to intermarriage is another factor tending to keep Jews and non-Jews apart. "Free association across ethnic lines," we are told by the authors of the study of Crestwood Heights, a Canadian suburb where conditions are not unlike those prevailing in the United States, "is permitted to pre-adolescents and to young children, but as adolescence is approached, with its ritualized dating patterns, the child is expected to conform to the communal norms." [29]

Prejudice against Jews and a desire to avoid intimate contact with them, of course, also plays a role. As one woman stated to the researchers of Crestwood Heights:

> Most of the Christians who do send their children to private school do so because of the Jews. I think all of them would be in private schools if the parents could afford it.[30]

In the most exhaustive study of Jewish suburbia yet undertaken, Albert I. Gordon reports that "invariably, Jewish residents of suburbia, when pressed for a more careful examination of Jewish-Christian relations, point out that Jews seldom come to know non-Jews any better in suburbia than they did in the big city." [31] Gordon sees the danger that inheres in this situation, and he asks, "Are Jews likely to become ghettoized in suburbia? Is the suburb in danger of becoming a gilded ghetto?" [32] The very posing of these questions, even if the author leaves them unanswered, indicates that suburbia has thus far produced little change in the relations between Jew and non-Jew.

Social segregation invariably results in residential segregation in the suburbs as well as in the cities. The history of the Jews in the United States may be written on the basis of the exchange of one area of compact Jewish settlement for another. There is a clear pattern in this exchange: first there is *concentration* in a given residential district, next there is *de*concentration after a certain period, and finally there is *re*concentration in a new district. This does not mean that individual Jews do not occasionally break out of the ghetto walls; but even when they do, they are able to rid themselves of all remaining ties to the ghetto only by severing every bond with the Jewish group in general. There are indeed some who go as far as this but they are the exceptions; the majority reject this kind of emancipation from the ghetto.

I have already discussed the socio-economic basis of the unfriendly relations among the various Jewish groups that arrived here on the three waves of immigration.[33] One more reason for this unfriendliness may be mentioned here. The more acculturated Jews feared that the unmodern Jews of eastern Europe would create a "Jewish problem" in America which the country might otherwise have avoided. From this stemmed the opposition of the German Jews to the mass immigration of Jews from Russia, Poland and Galicia. From this, too, stemmed, as we shall see, the German Jews' endeavor to regulate the economic pursuits of the newcomers. But the developments we have analyzed in previous chapters finally forced most of the Jewish "aristocracy" to change their attitudes. They came to realize that the view of the Jew as a "foreigner" in the United States had nothing to do with the country of his origin, as proven by the fact that a Jew whose American ancestry goes back four, five and more generations will still be considered by large numbers of Americans as an "alien." No matter how useful he may be to the country or how deep his roots here, he will be regarded differently from members of other ethnic and religious groups.

A general process is here reversed. The same America which so crudely and uncompromisingly demands the unconditional and immediate disappearance of other ethnic groups does not care to swallow the Jews. This America refuses to let the Jews disappear and at the same time cannot forgive them for remaining alive. "Whereas other European groups have generally gained respect as assimilation improved their status," writes Higham, "the Jews reaped more and more dislike as they bettered themselves. The more avidly they reached out for acceptance and participation in American life, the more their reputation seemed to suffer." [34]

Not at once and not willingly did the Jew who inclined toward assimilation come to realize the existence, in one form or another, of a Jewish problem, one which affected not only the immigrant, not only the Orthodox or nationalist Jew from eastern Europe. Wirth, himself not far from an assimilationist ideology, explains the feelings of such a Jew:

> The rebuffs administered by prejudice and exclusion serve to make the Jew keenly conscious of his separateness. He finds that the outer world

153

will not receive him as an individual, but insists upon attaching the obnoxious label "Jew" to him and his children, not taking cognizance of the fact that he feels himself no more a part of his people than they consider him a part of themselves.[35]

A man who feels at home nowhere must ask questions of himself and others concerning the meaning of his life. It is the tragedy of the Jews, says Kallen, that they have to forever justify their existence, in their own eyes and in the eyes of the world. Just like potential suicides, they must always be reminding themselves that they have something to live for. And Kallen adds:

> The more marginal the Jew—that is, the greater the number and variety of his relationships, actual and probable, with non-Jews—the greater his feeling of insecurity and his urge to "evaluate" his existence as Jew; the more deeply aware he is of "the Jewish problem." [36]

The very posing of questions relating to the roots of Jewish existence has an ethnicizing impact even on one who arrives at assimilationist answers. It should be emphasized that no organized Jewish group ever arose in America to preach dissolution as an answer to the Jewish question. Ideologies were indeed developed which objectively paved the way to assimilation, but subjectively no one ever presented it as a program, perhaps because anyone entertaining such ideas carried them out in his own personal life with little concern for the fate of the group as a whole. The overwhelming majority of the Jews, irrespective of social status, sought an answer to the Jewish question which would secure their collective existence.

It is therefore not correct, following Wirth, to regard the ghetto as the product of merely negative factors. There was, for example, no external pressure forcing the Spanish-Portuguese Marranos to revert to Judaism in America. The isolated German Jews who settled, in twos and threes and sometimes even singly, thousands of miles from the great centers of Jewish population, could all have merged with their surroundings, as many actually did, rather than lay the foundation for Jewish communal life in the most forsaken parts of the country. These individual Jews would have encountered no resistance to their complete assimilation. If they remained Jews, it was because they chose to do so. To remain in the Jewish camp meant to build

Jewish positions, and the ghetto threw an ethnic mantle around all these positions and made of them a secure structure.

It is also a mistake to see the ghetto only as a Jewish misfortune. It was indeed such when Jews were thrust into it as into a prison which enchained the body and oppressed the soul. But in its voluntaristic aspects, the ghetto was the place where the Jews, a minority everywhere, were the majority. It cannot be gainsaid, however, that even in America the voluntaristic aspects were only one side of the ghetto; the other side was supported by external pressure. The ghetto accompanied the Jew who wanted to remain a Jew from cradle to grave. The role of the cemetery in the formation of Jewish communal life in America cannot be overestimated. In a certain sense, it was even more important than the synagog. For though a Jew might live among Gentiles, he wanted to be buried among Jews. Thus, Jewish communal life everywhere began with a synagog and a cemetery. Sometimes the cemetery even preceded the synagog; to establish a synagog, a quorum of ten males was needed; to open a cemetery, only one dead Jew was required. A total of four Jewish families lived in Boston around the first quarter of the eighteenth century. There was no sign yet of any synagog; but two Jews, Michael Asser and Isaac Solomon, bought a piece of land to set aside as the cemetery of "the Jewish nation." The generally accepted date of establishment of the first synagog in Philadelphia is 1747; but a cemetery had already been opened there in 1738. The handful of Jews who arrived in New Amsterdam in 1654 and laid the groundwork for the first Jewish settlement in America had barely shaken foreign dust from their shoes when they began to concern themselves with establishing a Jewish cemetery. Jews who had thrown off the rigorous discipline enforced by the first synagog in America soon regretted their defection when they faced the threat of being buried among non-Jews. Hundreds of still extant *landsmanschaften* and similar societies owe their existence to the fact that they provide burial for their members in a Jewish cemetery. As Salo W. Baron says: "The cemetery appeared as second only to the synagogue among communal institutions. In fact, in view of the possibility of private congregational worship, many communities sought burial plots even before erecting a house of worship." [37] Baron has in mind the old Jewish communities of Europe and Africa, but his statement applies equally to the development of the Jewish community in the United States.

The ghetto is at once a physical institution and a source of spiritual sustenance. It exists simultaneously within geographic boundaries and in the psyche of Jews and Gentiles. The horizontal walls of the ghetto extend from the Sephardic Jews who sought a sanctuary from the Inquisition to the last German Jews who sought a haven from the Nazis. The vertical walls enclose Jews on the lowest rung of the social ladder and those who have risen as high as Jews can go in America. The center of the ghetto is the synagog, and on its periphery are all institutions which meet Jewish needs both at home and abroad. The ghetto is the home of local Jewish activity and the embassy in America of the Jews of other lands. It makes a community of isolated individuals and fragmented groups. In the ghetto, socially and economically differentiated Jews are consolidated ethnically.

There are those—H. G. Wells was one of them—who characterize the ghetto in America as a state within a state. This is a false conception. All state functions are in the hands of the American government, not the Jewish ghetto. Jews, like all other citizens, perform their duties to the country through the appropriate legal organs, and they enjoy the privileges of citizenship in the same way. The ghetto only serves the specifically Jewish communal interests of the Jews. The Jewish community in the United States does not possess the limited governmental prerogatives even in relation to purely Jewish matters which Jewish communities had, and still have in some cases, in other countries. The new element that America has introduced into Jewish experience is a free Jewish community which, though built entirely on voluntaristic principles, is nevertheless all-embracing and effective.

The ghetto is not homogeneous from a social point of view. On the contrary, it is differentiated and divided. Thus far, we have concentrated on one of its groups, that which we have included in the somewhat misleading term of "German Jews"; and we have analyzed the reasons for its failure to complete the process of thoroughgoing assimilation in the same manner in which comparable economic layers of other ethnic groups did. We must now examine the experience of the Jewish strata on the lower rungs of the ladder.

156

8 The Role of East European Immigrants in the American Jewish Community

Jewish immigration from eastern Europe soon overwhelmingly outnumbered both the Sephardic and the German Jews and in the space of three generations transformed the American Jewish community into the largest in the world. We would probably be understating the case if we placed the present proportion of East Europeans in the Jewish population at 85 percent. The ethnic achievements of East European immigration which have profoundly affected Jewish development in this country in the past seventy-five years were six in number:

(1) The retransformation of Orthodox Judaism into the majority religion of the Jewish community.

(2) The creation of a Jewish labor movement.

(3) The creation of a Jewish press, literature and culture in the Yiddish language and, to a much lesser extent, in Hebrew.

(4) The creation of a secular Jewish nationalism.

(5) The development of a Jewish intelligentsia which provided leaders, teachers and workers for the community.

(6) The democratization of Jewish communal life and the consequent broadening of the base of Jewish institutionalism.

The East European Jews accomplished all this by sheer numbers, by compactness, and by their folk character. This third wave of Jewish immigration carried with it not only individuals or families but whole villages and towns. Virtually an entire people emigrated, with its material poverty and spiritual wealth. The movement thrust forward with the furious force of a deluge, and just as uncontrollably. The opposition of the acculturated American Jews to mass-immigration was unceremoniously swept away, but not their fear that this immigration would bring trouble and upsets in its wake. What the acculturated Jews of German origin feared was precisely the compactness and folk character of the East European immigration; and if they could not stem the flood, they sought at least to regulate it.

Under the impact of this mass immigration, the German Jews quickly abandoned their determination to limit charitable activities to their own underprivileged compatriots. Reluctantly at first, then more resolutely, and finally even with enthusiasm, they extended every conceivable help to the new immigrants; but they were unable to free themselves of the misgivings aroused by this massive flood of new arrivals. Indeed, when the well established German Jews saw that entire sections of the larger American cities were assuming the appearance of Jewish *shtetlekh* (small towns) in Poland, their dread increased; and they tried, through their aid, to influence the living patterns and adaptation of the immigrants. The German Jews attempted to introduce a measure of planning into the chaotic torrent. Their chief concern was to disperse the mass immigration over the sparsely populated parts of the country and to settle large numbers of Jews on land.

ATTEMPTS TO SETTLE IMMIGRANTS ON THE LAND

The first such experiment, strange as it may appear to us today, was undertaken in 1837, when the Jewish population barely totalled fifteen thousand souls. In that year a society called Tzeiray Hatzon was founded in New York, with the objective of bringing Jews into agriculture. (Twenty years earlier, Mordecai Emanuel Noah had put forth a similar suggestion.) The only thing the society accomplished was to stimulate Congregation Anshe Chesed to establish the Jewish colony, "Shalom," in 1838, in Ulster County, N.Y. This colony lasted no more than three or four years.

In 1855, the Lebanon Lodge of B'nai B'rith, in New York, urged the creation of a society to help Jews settle on the land. The leader of the project, Sigismund Waterman, expressed ideas which closely resembled the theories propounded in the twentieth century by Chaim Zhitlowsky and other apostles of Jewish agrarianization. Jews, Waterman contended, were concentrated primarily in business and, to a very limited extent, in skilled labor. There were no farmers among them, and this evoked antagonism from the rest of the country, which considered them foreigners. If the Jews persisted in their traditional occupations, they would follow a course which ran contrary to the welfare of the country.

Endeavors of a broader scope were undertaken in the 1880's to thin out the compactness of the immigrant settlements. HIAS (Hebrew Immigrant Aid Society)—the first large-scale aid organization created by East European Jews, though with considerable support from German Jews—included among its tasks help and counsel to Jewish immigrants interested in farming. In fact, this society contributed significantly to the establishment of several Jewish colonies in Colorado and New Jersey. During the same period, several groups belonging to the *Am Olam*, an organization founded in Russia for the purpose of building Jewish cooperative settlements in the United States, came to this country. They established some colonies in Louisiana, Oregon and the Dakotas, which soon expired.

The most important and successful enterprise along these lines was the setting up of the Baron de Hirsch Fund, incorporated in 1891 with capital of $2,400,000. The settlement of Jews on the land was its chief, but by no means exclusive, object. The program of the Fund included other forms of employment allocation for Jews, all tending to disperse them over a broad geographical and economic area. In 1900, the Fund, in conjunction with ICA (the Jewish Colonization Association), founded the Jewish Agriculture and Industrial Aid Society.[1] The latter, though it took over all of the Fund's farming activities, was not, as can be seen from its name, an exclusively agricultural institution. The program of the Society included the following aims: "The encouragement and the direction of agriculture, the removal of persons from crowded cities, the grant of loans to mechanics, artisans and tradesmen, aid in the acquisition of houses in agricultural and industrial districts; the removal of industries from tenements and shops from crowded sections to country districts, and the encouragement of cooperatives and cooperative undertakings both agricultural and industrial." [2]

In order to organize its work more efficiently, the Society set up in 1901 an Industrial Removal Office, which took over its non-agricultural functions. The Removal Office rendered every manner of assistance to Jews who desired to settle in less populated areas. It strove to channel the arrival of Jewish immigrants into the country via Galveston, in the hope that they would remain in Texas and nearby states instead of gravitating toward New York.

All this testifies to the fact that there was no dearth of efforts to inject some sort of organized direction into the settlement of the Jewish immigrants. As noted, these efforts had a dual motivation: on the one hand, there was a sincere desire on the part of the affluent German Jews to be of help to their poor "co-religionists"; and on the other hand, there were lingering fears that the latter would create complications for all the Jews in the country.

The enormous efforts and the vast sums expended on the geographic deconcentration and economic redistribution of the Jewish immigrants were like water going through a sieve. Although nearly 1,500,000 Jews entered the country between 1901 and 1917, the Removal Office succeeded in settling only 79,000 of them in smaller cities.[3] It is not surprising that the Office closed down when the country entered World War I. The opinion is often heard that there would be considerably less anti-Semitism in America if the Jews were more dispersed throughout the country, if they were not so heavily concentrated in a limited number of economic pursuits, and if there were more of them in agriculture. This contention has never been proven and is, in my opinion, impossible of demonstration. In any case, it is irrelevant. The Jews were integrated into American life in consonance with the country's economic processes and with their own experience and tradition. Even governments have failed in their attempts at reversing the process of urbanization; it was not to be expected that improvised voluntary societies with limited means would have more success. However one may evaluate the consequences of the specific forms which Jewish integration took, from the standpoint of the non-Jewish attitude toward the Jews, there can be no question that these forms were decisive in molding Jewish ethnic cohesion. Without these particular forms, it is doubtful that the Jews could have retained, for a longer period than others, their ethnic dynamism. This is made strikingly clear by an examination of the various stages through which the acculturation of the East European immigration has gone.

SOCIAL FORMATION OF THE EAST EUROPEAN IMMIGRANT GROUP

Most of the third-wave immigrants came with one culture which consisted of two parts, one associated with Hebrew, the other with Yiddish. Both parts were exclusively Jewish, creations of the Jewish national genius. The proportion of those who were also rooted in the cultures of their native lands was incomparably lower among them than among either the Spanish-Portuguese Jews or German Jews. The East European immigrants at first found that, because of their extraordinary compactness, they could get along here almost entirely with their own culture. The Yiddish language, instead of being a hindrance, was actually an important means of adjustment. Whereas other groups became economically productive to the extent that they became Anglicized, the Jews became productive in and through Yiddish. And Jewish productivity at the end of the nineteenth and beginning of the twentieth centuries meant, as we have several times noted, proletarianization.

This economic transformation of an ethnic group is one of the most remarkable phenomena in American history. It was made possible solely because of the ghetto. Borochov defines a nation as a group which possesses not only a common past and culture, but a substantially segregated economy. From this point of view, one could speak of the American Jewish community as a nationality until just about World War I. Jewish laborers worked for Jewish employers, and the class conflicts between them were carried on in a Jewish ethnic environment within the framework of the ghetto. In cities like New York, Chicago, Philadelphia, and Baltimore, both workers and employers in the needle trades industry stemmed not only from the same countries, but often enough even from the same towns in Europe. A *landsmanschaft* spirit prevailed frequently in the shops; the Yiddish mother tongue was everyone's language there.

The Yiddish literature and most of the Jewish literature in English reflect the *shtetl*-character obtaining in the Jewish mode of production at the end of the nineteenth century and beginning of the twentieth. The selfsame spirit can be discerned in the demands which the needle trades workers pressed upon their employers in those days. For example, workers demanded time off in the shops to conduct the traditional afternoon and evening religious services. On another occasion, the demand was made that work be stopped earlier on Friday afternoons so that the Sabbath might not be desecrated. Since many of the shops were actually in the homes of the employers, and since the latter would in some cases try to follow the old-country practice of using their workers also as domestic help, the latter would, consequently, often demand that their union see to it that such practices be terminated. Abraham Cahan, father of the Jewish labor movement in the United States and longtime editor of the *Jewish Daily Forward*, relates that, on one occasion when he was settling a strike, a female worker insisted that the contract include a provision prohibiting the employer's wife from "beating up" the workers.

The non-Jewish immigrant worked at places far removed from his ethnic environment; there he would encounter an ethnic conglomeration and a babel of tongues. He would never meet or see the owner of the railroad, coal mine, streetcar line or factory where he worked, and he could communicate with his foreman only in English. At his place of work he would always be reminded of his backwardness and foreignness; his ethnic group would be a continual object of derision. Not so the early Jewish worker. Jewish immigrants who had succeeded in becoming small-time employers or contractors would meet new arrivals at the piers and persuade them to come to work for them. The Jewish immigrant immediately entered a milieu whose atmosphere resembled that of his birthplace far more than it did the prevalent general atmosphere in the United States. He could live in New York for years and not come into contact with the non-Jewish world or have need to use the English language. He arrived dreadfully impoverished; if he had taken something along from his old home, it had disappeared on the way here, a journey that took him through several European countries and lasted for weeks and sometimes months.

Bernard Weinstein, who came here in 1882 and later became an important trade union leader, described the situation which the East European immigrants found upon arrival:

> They had no friends or relatives, and so most of them, upon their arrival, had to remain at Castle Garden, at the edge of the ocean. At that time there was a big courtyard at Castle Garden and the German Yahudim persuaded the Commissioner of Immigration to allow the "greenhorns" to sleep there or on the barges that floated nearby.[4]

It is thus understandable why the tailors from the old country and the immigrants who were given the opportunity to become tailors readily went to work for the persons who met them at the ships. Aside from these encounters, workers and employers would often meet on the streets, in the *landsmanschaften*, synagogs and societies. Though some of the employers in the late nineteenth century were German Jews, the industry quickly fell almost entirely into the hands of East European Jews. Weinstein describes a tailorshop of that period:

> The boss of the shop lived there with his entire family. The front room and kitchen were used as workrooms. The whole family would sleep in one dark bedroom. The sewing-machines for the operators were located near the windows of the front room. The basters would sit on stools near the walls, and in the center of the room, midst the dirt and the dust, were heaped great piles of materials. There, on top of the soft piles, several finishers would be sitting. . . . Old people . . . using gaslight for illumination, would stand and keep the irons hot and press the finished coats, jackets, pants and other clothes on special boards.[5]

Max Pine, one of the most important union-builders in American Jewish labor history, relates how he became a tailor:

> I looked over the place. The little rooms which constituted the "factory" served as both a shop and a dwelling place. There was a sort of kitchen near the entrance, and a dozen pressing-irons glowed on an oven there. A tall, thin Jew with a little black beard was pressing pants, breathing and moving jerkily.
>
> In the next room, the largest, there were about nine or ten machines, set so close to each other that it looked as if the operators had been squeezed into their places.

The contractor approached me, looked me up and down, and a satisfied little smile appeared on the heavy lips under his thick, yellow mustache.

"A healthy specimen," he declared, "red cheeks, clearly a good eater. You'll do all right in America!"

So we arranged our "bargain," standing right there. I was to pay him $25 and work unpaid for three weeks. And after I had finished my apprenticeship, I would be on my own.[6]

Weinstein, who had become Secretary of the United Hebrew Trades, joined with the noted Protestant clergyman-reformer, Charles H. Parkhurst, in an inspection tour of the shops where Jews were employed late in the nineteenth century. They came to a shop, Weinstein relates, where old rags were being sorted. The filth and dirt, the darkness and neglect were unbearable. Old people and young children worked there.

I asked the workers how it happened that so many Jewish laborers worked at sorting rags. Their answer was: there are a great many elderly Jews who have to earn a living and can't find employment at any other work —so they are reduced to sorting rags. Both the employers and the workers here are Orthodox Jews. They work on Sundays rather than on the Jewish Sabbath; and many pious parents would rather that their daughters work in such establishments so as not to desecrate the Sabbath.

In another desolate spot we found a synagog in the midst of the sweatshops. Jews worked there during the week and conducted services there on Friday nights and Saturdays.[7]

The needle trades were not then, and are not today, the sole base of Jewish industrial wage-earning in the United States. Substantial numbers of Jewish workers were also employed in the tobacco, construction, metal, watchmaking, jewelry and transport industries. And in the old days, the number of Jewish workers engaged in unskilled labor was also not small. But these were all branches of the tree of proletarianization; the trunk of the tree was, and remained, the clothing industry. We must examine the workings of this industry more carefully if we are to understand how Jewish culture enabled the Jews to root themselves economically in American life.

THE NEEDLE TRADES AND THE FOUNDING
OF THE JEWISH LABOR MOVEMENT

Though the bulk of the other "new" immigrants did not work in sweatshops, their income and working conditions were certainly no

better than those of the Jewish needle trade workers. The difference
between the proletarianization of the Jews and that of the non-Jews
can therefore not be found on the level of earnings. The difference, as
has been noted, lay chiefly in the fact that among non-Jews capital and
labor for the most part belonged to different ethnic communities,
but among Jews both belonged to the same ethnic colony. Non-
Jewish workers had no social or cultural points of contact with their
employers, but Jewish workers and employers were part of the same
community and drew their spiritual sustenance from the same cultural
sources. In Chapter 2 we noted that industrial enterprises which
employed immigrant labor frequently had to sponsor courses in English to help their workers avoid accidents in the factories. Jewish
employers never had such a problem. The workers generally had no
need of English, and only the tiny percentage of employers who also
engaged in selling needed to know the language. Many of the entrepreneurs in the shops did not produce for the ultimate consumer;
they were, and still are, in New York and other large cities, contractors
who produced goods for others to sell. Naturally, they had no direct
contact with the consumer, and their economic dependence on English
was quite small.

In these circumstances, Jewish workers would organize themselves
only into Jewish unions. Other foreign-language workers had, as we
have seen, their own locals; and only the Germans had some national
unions and even a central trade union organization of their own—the
source of the name, *Gewerkschaften*, which the Jewish workers later
adopted. The Jewish needle trade unions, on the other hand, were at
the time of their formation entirely ethnic organizations, for that part
of the apparel industry which was organized was not only in Jewish
hands, but in Yiddish-speaking hands. The founders of the Jewish
unions actually had very little ideological interest in Jewish culture;
but it did not take them long to learn that if they wanted to organize
the Jewish workers economically and politically, they would have to
use the Yiddish language.

These founders were, with rare exceptions, immigrants from Old
Russia. They came mainly from middle-class homes and first became
workers in America. They did not draw their social theories from their
own environment: there was not yet a Jewish labor movement in the
old country they left, and precious little inspiration could be drawn

165

from the Jewish proletariat in this country in the 1880's and 1890's. The pioneers of the Jewish labor movement in the United States were thus almost without exception under the influence of the Russian revolutionary movement and West European, chiefly German, socialism. Their objective was not to create a *Jewish* labor movement in this country, but rather to attract Jewish workers to the *American* unions and to the *American* Socialist Party. It was no accident, therefore, that Jewish socialist activity in the United States began in New York with the creation, in 1887, of the Eighth Branch of the Socialist Party and of the Russian Progressive Club a year earlier.

When the time appeared ripe for the organization of the Jewish immigrant workers, the Jewish socialists were the only ones capable of undertaking the task. Their great achievement was that they transformed these degraded Jewish immigrants into a social force which not only altered the course of Jewish history in the United States, but left its mark on the country's entire labor movement. The remarkable thing was that these beaten-down laborers, who worked under such abominable conditions, who were not part of a tradition of independent trade union action, who were worlds away from a proletarian psychology, and who were, perhaps in their majority, Orthodox in religion, founded their first trade unions as socialist organizations. The socialist ideology of the leaders found a warm response in the sense of social justice that lived in the soul of the ordinary Jew—a sense that derived from a combination of the prophetic vision and his unjust treatment at the hands of the non-Jewish world.

The pioneers of the Jewish labor movement were not nationalistically oriented Jews. On the contrary, almost all of them tended toward assimilation, which for them represented the cosmopolitan idea of universal brotherhood. They had just recently left the *Yeshiva* (Jewish religious academy), and their first revolutionary act was to break with Orthodoxy, which bitterly combatted every form of secularization in Jewish life. The pioneers were therefore not religious, and among them could be found many who were militant atheists. Unlike the German Jews, who saw the Jews as a religious group which they sought to perpetuate, the first Jewish socialists saw Jewish collective existence as a plant that could flourish only in conditions of oppression and persecution and that would wither away under the warmth of democratic life. Their objective was therefore not divorcement from the non-Jewish workers, but the closest integration. However, in the very process of initially injecting a socialist spirit into their unions, they created a gulf between the Jewish labor movement and the general labor movement in the country. The latter, as we know, was far removed from a class approach to social problems and did not seek radical changes in the existing social order; hence, the Jewish unions did not model themselves on their American counterparts but on European socialism. And though the Jewish trade unions affiliated themselves with the American Federation of Labor, they did not march in step with it. It was precisely the social ideal of universal human unity at the heart of the Jewish labor movement that objectively reinforced, against the subjective intentions of its founders and leaders, its tendency toward ethnic separatism.

This tendency was strengthened by the fact that the young Jewish labor organizations, drawing their inspiration from European social struggles, made it one of their central tasks to be the support of the anti-Tsarist revolutionary movement in Russia. This in itself deepened the impact of ideologies on the Jewish immigrants; and as pointed out previously, ideological consciousness has always been a solidifying factor among ethnic groups. Social ideology had a dual influence on the Jewish masses. In the minds of those who retained a conscious concern for the survival of the Jewish people, it bolstered the national impulse toward ethnic identity with social objectives. And for those Jews who had lost their ties with Judaism and did not possess any Jewish national aspirations, socialist principles led to a demand for organizational separateness, so as not to become ideologically lost in the larger environment.

In this fashion, the trade unions, which were for all other workers second in importance only to the school as an assimilating factor, became for the Jewish workers the most important instrument of ethnic cultural advance in the Yiddish language. An extensive Jewish culture developed parallel with the rise of the Jewish labor movement and in large measure as a result of it. A Yiddish literature of great scope was created, the most important non-English literature ever to arise in the United States. The Yiddish theater, the Yiddish press,

Yiddish schools for children and courses for adults, all these and more were largely the outgrowth of the Jewish labor movement. Around the relative economic isolation there was built a cultural structure in the very center of the ghetto. Add to this the fraternal, mutual aid and social institutions, on the one hand, and the Jewish sections and federations of the socialist parties and other groups, on the other hand —and it becomes clear why the Jewish worker did not have to leave his Jewish environment in order to satisfy any of his socio-communal needs. He lived in a sort of social autarchy.

It would be a mistake to assume that the mass of Jewish workers were, like most of their leaders, either antagonistic or indifferent to religion or Jewish collective existence. Quite the reverse. It was they, in their great numbers, who crowded the Orthodox synagogs that were opened after 1882 by the scores and hundreds. Out of their ranks also came the supporters of the secular nationalism that arose among the masses of East European immigrants—a nationalism, that is, which viewed the Jews not merely as a religious community, but also as a people, and which aspired to Jewish continuity on the basis of a normal national existence. This, however, was the view of the Jewish workers as individuals; the organized Jewish labor movement set itself social, rather than national, goals. The whole extensive cultural life which the movement carried on was not grounded in any desire to hew out for itself a leading role in the life of the Jewish group; it derived from the demand to strengthen its class positions in the struggle against the bourgeoisie and anti-labor ideologies.

THE CLASS CONFLICT IN AMERICAN JEWISH LIFE

Since Jewish laborers worked for Jewish employers, the ghetto became the arena of class conflict in American Jewish life. We have already discussed the economic aspect of the conflict; its political aspect played an even greater role because of the socialist spirit of the first Jewish unions. And not merely as a result of the fact that the employers were Republicans and Democrats—and the workers, socialists; cultural factors were involved, too. Even in the old country, the workers had sought to liberate themselves from the hegemony of the Orthodox leadership, and here they found that their bosses were at the helm of the synagogs and temples; the latter, moreover, did not scruple to use religion as a weapon against the workers on the economic and political levels. As Elias Tcherikower, editor of two volumes on the early history of the Jewish labor movement in the United States, has written:

> The Jewish worker was employed almost exclusively by a Jewish entrepreneur, exactly as he had been in the old country. This situation had to—and did—play no small role in the development of the social conflicts in the Jewish community here. Furthermore, the manufacturer was, especially in the early years, generally a successful German Jew, whereas the workers were newly arrived East European Jews, mainly *Russians*. But the Jewish worker did not have a direct, face-to-face relationship with the large manufacturer and his inside shop. Between these two social classes stood the contractor. (Tcherikower's emphasis.) [8]

Here we see the convergence of all the social, economic, cultural and spiritual divisions which set the ghetto off into conflicting subgroups. Had the Jewish labor movement existed on the same ideological plane as the rest of American labor, the conflict inside the ghetto would not have been so embittered. But the socialist spirit of the Jewish unions speedily put an end to the idyllic Jewish *landsmanschaft* character of the production in the tailor shops after East European Jewish entrepreneurs had taken them over. At a time when the unions of America pursued the policy of the AFL—"a fair wage for a fair day's work"—the Declaration of Principles of the United Hebrew Trades in 1890 proclaimed "that all the wealth and means of production are created through labor, and therefore the worker has the full right to enjoy the fruit of the labor which he creates." The Declaration proceeded to list the injustices of the capitalist system and added with emphasis "that this kind of system is an unjust one and must be overturned, and in its place must be built a truly humane society where everyone will receive the proper return for his work." The authors of this Declaration of Principles were convinced that "there can be no peace between capital and labor in the prevailing social system." [9]

If this was the outlook of the weak Jewish unions of the last decade of the nineteenth century, unions that consisted of former petty bourgeois, handicraftsmen, *luftmenschen,* and workers without previous union experience, can there be any wonder at the even more outspoken socialism of the unions during the first two decades of the twentieth century? By then, these unions already had, in both their leadership and membership, substantial cadres of workers who came here with years of socialist activity behind them in the old country. For in 1897, the Bund, the first Jewish labor party in the world, was founded in Russia. Several years later, the Poale Zion and Socialist-Territorialist parties were established. However mutually antagonistic these groups might have been in their objectives and programs, they had one unifying principle in common: they were all socialist organizations that taught their members not to barter historic social goals for temporary improvements. So we find that the preamble to the Constitution of the International Ladies' Garment Workers' Union pledged the union to the mission of creating "a system of society wherein the workers shall receive the full value of their product," this mission to be realized only with "the aid of the political party whose aim is the abolition of the capitalist system." [10] Until 1924, the ILGWU forbade its members to run for political office on the ballots of non-labor or non-socialist parties.

The Constitution of the United Hatters, Cap and Millinery Workers International Union declared that "the concentration of wealth and power in the hands of the capitalist class is the cause of the workingman's economic oppression." [11] The Constitution of the Fur Workers Union spoke of the struggle "going on in all nations of the civilized world between the oppressors and the oppressed of all countries, a struggle between the capitalist and the laborer, which grows in intensity from year to year." [12]

The Amalgamated Clothing Workers of America, established in 1914, declared in its Constitution that "industrial and inter-industrial organization, built upon the solid rock of class knowledge and class consciousness, will put the organized working class in actual control of the system of production, and the working class will then be ready to take possession of it." [13] In 1920 the New York clothing manufacturers brought suit in court for the dissolution of the Amalgamated on the ground that it was not a labor organization, but a conspiracy against the government, citing this clause in the union's Constitution as their proof. The suit was dismissed.

The Jewish unions viewed the workers as a separate class, but they did not, as we have noted, recognize the existence of the Jewish people. On October 4, 1890, a national conference of all Jewish labor organizations in the United States and Canada opened in New York. One of the placards which decorated the walls of the meeting-hall read: "The world is our fatherland, Socialism our religion." Poznanski's slogan, "America is our Zion and Washington our Jerusalem," received here a proletarian twist. The conference created the Jewish Labor Federation, which adopted the goal of "raising the Jewish worker to a status of equality with his American brothers and helping him understand the labor question—the question of the enslaved class to which he belongs; teaching him to fight for and contribute to the coming victory of laboring humanity." As for Jewish matters, the conference found it necessary to emphasize: "We have no Jewish question in America. The only Jewish question we recognize is the question of how to prevent the rise of such 'Jewish questions.' " [14]

This being the case, why a separate Jewish labor federation? The conference answered:

> Only because we, Yiddish-speaking citizens, can influence Jewish workers, only because we speak their language and know their life—only for these reasons have we created this special Jewish organization. The Yiddish language is our instrument; the elimination of all barriers between Jew and non-Jew in the labor world is one of our goals. [15]

Other immigrant workers were for a period of time cut off within an isolated ethnic environment because there developed among them a *nationalism* bound up with the lands of their origin; the Jewish workers remained separate because of their *internationalist ideology,* which the American labor movement did not share. And though they regarded the Yiddish language as a means rather than an end in itself, they nevertheless became the most important bearers of the extensive Yiddish culture in this country.

So unique has the productivity of Jews been in the United States that both capitalist and worker have been influenced by ethnicizing tendencies yielding objective results running counter to the subjective programs of their respective leaders. On the one side, we have found the Jewish bourgeoisie blockaded, through social and economic discrimination, within a Jewish environment. On the other side, we see organized Jewish labor, moved by its ideal of assimilationist universalism, creating national Jewish values and providing secular reinforcement for Jewish ethnic cohesion in the United States at a time when the latter's religious bulwark was weakening.

Until World War I, organized Jewish labor was Jewish in terms of history and environment, but not in terms of philosophy and objectives. As a result, the Jewish labor movement did not participate in general Jewish activities; at best it remained indifferent to them, and not infrequently its attitude was antagonistic. Not only did the movement create its own economic and political institutions, its own network of schools, its own press, its own self-help and mutual aid organizations, but, whenever possible, its own philanthropic institutions as well. It is one of the ironies of Jewish communal development in the United States that precisely at the time when there existed a virtually independent Jewish labor movement, this movement adopted, because of its extreme class conceptions, a nihilistic attitude toward general Jewish problems and remained unintegrated within Jewish communal life. Conversely, Jewish workers became active in general Jewish undertakings only at a time when the Jewish labor movement had ceased to exist as an entity and had become an integral part of the American labor movement.

9 Upward Economic Mobility and the American Jew

ASSIMILATORY TRENDS

If the unique forms of Jewish industrial wage-earning played so decisive a role in solidifying Jewish ethnic identity in the United States, then Jewish drift away from wage work which, as we saw earlier, brought the Jews into commerce, the professions and the white-collar occupations in higher proportion than any other group of the "new" immigration, should have had a disintegrating effect on the Jewish community. In many respects, this was actually the case. The worst victim was the Yiddish language. Its position was weakened in large measure as a result of the fact that the Jews lost their commanding position in the clothing industry in the large cities. In the first place, the number of Jewish workers in the industry decreased in absolute terms; and this contributed substantially to the shattering of Jewish economic compactness, which had been such an important ethnic factor. Secondly, the relative weight of those Jewish workers who remained in the industry—and they are still to be numbered in the tens of thousands—dropped in comparison to the total number of workers in the needle trades, leaving the Jewish workers as a diminishing minority both in the industry and in the unions.

The socialist character of these unions disappeared along with their

Jewish majorities, and the unions adapted themselves to the spirit of the general trade union movement. By the 1930's, there was not one needle trade union that had not stricken from its constitution the socialist preambles adopted at the time of its founding. These unions, virtually Jewish bodies at their inception, thus broke out of the ghetto walls. The last of the many periodicals that had been published directly by these unions in Yiddish ceased appearing in 1958; Yiddish is still the language of only a tiny handful of union locals, and it is only a matter of time before they too will transfer to English. Because of their tradition and Jewish leadership, these unions still participate in certain Jewish activities and make financial contributions to Jewish causes, but they are no longer Jewish organizations.

The Yiddish language has thus lost its most important position of strength and is now caught up in a process of disintegration which will probably never be stopped. But linguistic assimilation does not lead to the degree of national assimilation among Jews that it does among other ethnic groups, although it does tend to weaken the foundation upon which the Jewish ethnic structure rests. For nearly two thousand years Jews have created Jewish culture not only in their ancient Hebrew and not only in Yiddish, mother tongue of the vast majority of the Jews in the world prior to World War II, but in the languages of the countries where they resided as well. They have also produced a considerable Jewish culture in English—practically the only substantial ethnic culture in English—thus mitigating the effects of linguistic disintegration and reducing the impact of the assimilatory pressures.

We are again witnessing the old interplay of positive and negative forces which gives the relations between the Jewish minority and non-Jewish majority such a unique direction. An examination of the economic mobility of the Jewish population since it has become of predominantly East European origin will provide additional evidence of the results of this uniqueness.

ISOLATING EFFECT OF EDUCATIONAL DISCRIMINATION

In business, the later Jewish arrivals encountered the same difficulties and discriminations as their predecessors, but in greater measure and, for reasons to be established later, in more intensive form. In the social boundaries beyond which the wealthier Jews could not pass we have isolated the factors that have prevented assimilation among them from assuming the scope and tempo it has assumed among elements of comparable status in other ethnic groups. A similar situation has obtained among Jewish intellectual elements, whose counterparts among other ethnic groups were quickly assimilated into the prevailing milieu. To the extent that there has been a deliberate policy in the United States to close the doors to certain positions for Jews as Jews, this policy applied not only to the wealthier clubs, resorts and hotels, but to the colleges and universities. At the very time the younger generations produced by the third immigration had qualified materially to flow into the country's cultural mainstream, they were made to realize that there was such a thing as a Jewish question even in the United States. Jewish youth learned this in two stages: first, when they discovered that it was much more difficult for a Jew than for a non-Jew to enter a higher institution of learning, and then, when those who had made their way into the institutions found the doors of the student organizations closed to them.

Until the first war, only a few of the most aristocratic colleges had restrictions against Jewish students, and not openly at that. Thereafter, the restrictions became more widespread and more open. Until just recently, it was not easy to find a private university that had not adopted some kind of a quota system for Jewish students as well as for Negroes and other minorities. The schools pursuing this practice hardly made a secret of it. It reached the point where a certain number of Jewish students who wished to study medicine had to go abroad to find admittance. A study made by the B'nai B'rith Vocational Service in 1935 and again in 1946 makes it possible to establish the results of the discriminations and quota norms in the colleges. Thus we learn that though the proportionate relation of the Jewish students to the general student body in the colleges remained virtually stationary in those eleven years—8.8 percent in 1935 compared with 9.0 percent in 1946—the proportion in the professional schools did change. In 1935, Jewish students constituted 8.8 percent of the student body in the professional schools, but no more than 7.0 percent in 1946. The B'nai B'rith study could find no other reason for this except discrimination. In 67 medical schools the percentage of Jews fell from 15.9 to 12.7. While the total number of students in these schools increased from 20,039 in 1935 to 21,575 in 1946, the number of Jewish students dropped from 3,179 to 2,737.

In 31 schools of dentistry, the proportion of Jewish students decreased from 28.2 percent to 18.9; in 38 pharmaceutical schools, from 24.5 to 15.1; in 77 law schools, from 25.8 to 11.1; in 7 veterinary schools, from 11.1 to 1.8; in 62 schools of engineering, from 6.5 to 5.6; in schools of architecture, from 8.5 to 4.4; in schools of social work, from 13.6 to 11.1; in schools of commerce, from 16.7 to 10.7; and in art schools, from 15.5 to 8.4. A proportionate increase in Jewish students occurred in such professions as osteopathy, nursing, military science, education, theology, etc. The increase in military science students was certainly a concomitant of the second war; and as for the categories of education and theology, these were essentially related to the internal needs of the Jewish community, that is, the number of rabbinical students increased, as did the demand for teachers in the Jewish educational system.[1]

That discrimination was the main, albeit far from the only, factor in the declining ratio of Jews in the general student population is further attested by the third Decennial Census conducted by the B'nai B'rith Vocational Service in 1956, to the findings of which we have referred earlier. That census revealed that while enrollment in the colleges of the United States and Canada rose from 2.1 million in 1946 to 2.7 million in 1955, the number of Jewish college students remained at the 200,000 figure, thus reducing the proportion of Jews in the college community from 9.0 percent in 1946 to 7.5 percent ten years later. These figures reflect the tremendous drift toward higher education among the general population on the one hand, and the fact that the Jewish population has lagged behind the country as a whole in numerical growth on the other hand.

No discrimination is to be inferred from these statistics. On the contrary, close scrutiny will find them disclosing a diminution in the practices which tended to hold down the number of Jews in the colleges in former years. There is no question but that court rulings, federal government policy, fair educational legislation and fair employment practice laws enacted in a number of states, and the more enlightened attitudes of the American public have all had the effect of reducing discrimination. The results point up the existence of discrimination in previous years. With the relaxation or abolition of the quota system in education and the lessening of discrimination in employment, there is to be observed among Jewish students a tendency to enter in greater numbers the study of professions in which Jews were formerly sparsely represented. Correspondingly they are showing less inclination toward the professional courses with which Jewish students were formerly more closely identified. Thus we find the proportion of Jewish students taking courses in education rising from 17.4 percent of the total number of Jewish students in the professional fields in 1946 to 18.9 percent in 1955. In engineering, the percentage rose from 16.9 percent to 17.6; in law, from 6.1 to 8.2; in medicine from 5.3 to 7.6; and in pharmacy, from 3.2 to 5.2. On the other hand, there has been a drop in dentistry from 2.5 percent in 1946 to 1.8 in 1955; in music, from 3.3 percent to 1.5 and in optometry, from 1.8 percent to 0.6.

Should discrimination in education and employment continue to abate, it will, of course, in time materially alter the economic picture of American Jewry, but the American Jewish community of today has been shaped by processes operating during past generations, and it would take more than a few years to change the patterns those processes have produced. Basic in these patterns is the preference of Jews for intellectual pursuits which offer the greatest opportunity for self-employment and in which discrimination is less prevalent. These patterns are followed by the Jew in the colleges today as they were followed ten and twenty years ago. In 1955 the B'nai B'rith Vocational Service found "25.2% of all Jewish students reported for specific professions were in seven of these [self-employing and less discriminating] fields. If we add to this the figure for business administration, which includes a great many accounting students and those preparing to enter family business enterprises, we have accounted for more than half of the total." [2]

Those who sought to free themselves from the ghetto encountered their first disappointment in seeking entry into the colleges. Once admitted, they experienced their second disappointment: non-Jewish students did not want them in their fraternities, sororities and clubs.

Jewish students were consequently forced to form their own, exclusively Jewish societies and clubs—a new ghetto. For many Jewish young people, the student society was their first affiliation with a Jewish institution, a kind of introduction to Jewish communal life. The school of higher learning, which intensified the trend toward assimilation among students of other ethnic groups, accentuated for the Jewish students their ethnic separateness.

ISOLATING EFFECT OF PROFESSIONAL DISCRIMINATION

But it was only when the Jewish boys and girls had concluded their education and sought to enter the professions that they were confronted by the full measure of Jewish otherness, a quality which they perhaps did not want to acknowledge but which was imposed upon them from outside. If they looked for employment, they encountered discrimination in non-Jewish enterprises; if they decided on self-employment, they could count on only a small number of non-Jewish clients. On the whole, therefore, they were dependent on either Jewish employers or Jewish clients: in both cases, they found themselves encircled by the Jewish community. And this was bound to retard substantially the assimilatory trend which education normally hastens.

There are a number of surveys which demonstrate the extent to which Jews in intellectual occupations are dependent upon the Jewish environment. About a quarter of a century ago, the Conference on Jewish Relations (now Conference on Jewish Social Studies) sponsored a study of Jewish lawyers in New York, the results of which were published in 1939.

Of the 511 Jewish attorneys who earned their living by working for other lawyers, 323 were employed by Jewish lawyers or in exclusively Jewish legal firms. An additional 79 worked for firms most of whose members were Jews. In other words, nearly eight out of every ten employed Jewish lawyers in New York worked for Jews, one worked for a partly-Jewish firm, and only one for a firm that was predominantly non-Jewish.[3]

The situation of the self-employed attorneys seemed somewhat better. Nevertheless, of the 2,968 self-employed Jewish attorneys, 1,621 (54.26 percent) had a clientele that was more than one-half

Jewish; 1,113 (37.50 percent) had more than one-half non-Jewish clients; and 234 (7.88 percent) did not specify. We shall have more to say about the non-Jewish clients of Jewish professionals.

In 1950, the B'nai B'rith Vocational Service Bureau conducted a survey among lawyers who were graduated from law school in 1946 and 1947. Questionnaires were sent out to 2,325 graduates throughout the country who were previously identified as Jews or non-Jews. The findings, as summarized in a memorandum submitted by the World Jewish Congress to the International Labor Office, follow:

> Jewish law graduates of those two classes earned less than their non-Jewish classmates; three times as many non-Jews as Jews began their legal careers as attorneys in private industry; the common belief that a higher percentage of Jews than non-Jews entered legal work in government was not true; proportionately more Jews than non-Jews failed to go into legal work following graduation from law school; of all Jewish lawyers in law firms, 63 percent were connected with firms in which all of the partners were Jewish and another 21 percent were connected with firms in which some of the partners were Jews; half of the non-Jewish lawyers earned under $3,170 in 1948, whereas half of the Jewish lawyers received under $2,950.[4]

The Conference on Jewish Relations sponsored a study of Jewish doctors in the United States, the results of which were published in 1939.[5] The study provides a picture of the extent of discrimination against Jews in medical schools. Thus, of the 1,346 Americans studying medicine abroad in 1937–38, over 1,200 (90 percent) were Jews, most of whom presumably had failed to gain admission to American medical schools. The study, which embraced 16,000 Jewish doctors throughout the country, brought out that in the smaller towns their practice was much less restricted to Jewish patients than in the larger centers. But it should be remembered that in 1936 three-quarters of all Jewish doctors were to be found in six states—New York, Illinois, Pennsylvania, New Jersey, Massachusetts and California. New York alone contained nearly one-half of all Jewish doctors. This proportionate division of Jewish doctors, clearly reflecting the distribution of the Jewish population, points up the fact that Jewish physicians earned their living mainly from Jewish patients.

A later study by Alfred I. Shapiro numerically authenticated the presence of discrimination against Jews in the medical profession. The same study also proved that "great numbers of Jewish physicians are found only where the Jewish population of a given community is unusually large," confirming the thesis that Jewish doctors draw their patients primarily from the Jewish community.[6]

In 1938, Lee J. Levinger undertook a study of the position of Jews in the professions in Ohio,[7] covering the following occupations: doctors, dentists, lawyers, teachers, druggists, engineers and architects. Levinger concluded that the clientele of Jewish professionals was not generally, or even primarily, Jewish. As proof, he cited the fact that there were a great many more non-Jews for every non-Jewish doctor, dentist or lawyer, etc., than there were Jews for every Jewish professional of the same category. The following table, based on Levinger's statistics, shows the proportionate difference in the number of professionals in the Jewish and general communities.

Table 13.—Number of people for each professional in Ohio in 1936

PROFESSION	NO. OF PEOPLE PER EACH PROFESSIONAL IN THE GENERAL POPULATION	NO. OF JEWS PER EACH JEWISH PROFESSIONAL
Doctors	756	231
Dentists	1,603	469
Lawyers	682	147
Teachers	162	318
Druggists	1,179	303
Engineers and Architects	944	1,100

Levinger's study shows, as do the studies of Jewish lawyers in New York and of Jewish doctors in the United States, that among Jewish professionals there is a much higher proportion of self-employed than among non-Jewish professionals. In this, a large role is doubtless played by the discriminations against Jews seeking employment. Levinger also shows that while Jews comprise only 2.5 percent of the total population of Ohio, they account, in 56 cities with a population of 10,000 or more each, for 8.1 percent of the doctors, 10.6 percent of the dentists, 13 percent of the lawyers, and 13.1 percent of the pharmacists. If these statistics are examined out of context, it is easy to arrive at Levinger's mistaken conclusion that Jewish professionals have a much greater proportion of non-Jewish clients than they actually have.

To avoid this mistake, two facts must be taken into account. First, that the table includes a city like Cleveland, with a population of close to a million, 9 percent of whom are Jews—and small towns of no more than 10,000 each, where the Jews are no more than 1.5 percent of the population. The smaller the city, the smaller the Jewish population; and the smaller the Jewish population, the closer is the number of professionals it produces to its proportion in the general population. Likewise, the larger the city, the larger the Jewish population and the higher the percentage of Jewish professionals in relation to the general population. The second fact to be remembered is that the professions cited are all of a type in which the proportion of self-employed is very high. Both facts make it clear that Levinger generalized too much and unwarrantedly when he inferred from the smaller number of Jews per Jewish professional that Jewish professionals have a large percentage of non-Jewish clients. A likelier conclusion would be that Jewish professionalism was more concentrated within rather than without the Jewish community. Jews, who were heavily concentrated in small and medium-sized business and in real estate, were in greater need of lawyers than other groups who had a higher proportion of workers. This, indeed, accounted for the greater number of Jewish lawyers; but, as the New York study showed, Jewish lawyers generally earned less than their non-Jewish colleagues and engaged to a greater extent than the latter in side occupations. It is therefore clear that the greater number of Jewish lawyers was more an indication of an overpopulation of this profession among Jews than of the greater demand for their services among non-Jews.

As for doctors, it is well known that Jews seek medical advice more than do non-Jews; here too, then, the smaller number of Jews per Jewish doctor is chiefly the result of conditions in the Jewish environment itself rather than of the fact that Jewish doctors have a very high proportion of non-Jewish patients. Further confirmation of this thesis is seen in the smallness of Jewish participation, in Ohio, in such professions as education, engineering and architecture. These are professions that have a very small percentage of self-employed, and their clientele more closely corresponds to the general population than to any particular part of it. In other words, the clientele of these professions, especially education, is not as selected and segregated as that of medicine or the law. And in fact we find that Jewish participation in them is lower than the Jewish proportion of the population. This proportion, as noted, is around 2.5 in Ohio, but, in that state Jews constituted only 2.1 percent of the engineers and architects, and no more than 1.3 percent of the teachers.

A study carried out by the B'nai B'rith Vocational Service Bureau among persons graduating from college courses in business administration and accounting in 1946 and 1947 resulted in the same finding: Jewish graduates were generally employed in Jewish-owned firms, earned less and had a harder time finding employment than their non-Jewish colleagues.

In short, education does not lead nearly as high a percentage of Jewish professionals out of the ethnic environment as it does professionals of other ethnic groups. One more very important fact must also be borne in mind. A large proportion of Jewish professionals who are not economically dependent on Jewish clients do not, for the most part, earn their living from the non-Jewish "aristocracy," but from other minorities. The implications of this fact are readily at hand. The process of assimilation always moves in the direction of the dominant group, never in that of an ethnic group which is itself underprivileged or on the way to dissolution. Had Jewish professionals—we speak of those who are not dependent on Jews themselves—greater entree to the "Nordic" elements of the population, their urge to dissolve within those elements would be enormously strengthened; but access to Italians, Poles, Ukrainians, Puerto Ricans, Negroes, and other minorities cannot stimulate such a desire.

Jacob Lestchinsky has shown the high proportion of clients of Jewish professionals and merchants among the non-Jewish immigrants from eastern Europe and their children—for the latter came from areas where the population was accustomed to dealing with Jewish storekeepers, doctors, dentists, and pharmacists. His generalizations are indeed too wide-ranging and his conclusions therefore rather extravagant; but that non-Jewish immigrants and their children constitute a large proportion of the clients of Jewish professionals is a fact that is unmistakably manifest wherever any substantial immigrant colony is to be found. One can even go so far as to assert that a not-inconsiderable proportion of those who deal with Jews come from non-Jewish lower socio-economic strata. This is evident among the Slavic elements in the Atlantic states, among the Negroes and poor whites of the southern states, and among the Mexicans in the Pacific states. Compared with these groups, the Jews represent a higher social stratum; consequently, any tendency among Jews to assimilate with these groups must be small indeed. In this fashion, the assimilatory tendency of upward economic mobility and education is considerably neutralized. If economic dependence on Jews keeps a large segment of Jewish merchants and professionals within the ghetto, that segment which is dependent on socially depressed non-Jewish groups has little motivation for leaving the ghetto. There still remains a segment, whose size is impossible to estimate, which does have economic contact with "higher" social elements and even with the "aristocracy," and is materially dependent on them; and it is this segment which is the chief source of the trickle of defection that runs from the ghetto to the non-Jewish environment. This trickle is of sufficient force to create a problem among Jews, but it is quite insignificant in comparison with the flood of defection of parallel elements among other ethnic groups.

As we pointed out several times, discrimination in the schools and professions is on the decline. Should it continue to diminish, it will in time undoubtedly facilitate Jewish assimilation. At present, however, the decline has not produced a sufficient change of situation to warrant a revision in our conclusions even if some of the statistics we have cited are somewhat dated. The quicker tempo of participation in general economic processes has not had the effect of correspondingly undermining Jewish group solidarity; in a sense this quicker tempo has even strengthened Jewish communal life in this country.

PATTERNS OF INTERMARRIAGE

Intermarriage, we have observed earlier, is one of the longest steps in the direction of ethnic dissolution. It begins to assume significant proportions after a measure of economic and social progress has been

achieved. Has an increase in intermarriage followed upon the upward
social and economic mobility of the American Jews?

We lack the kind of exhaustive statistics on mixed marriages among
Jews in the United States as exist for Canada; but there are enough
figures available to allow a definite conclusion, particularly when this
conclusion is corroborated by the writer's long-term personal observations in all the major cities of the country. Although it was to
be expected, because of the factors analyzed above, that there would
be a very sizable increase of intermarriage among Jews between the
two world wars, such an increase did *not* occur. This is not to say
that the number of mixed marriages involving Jews did not grow;
rather, that the increase in no way corresponded to the potentialities
and the favorable conditions that created a situation conducive to
intermarriage. Mixed marriages are certainly a problem for Jews, but
they are far from constituting a serious threat to the continued existence of the Jewish community in the United States.

The most important study in this field is still the one conducted by
the late Julius Drachsler in New York after World War I, the non-
Jewish aspects of which were dealt with in Chapter 2 of this book.
As regards the Jews, Drachsler found that in the period 1908–1912
mixed marriages amounted to slightly more than 1 percent (1.17%)
of the total number of Jewish marriages. Only in marriages between
white and Negro was the percentage lower (1.08%). Even at that
time it was clear that intermarriage grew in proportion to the secular
advancement of a particular Jewish group. Thus, for example, among
Rumanian Jews less than one-half of 1 percent of the total marriages
were mixed, among Russian Jews—barely two-thirds of 1 percent;
while among English Jews the percentage of mixed marriages was
3.47; among German Jews, 5.16; and among French Jews, 6.54
percent. Native-born Jewish children of native-born parents had 4.26
percent mixed marriages.[8] This demonstrates that the trend among
the native-born generations is in the direction of a higher rate of
mixed marriages. When one takes into account that these statistics
are for New York City, which contains more than two-fifths of the
American Jewish population, and that they cover the period of the
largest Jewish mass immigration, when great numbers of Jews could
live out their entire lives without any contact with non-Jews, it

becomes clear why it was possible then to predict with certainty a huge rise in the rate of intermarriage, particularly in the smaller cities. The actual increase in no sense confirmed the prediction, except for the very small towns with a handful of Jewish families.

No research comparable in scope to Drachsler's study in New York was ever undertaken for the country as a whole, or even for New York, at a later period. Comparisons are thus impossible to make, but one can get a conception of the dynamics of intermarriage from isolated figures that crop up in various studies. For example, Barnett Brickner found that Cincinnati, the stronghold of Reform Judaism, which attracted a relatively small amount of Jewish immigration in the early twentieth century and where the Jewish population attained a high degree of nativization, had 21 mixed marriages out of a total of 582 Jewish marriages during the years 1916–1918—barely 2 percent: a figure nearly identical with Drachsler's for New York.[9] An even smaller proportion was discovered by Bessie Bloom Wessel in Woonsocket in 1926—only about 1 percent of marriages among Jews were mixed.[10] In another of her studies, Mrs. Wessel noted that in only 27 of the 517 Jewish families in New London was one of the parents a non-Jew in 1938.[11] Koenig found a higher proportion of mixed marriages in Stamford the same year. Of the 823 Jewish couples, 59 (7.2 percent) were mixed—or, if individuals rather than couples are counted, 3.7 percent.[12]

In 1953 Aaron Antonovsky conducted a study of the Jewish community in New Haven. He found that 7.9 percent of the 127 men comprising his sample were married to Gentile women. Considering that more Jewish men are involved in intermarriage than women, Antonovsky is justified in seeing in these figures a confirmation of Ruby J. R. Kennedy's findings that the total rate of intermarriage among New Haven Jews was 6.3 percent in 1940 and 5.1 percent in 1950.[13]

Studies made in the highly Americanized community in San Francisco at about the same time show that one Jewish family out of ten had a non-Jewish member.[14] In the even more Americanized and considerably assimilated community of New Orleans, the only city in the country with a general population of over 100,000 which has more Reform than Orthodox Jews, Julian Feibelman found that one out of every 17 Jewish families had a non-Jewish member in 1938.[15] A survey carried out 15 years later established that 7 percent of all individual married Jews in the city had non-Jewish spouses and that 10 percent of the Jewish households included non-Jewish members.[16] This would indicate an appreciable increase in the rate of intermarriage over Feibelman's figures, but at least part of the increase may be attributed to the difference of classification in the two studies.

Jacksonville, Fla., had 10 intermarriages in every 100 Jewish families in 1946, and 6.5 in every hundred in 1954.[17] A survey conducted in 1951 by the Jewish Community Council of Los Angeles disclosed that from 5 to 8 percent of the Jewish adult population had taken marriage partners from another faith.[18] In Washington, D.C., with a Jewish population of over 81,000, 11.3 percent of 27,000 households had either a Gentile husband (7.8%) or a Gentile wife (3.5%) in 1956.[19] In Charleston, S.C., there were 8 or 9 intermarriages in every 100 marriages among Jews.[20]

A study published in 1957 by Benjamin Kaplan covering the Jewish communities of Clinton, Opelousas and New Iberia, all in the State of Louisiana, throws interesting light on Jewish-Gentile relationships in very small towns during the latter part of the nineteenth century. In Clinton, the Jewish community, never numbering more than 100 persons and now extinct, was as thoroughly integrated into the social fabric of the general society as any Jewish settlement had ever been. Jewish children all attended public schools, and many young people frequently attended Christian churches and even partook in their services. And yet "there were only two cases of intermarriages before 1900," Kaplan tells us.

The Opelousas community, with only 16 Jewish families comprising 36 individuals at the time of the study, is losing a valiant struggle to maintain itself. This community shows the effect of a very high rate of intermarriage. On the other hand, there is New Iberia with only 37 Jewish units composed of 76 individuals where only three men married Christian wives, and they all retain their Jewish identification.[21]

The best estimates for the country as a whole place the intermarriage rate at the beginning of 1958 at between 7 and 10 percent. Hershel Shanks placed the figures at between 5 and 10 percent in

1953.[22] The 7 to 10 percent estimate finds confirmation in the answers to a voluntary question regarding religious affiliation contained in a Census report for 1957. From a sample comprising 35,000 households in 330 areas, the following table was constructed:

Table 14.—Married couples by religion reported for the U.S. civilian population, March, 1957 [23]

RELIGION	NUMBER OF COUPLES	%
All Married Couples in Major Religious Groups [1]	36,576,000	100.0
Husband and wife in same religious group	34,223,000	93.6
Husband and wife in different groups	2,353,000	6.4
Either or both spouses Protestants:	26,916,000	100.0
both spouses Protestant	24,604,000	91.4
one Roman Catholic	2,255,000	8.4
one Jewish	57,000	0.2
Either or both spouses Roman Catholic:	10,657,000	100.0
both Roman Catholic	8,361,000	78.5
one Protestant	2,255,000	21.2
one Jewish	41,000	0.4
Either or both spouses Jewish:	1,356,000	100.0
both Jewish	1,258,000	92.8
one Protestant	57,000	4.2
one Roman Catholic	41,000	3.0

1. As used in this table, the term "major religious group" includes Protestant, Roman Catholic and Jewish faiths.

The number of married Jews in the country totalled 1,356,000. In 1,258,000 or 92.8 percent marriages both spouses were Jews; in 4.2 percent cases a Jew was married to a Protestant and in 3.0 percent marriages one spouse was a Roman Catholic. These particular figures in the Census must be taken with great caution; however, the 7 percent rate of intermarriage that they reveal is too close to the findings in the various population studies we have cited in this chapter not to be accepted as a corroboration of the general conclusion at which we have arrived for the country as a whole.

The 7 to 10 percent rate is quite a jump over the 2 percent rate Drachsler established for the City of New York fifty years earlier, but, considering the degree of acculturation to which the Jewish community has attained during this period, the surprise is not that the increase has been so big, but that it has been so small. Not only has the rate of intermarriage among American Jews been lower than among other white ethnic and religious groups; it has also been considerably lower than among Jews in other western lands as the following figures, based on studies by the late Arthur Ruppin, Uriah Zevi Engelman and Jacob Lestchinsky show:

From 1921 to 1929, the number of mixed marriages in Germany increased from 29.4 for every 100 homogeneous Jewish marriages to 59.0 for every 100. In Switzerland in 1920, there were 13.2 mixed marriages for every 100 homogeneous ones; in 1930, 19 for every 100. In Hungary in 1933, there were 32 mixed for every 100 homogeneous marriages; in Austria in 1931, 29.6 mixed for every 100 homogeneous; in Czechoslovakia in 1933, 11.3 for every 100. One-third of all marriages involving Jews in Copenhagen during the first third of the twentieth century have been mixed. In Amsterdam, the percentage of mixed marriages increased from 5 at the end of the nineteenth century to 70 in 1933. In Trieste, the percentage grew from 17.9 in 1903 to 56.1 in 1927.[24]

No reliable figures are available for western Europe and Central and South America, but scattered reports give a fairly clear indication that intermarriage is on the rise throughout and assumes almost mass proportions in some countries. Both old and stabilized Jewish communities, like the one in England, and relatively young communities, like those in Argentina, go through the same experience.[25] In Canada, where the Jewish community is considerably younger than in the United States, the intermarriage rate was nearly 12 percent at the end of 1956.[26] Not only is the rate of intermarriage smaller in the United States, but the tempo of increase is also slowest here.

Figures do not reveal the full effect of intermarriage upon the American Jewish community. We know that the number of Jewish men marrying non-Jewish women is throughout higher than the number of Jewish women marrying non-Jewish men. Inasmuch as there is a greater tendency for the wife to adapt herself to the environment of the husband than vice versa, it is safe to assume that the number of non-Jewish spouses brought into the Jewish community is not insignificant in proportion to the number of intermarriages. To be sure, the number of Jews leaving the Jewish community after marriage to a non-Jew is higher than that of the non-Jews entering the Jewish community after marriage to a Jew; still, the process is by no means a one-sided one. The surest indication of this is that nearly all Reform temples have members of non-Jewish descent. Conservative synagogs also have their share, and new Jews are even to be found in Orthodox synagogs. In the light of the earlier established fact that in a mixed marriage the Jew does not gain social status and the non-Jew loses it, the wonder is that the path from the non-Jewish to the Jewish community is not wholly barred.

Two generalizations will sum up the intermarriage situation among American Jews: (1) the substantial growth of the Jewish population, the upward economic mobility leading to social stabilization, the ghetto, and the softening of status conflicts within it are factors that diminish the Jew's need to seek a marriage partner outside the Jewish environment; (2) the intensified urge for Jewish belongingness, stimulated by the Hitler tragedy on the one hand and the rise of the State of Israel on the other, tends to slow the pace of intermarriage. In any event, one may venture the prediction that intermarriage will increase in numbers in proportion as acculturation deepens but will not assume, in the foreseeable future, such proportions as to threaten the existence of the Jewish community in this country.

10 Inner Solidification of the American Jewish Community

INFLUENCE OF AMERICAN CONDITIONS UPON RELIGIOUS AND SECULAR INSTITUTIONS

Further major growth of the American Jewish community by outside accretion is no longer to be expected; the community is increasingly a native one. We have before us, then, a more or less stabilized community. It is far from having lost its mobility, but it has already reached a high degree of consolidation. And if the prevailing situation in the country at large does not change radically, basic changes in the material dynamics of the Jewish community are not to be expected: whatever changes do occur will proceed in the direction that has been largely set. When other ethnic groups have attained the stage of development occupied presently by the Jewish community, they have revealed unmistakable signs of ethnic disintegration; but for the Jews this point has served as a starting place for inner solidification.

Earlier, we saw that the wealthier Jewish elements had come to a standstill on a rung of the social ladder beyond which they could not move. This allowed later arrivals an opportunity to overtake them. Thanks to the economic and cultural changes to which all Jewish elements were subjected, the sharpness of the initial conflicts among them has toned down, although it has not entirely disappeared. The social differences between the immigrants from eastern and western Europe are not as striking among their children, and even less so among their grandchildren; they no longer exist among the great-grandchildren of the immigrants. These differences diminish in direct proportion to the growing nativization of the American Jewish community. The descendants of the Sephardic immigration are too few in number to be a substantial factor in Jewish communal life. The descendants of the German immigrants still play a significant role, but their influence is waning while that of the East Europeans grows. Because of their greater numbers and their deeper moorings in the Jewish heritage, the latter provide almost the whole of the Jewish intelligentsia in this country. This intelligentsia includes the rabbinate and other religious functionaries, editors of the Anglo-Jewish press, teachers, journalists, authors, lecturers, and other Jewish professionals. The Reform temple, once the religious citadel of the wealthy Jews of German origin, today has the majority of its membership consisting of native-born descendants of immigrants from Russia, Poland, Galicia, Lithuania, etc. And the Reform rabbi, the guardian of the old citadel, today comes, as like as not, from New York's lower East Side—often enough he is the son of a cloakmaker or men's tailor. The B'nai B'rith, which once hesitated to accept East European Jews as members, is now the organization of the Jewish petty and middle bourgeoisie, which is overwhelmingly recruited from the third immigration wave.

This explains why the breach between the various Jewish religious groups did not become deeper, but has instead lost much of its former acerbity. Alongside Reform and Orthodoxy there arose the Conservative movement, which retained a good deal of Orthodoxy's traditionalism and borrowed many of the outer manifestations of Reform; and all three groups now coexist peacefully and are even united in one Synagogue Council of America. Among other ethnic groups, religious splits widened in the measure that the groups became acculturated. The very opposite occurred among the Jews: the deeper the roots struck by the Jewish community in America, the closer the various religious groups came to each other. True, in the course of time, the Orthodox synagog has modernized itself considerably and is gradually passing into the hands of American-born rabbis; but during the same period, the Reform temple has also reverted to more traditional ways. For example, it has almost universally abandoned Sunday in favor of the traditional Jewish Sabbath as the day of worship; it has reintroduced a good deal of Hebrew into its liturgy and readopted much of the ritualism that classical Reform discarded. The contemporary Reform rabbi comes from the same social background as the Conservative and native-born Orthodox rabbis; and, as a result, the three can often be seen working together not merely in Jewish communal activities, but in larger American undertakings. The former embittered anti-Zionism of Reform has almost entirely vanished; the overwhelming majority of the rabbinate of all three groups is pro-Israel today. In general, the Orthodox synagog and the Reform temple today resemble the two points of a half-moon, with the Conservative synagog in the middle, moving ever closer toward each other. It is by no means excluded that in time they will all converge and form a single circle embracing the entire religious segment of American Jewry. As Rabbi David de Sola Pool of New York's Congregation Shearith Israel has written:

> . . . as East European Orthodoxy yields its rigidity under the impact of American life, and as Reform encompasses more of the cultural and historical aspects of Judaism, there should emerge a more unified Jewry, characterized by greater understanding and co-operation.[1]

It should be noted that suburbia has in some respects again deepened the division between the various religious denominations and, in many a case, reintroduced a spirit of parochialism in the social activities of the synagogs, with each group trying to establish itself in the community as an all-inclusive Jewish agency. Orthodox, Conservative and Reform congregations will frequently come up in new areas before there are enough Jews there to maintain one sizable synagog. The Hebrew schools conducted by the various congregations will more often than not be open to the children of their respective memberships only, and so will the other facilities of the synagogs. However, the division is predicated primarily on institutional considerations and has little ideological basis. In form and content, there is even greater similarity between the synagogs in the suburbs than in the cities. It is therefore safe to predict that the similarity will in time break down the parochialism. There does not seem to exist enough social, economic or cultural difference to sustain separatism for a long time once the impetus of building new establishments has spent itself.

We shall yet see that the increasing similarity of the various religious groups is not only the effect of "the impact of American life." It has been brought about mainly by the numerical, economic and social upsurge of the East European immigrants and their offspring, and by their growing acculturation. We should not, however, minimize the fact that the descendants of the German Jews gradually lost their snobbish attitude toward the "Russians." This happened as the result of three factors working in concert: (1) the discrimination which all Jews have experienced in this country; (2) the impact of America's democratic processes; and (3) the events in Europe and their repercussions in the United States. These factors had a consolidating effect on Jewish secular institutionalism even more than on the synagog.

Jewish institutionalism is a barometer that at any given moment accurately registers the climate of the Jewish community. Actually, it is only in our own time that one can speak of a consolidated Jewish institutionalism, which, with the synagog, is the most important communal possession of the Jews in America. Previously, there had existed only Jewish institutions, which, as we have noted, carried on in a parochial manner and had little to do with each other. These institutions, which, among other ethnic groups, were largely a phenomenon of the immigrant generation and dissolved in proportion as the groups became Americanized, grew stronger, more influential and more respected among Jews precisely because the Jewish community turned more indigenous. Originally created as sectarian organs to provide financial, cultural and communal help to the needy of the separate Jewish subgroups, the institutions are today the best organized, the most consolidated and most firmly integrated sector of Jewish ethnic solidarity in the United States.

The discrimination from the outside that all Jewish strata had to cope with broke down the internal discrimination which one Jewish subgroup practiced against another. Such was the effect of the negative factors of American reality; but the positive elements of that reality played no less a role. The democratic American spirit, for which personal qualifications rate higher than the prestige of social origin, helped to modulate the sharpness of status conflicts in the Jewish community. Though voluntary communal activity, particularly its philanthropic phase, cannot be entirely democratic, and though the influence of the wealthier Jews is still the dominant one in Jewish communal institutions, a marked tendency toward broadening the base of these activities is increasingly discernible. If the "classes," under the influence of American conditions, have adopted a more democratic approach, the "masses," under the same influence, have learned to cooperate with the former in common endeavors. The Jewish workers, for whom such cooperation would have spelled betrayal of the class interests of the proletariat during the period of their estrangement from the general American labor movement, lost their class sectarianism when they became an integral part of that movement. They came to understand that participation in communal activities strengthens rather than weakens the influence of labor. Currently, workers, both as individuals and as members of organized groups, are among the most energetic figures in general Jewish activities.

American utilitarianism affected the Jewish community no less than it did the other segments of the American population. It had a dual effect on Jewish institutionalism. First, in the direction of conservation of time and money. The hundreds of separate fund-raising campaigns that used to be conducted in the Jewish community not only ran up great amounts of unnecessary expenses, but consumed a vast reservoir of communal energy. The enormous sums which American Jewry has been called upon to raise in the last few decades would never have been collected had the Jewish institutions not united and applied the most modern methods to their fund-raising. Nor would there have been enough communally active persons to go around had they had to spread themselves over countless separate campaigns. In addition, those who gave money began to complain of being asked for contributions so often and categorically demanded reforms. The consolidation of fund-raising campaigns became indispensable.

The second and more fundamental effect of utilitarianism was that it taught American Jews to evaluate organizations and their objectives not in terms of their ideological consequence, but in terms of their practical usefulness. If a movement or an agency displays a tendency to strengthen Jewish group solidarity or to stimulate spiritual creativity, it earns the support of the community. Only the future will determine whether a given institution or cause possesses historical truth; what is of immediate importance is its constructiveness and its ability to bring into the Jewish arena individuals who, without the stimulus of a particular organization, might have remained outside the community entirely. And if a particular group finds that on occasion it must make concessions in its financial support, it is compensated by concessions made to it by another group.

In this fashion the ground was prepared for the communal consolidation of American Jewry. Nevertheless, this consolidation would not have assumed the mass character it did and would not have proceeded at so rapid a pace had it not been for powerful stimuli from Europe and Israel.

INFLUENCE OF CONDITIONS IN EUROPE AND ISRAEL UPON THE AMERICAN JEWISH COMMUNITY

We have seen that the status of a people outside the United States affects the descendants of that people in this country. The worse off that people is, from a national point of view, the more closely knit here the ethnic group springing from it. By the same token, the solidarity of the group here melts away in the measure that conditions abroad improve; this is particularly true of the immigrants and their offspring stemming from oppressed nations.

The Jews derived from the most oppressed of peoples, and there was never a moment in the entire history of the American Jewish community when it was altogether free of concern for Jews in other countries and for the status of the Jewish people on a world scale. Moreover, while the position of other oppressed peoples generally improved in the course of time, thus diminishing the responsibility for their welfare among the corresponding ethnic groups in the United States, the situation of the Jews steadily deteriorated on both local and international levels. Help for needy brothers throughout the world was one of the cardinal principles of Jewish collective existence over thousands of years, and American Jewry abided by this principle to an extent that has no parallel anywhere else. Even the Spanish-Portuguese Jews, who considered themselves an aristocratic caste, dispatched relatively substantial sums for Jewish needs in Europe and Palestine, though they were not eager to welcome emissaries, who were usually Ashkenazic Jews, from those parts of the world. Such emissaries nevertheless did come from time to time and contributed, along with Jewish philanthropic work in general, to the creation of a bridge between the Jews in America and their co-religionists abroad, and thus to the integration of the young Jewish community within the orbit of world Jewish interests. In the words of Grinstein: "Every call for aid from stricken Jews in other parts of the world revivified Jewish life in New York by reminding New York Jews of their own people." [2] The same can be said of later Jewish communities in all other American cities.

The needs of Jews abroad constantly increased and with them the commensurate responsibilities of the Jewish community in the United States. Even Jews who had become estranged from Jewish values and were perhaps even close to defection could not resist the pressure of the ancient Jewish tradition of helping a brother in distress. The number of Jews who could have left the ghetto but remained because of the force of that tradition is quite large. There are naturally no statistics on it, but the influence of this factor can be felt in every corner of Jewish life in America. An enormous percentage of Jewish leadership first entered communal life as a result of the call for help from abroad. This group responded initially out of a feeling of pity, but in time pity was transformed into a sense of national duty which carried over into the constructive, non-philanthropic aspects of communal activity. It would otherwise have been impossible for American Jewry to have raised the fantastic sums of money which their work in behalf of the Jews of Europe and Palestine-Israel has called for since World War I. For just the United Jewish Appeal alone, which comprises help for the Jews of Europe, construction in Israel and the integration of Jewish refugees in the United States, American Jews raised $103,000,000 dollars in 1946, $125,000,000 in 1947, and $150,000,000 in 1948. From 1948 to 1955 there was a steady decline in the amounts raised. The decline was arrested in 1956 under the impact of the threatening situation in which the State of Israel found itself. The total spent by the Jewish community on Jewish causes outside this country never fell below $100,000,000 a year, since the end of World War II.

But American Jews have not confined themselves to financial help in their assistance to less fortunate brethren in other countries. They have also given political help in countries where Jews suffered religious persecution and economic boycotts and where the very physical existence of the Jews was in jeopardy. Characteristically, the first time American Jews operated as an organized community was over a century ago in connection with the Damascus Affair in 1840.

In its essence, this sort of incident was not new to Jewish history, but it was the first time a modern democratic country was involved. A Christian monk in Damascus disappeared one day. His brother monks soon spread the charge that the Jews had murdered him for their ritual needs, and the French consul in the city helped disseminate the ancient blood-libel. A number of Jews were arrested and they "confessed" under torture. Later, the entire falsehood was uncovered, and those Jews who had not died in prison were freed—but only after the most strenuous efforts had been made by the Jews of the free countries, under the leadership of Moses Montefiore in London and Adolphe Cremieux in Paris.

The Damascus Affair reverberated throughout the Jewish world. It brought together the Jews of America as no other event had theretofore succeeded in doing. Since then, activities on behalf of Jews in other countries have always proven to be a more effective means than any other of uniting American Jews. In 1859 the Board of Delegates of American Israelites was founded as "a national organization for the purpose of securing and maintaining like rights at home and abroad." The Kishinev pogrom in 1903 led to the formation of the American Jewish Committee in 1906. It is no wonder, then, that World War I brought a revolutionary change into American Jewish communal activity. If the Jewish population entered the war as a conglomerate of fragmented bodies and circles, it emerged a consolidated community.

The time was ripe for such crystallization. All the internal and external factors that stimulated Jewish ethnic identity converged to create a situation with which American Jews could cope only through the cooperation of the various groups and strata. The time had passed for *ad hoc* or spontaneous action; the hour for organized planning had arrived. Developments inside the United States and, even more, the Jewish situation throughout the world demanded it. On the one hand, the war brought devastation to Jewish life in Europe and left hundreds of thousands of Jews in a critical condition from which they could be rescued only with the help of their brethren in the United States; on the other hand, the war led to the issuance of the Balfour Declaration, which for the first time in the history of the Dispersion presented a realistic prospect of a Jewish return to Palestine and the creation there of a normal national life. Both tasks required enormous financial resources; both also required maximal political support. The American Jewish community was already far enough advanced, economically, to be able to undertake the financial burdens; and it had already sunk roots deep enough in American soil to be able to extend the political help of which the Jewish people as a whole was in need. This help included support for Jewish demands in Europe, intervention in behalf of Jewish aspirations in Palestine, protests against the violations of Jewish rights in other countries, and similar actions. All this required Jewish unity in the United States.

It was easier to establish unity in the fields of aid, reconstruction and social services than in those fields which affected ideology—and so it was that Jewish institutionalism became the center of Jewish ethnic cohesion in this country. First came the movement to unite local Jewish philanthropic institutions into one central organization that would provide the necessary budgets for all of them out of one fund-raising campaign, and would supervise their administrative functions without impinging on their ideological autonomy. The organized expression of this movement was the federation. Although the first local federation was created in Boston in 1895, the federation movement was largely the product of the war period. The psychological sentiment for unity and the social changes that created a basis for it led to the formation of federations in every city with a sizable Jewish population.

But while the federations provided for the purely local needs of American Jews, the call for help from abroad became ever more insistent. The response came in the form of the American Jewish

Joint Distribution Committee and other such agencies. But this only led to an increase of fund-raising campaigns, whereas the cry was for a smaller number of better-organized campaigns. Then the rise of Nazism threw upon the shoulders of American Jewry responsibilities in comparison with which all their previous undertakings had been puny. New organizational forms became the order of the day, and the welfare fund was created.

From a financial point of view, the welfare fund takes up where the federation leaves off. The welfare fund comprises all causes, institutions and movements that go beyond purely local needs, though there are many welfare funds that also function as federations. But the welfare funds are more than just instruments for collecting larger sums of money at less expense: they are also centers of Jewish communal consolidation and strongholds of group identity. They are the arenas where all Jewish elements and strata converge for both practical endeavors and a meeting of minds on ideological differences. They are the most important organizational expression of the spirit of utilitarianism and pragmatic philosophy in the Jewish community. Welfare funds extend into practically the entirety of American Jewry outside New York City, and even here a welfare fund will inevitably arise.

The renewed parochialism in the suburbs creates difficulties of a dual nature for the federations and welfare funds. First, the suburbs disperse geographically the constituencies of the established agencies and, second, they produce a multiplicity of independent campaigns for capital funds to build new synagogs, community centers, Hebrew schools, etc., thus endangering the centrality of welfare fund and federation fund-raising. They also raise the additional problem of making many institutions maintained by the central agencies obsolescent in proportion as Jews move out of the old neighborhoods. But here, too, there is reason to believe that a new stability in the direction of coordinated effort will be achieved after the transitory period has elapsed.

A further development of the federations and welfare funds is the Jewish community council. Owing existence to the appearance of Nazism on the international scene and its effects in the United States, the community council has since become a basic institution in organized Jewish life. Starting out as a defense agency to combat anti-Semitic manifestations in this country, it has in recent years veered toward a more positive approach to Jewish problems and toward affirmative action within the Jewish community itself. Three types of council crystallized by the 1950's. There is, first, the original type, still almost exclusively engaged in civic defense work and the promotion of interfaith good will. A community council of this type is, for the most part, made up of individuals or of the local representatives of the national community relations bodies,[3] and functions as an adjunct to the federations or welfare funds. Next there is the representative community council concerning itself with all aspects of collective Jewish life whether they be of an internal or external nature. Although democratically organized, a community council of this kind usually lacks financial independence in that it has to turn to the welfare fund or federation for its budgetary requirements. And finally there is the community council which also operates as a federation and welfare fund. A council of this type is the closest thing in this country to the traditional *kehilla,* the legally constituted council administering the internal affairs of the Jewish community and acting as its recognized spokesman, which operated in eastern Europe and still operates in a number of lands in western Europe and South America. Such a community council has neither the legal standing nor the enforcement power that the *kehilla* had, but its moral authority is voluntarily recognized by every Jewish individual identifying himself with the Jewish community. The trend is toward the growth of this type of council. In cities with a Jewish population of up to twenty thousand it is already the prevailing type; and the larger cities are heading the same way. Already federations and welfare funds have merged their fund-raising into central campaigns in the most important communities outside New York, with the proceeds allocated by unified governing bodies. All community councils, without exception, are active in the struggle for civil rights for all parts of the American people.

EFFECTS OF ANTI-SEMITISM AT HOME AND ABROAD

The rise of Nazism led not only to the intensification of American Jewish efforts to help their brothers suffering under Hitler's persecution. Nazism suddenly confronted American Jews with the fact that

201

Jewish life is nowhere fully secure, that there is no land immune to Jew-hatred. At the very time when all the objective conditions seemed conducive to a speed-up of the processes of assimilation of the Jewish population, when movement out of the working class towards business and the professions was in full swing, and the community was on the way to full nativization, when native-born Jews were becoming increasingly indifferent to Jewish culture and the Yiddish language was losing position after position even among immigrants —just at that time an organized anti-Semitic movement arose in the United States. It would be wrong to assume that anti-Semitism is always an importation into the United States: discrimination against Jews and manifestations of Jew-hatred existed here prior to the rise of Nazism in Germany. But Hitlerism in Europe stimulated hysteria here of a kind previously unheard-of in this country. It was not the fulminations of hate groups that made the situation alarming, but rather the attitude of "respectable" isolationist elements who, while publicly disavowing any connection with the lunatic fringe, accused the Jew of warmongering. They made a deep impression, not alone because they occupied a prominent place in social and economic circles and in public life, but also because they operated with American slogans, appealed to American traditions and addressed themselves to the peculiarities of the American mentality.

Certain characteristics of that mentality, discussed in Chapter 1, make it susceptible to anti-Semitism. There is, first of all, the heritage of the frontiersman, who, admiring ingenuity and resourcefulness in the fight for material advancement, was suspicious of otherness in spiritual matters. Then there is the influence of populism, lingering on long after the populist movement had disappeared from the American political scene. Strongly anti-immigrationist and anti-urbanistic, many populists saw in the Jew the incarnation of everything that was evil in big city life, the symbol of economic exploitation by the banking interests, and the alien power deflecting American political life from the road of righteousness.

Even more decisive in making the American mentality vulnerable to anti-Semitic propaganda is the tradition of isolationism, which, as Selig Adler puts it, "has been woven into the warp and woof of the American epic." [4] It was this tradition that made it possible for some isolationist leaders in the late 1930's and early 1940's openly to embrace anti-Semitism as part of their America First program. "The three most important groups which have been pressing this country toward war," said Charles A. Lindbergh in a speech delivered in Des Moines, Iowa, three months before Pearl Harbor, "are the British, the Jewish, and the Roosevelt administration." And regarding the Jews he added, ". . . their greatest danger to this country lies in their large ownership and influence in our motion pictures, our press, our radio, and our government." [5] Mention has already been made of the fact that polls taken at the time disclosed a majority of the American people sharing the view that Jews possessed too much political and economic power. America became Jew-conscious as it had not been before and has not been since.

The Jewish question was exacerbated by the reaction of the Jews themselves. They were frightened and for the first time became uneasy about their own security in this country.

The climate in America began to change. The quotas in the colleges, the exclusion of Jews from certain social institutions and occupations, all the things that had been practiced before in a limited fashion and somewhat shamefacedly, loomed larger in nativist thinking and, correspondingly, in the emotional reaction of the Jews. Active anti-Semitism became a problem in the United States, and in certain circles there could be discerned a clear tendency to present the Jews as those most responsible for whatever was unsatisfactory in the country. This tendency has throughout the ages brought political anti-Semitism in its wake, and it might well have led to the same results here had not World War II intervened.

There were indeed many things to cause uneasiness among the Jews in the United States on the eve of the war. The rise of Nazism in Germany had coincided with the economic crisis that began in the United States in October, 1929. The Jews were not more adversely affected by the crisis than were other parts of the population, and certainly much less than the Negroes and other racial minorities; but they suffered more in a psychological sense than any other group. For the first time, the Jews felt concern about their safety here.

Jews could never dream of becoming a majority in the United States, and so they were never a threat either to the dominant religion or to the dominant social group. This explains why their development here has been in many respects quieter and smoother than that of the Catholics, who do aspire to become a majority. In the eyes of the seventeenth-century Puritans and other religious groups belonging to the majority, Jews in general occupied a more estimable position than did the Catholics and Protestant dissidents. This does not mean that Jews were treated as equals, but rather that they were tolerated. Gustavus Myers, referring to conditions in the first quarter of the nineteenth century, wrote:

> In the larger contests going on they [the Jews] were subordinated to an obscure position except in one respect which seemed to furnish a sufficient outlet for lurking bigotry. If a Congregationalist, Baptist, Methodist, Episcopalian, Catholic or other Christian embezzled or otherwise committed felony, no mention was made in the published reports of his religious faith or connections. But let a Jew slip even into a misdemeanor, the fact that he was a Jew was prominently heralded.[6]

The pattern of holding the Jewish community responsible for the behavior of an individual Jew runs through the whole history of the Jewish Dispersion, in the New as well as the Old World. Here too, in colonial times, the Jews had to fight for their citizenship rights, and after the Revolution—against economic and social discriminations. These battles were themselves ethnicizing factors, for the disabilities contended against affected all Jews. But the important thing was that, despite these disagreeable encounters, American Jews felt secure in their adopted home. The anti-Jewish manifestations were not frequent or dangerous enough to warrant the establishment of special instrumentalities to defend the rights of Jews in America. If these rights were occasionally attacked in former years, the battle was taken up by organizations that had been created to defend the rights of Jews in other countries. It is only since the rise of Hitlerism that American Jews have found it necessary to maintain agencies whose chief purpose is to combat anti-Semitism in the United States itself.

It is no wonder, then, that Jewish nationalism was greatly reinforced among American Jews during the period between the wars. Once again, the Jewish experience was different from that of the other ethnic groups. The longer the latter lived here, the more they discarded their old-country nationalism, frequently to the point of its complete abandonment; among the Jews, nationalism waxed and grew stronger, coming in time to gain the sympathy even of those elements which had originally combatted the very notion of a Jewish national renaissance. They included those who came under our rubric of "German Jews" as well as many socialistically oriented Jewish workers. With very few exceptions, they are today all active in the process of building Israel. Every objective study has confirmed the fact that more than 90 percent of American Jewry is pro-Israel oriented, and can see in this orientation no contradiction to its loyalty or patriotism to the United States. American Jews are convinced that, even as they have happy homes as individuals here, so must the Jewish people as a people have a national home if it is to survive and live a normal and creative life.

It is for this reason that there has developed such close collaboration among the various Jewish groups in recent years. An interest in Jewish affairs has been aroused even among those Jews who never possessed it before or in whom it had virtually disappeared. Charitable activity has contributed no little to the democratization of Jewish community life, because for Jews, as pointed out several times in this study, charity has never had a purely philanthropic character. Even those who came to Jewish communal activity by way of philanthropy ultimately arrived at a positive appreciation of Jewish spiritual values and a determination to preserve them.

11 Continued Development and Strengthening of the American Jewish Community

However one approaches the development of the Jewish community in the United States, one must arrive at the same conclusion: the Jews may occasionally have proceeded in their own path and always at a more rapid pace but invariably in the same direction as the country as a whole. They absorbed all the influences of the American environment; they accommodated themselves to American conditions faster and more fundamentally than others; but because of internal and external reasons, both positive and negative factors, these processes affected them differently from others. The Jews are the single white group whose ethnic solidarity is not disappearing in the United States. This solidarity is compounded of a host of impulses and motivations, historical, cultural, social, economic, religious and national. The Jews as a group cannot be placed in any one of the categories into which the American population is normally divided. They are neither immigrant colony, political minority, nor racial caste.

The famous Hansen thesis to the effect that the grandchildren of the immigrants want to remember that which the children want to forget is true, as we have seen, only in the sense that the grandchildren, being twice removed from, and hence more indifferent to, the immigrant generation are more objective in their attitude to the values that the immigrants had brought over from abroad. The grandchildren, in other words, are completely emancipated from an ethnic heritage which the children still regard as an obstacle to their Americanization. The children reject this heritage precisely because they are emotionally and psychologically closer to it; and the grandchildren assume a more tolerant and understanding position precisely because they are no longer tied to the way of life of their grandparents. Alone of all the white ethnic groups do American Jews supply proof for the correctness of the Hansen thesis. Only among them do the grandchildren manifest a greater desire to be part of the community than the children of the immigrants. This is a fact which is subject to statistical substantiation. — *We innot rec.bee. wish to-*

GROWTH IN SYNAGOG MEMBERSHIP SINCE WORLD WAR II

We have first of all the amazing growth of synagog membership since World War II. In determining the trend in this area, we find the figures of the religious census conducted in 1926 and 1936 of little value because Harry Linfield, Jewish director of those censuses, assumed a synagog membership for every Jew in the United States. Since he exaggerated the size of the Jewish population in the country, he arrived at membership figures which, in the aggregate, exceeded the total number of Jews in the United States. That there was no basis for these figures was attested by every observer of Jewish life. The Beards asserted that congregational belonging comprised no more than one tenth of American Jewry in 1926.[1] This was probably an understatement, but, by a smaller percentage than that by which Linfield's statistics were overstated. The situation had not changed greatly in 1936, as several samplings proved.

In his Stamford study, Koenig noted that whereas 100 of the 150 Jewish families in the city belonged to the Orthodox synagog in 1908, only 148 of the 960 Jewish families belonged to it in 1938. And though a Conservative synagog was established there during that thirty-year period, it failed to attract even a small portion of those who had left the Orthodox synagog.[2] In San Francisco, only 18 of every 100 families in 1938 had one or more of its members affiliated with a synagog.³ The study of the youth of New York, referred to above, queried its subjects as to whether they had attended a church or synagog in the week prior to the inquiry. Their answers were as follows: 60.5 percent of the 2,092 Catholic boys and 37.8 percent of the 739 Protestant boys had been to church, but only 10.8 percent of the 1,324 Jewish boys had attended synagog that week; similarly, 69.5 percent of the 2,229 Catholic girls and 42.2 percent of the 844 Protestant girls answered affirmatively, as against a mere 6.6 percent of the 1,465 Jewish girls.⁴ On the basis of the research studies conducted in 1945–46, the Brooklyn Church and Missionary Federation ventured the opinion that a maximum of one-quarter of the one million Jews who lived in Brooklyn belonged to a synagog.⁵ Many similar examples can be cited to confirm the fact that a majority of American Jews were not affiliated with a synagog as late as the mid-1940's.

The picture is drastically changed by the mid-1950's. All community surveys register a constantly rising local rate of affiliation. On a national scale, the reports of the synagog associations point in the same direction. Thus we find the Union of American Hebrew Congregations, central body of the Reform group, increasing its constituency from 312 temples in January 1945 to 548 in April 1958, with the membership trebling during this period and estimated to be over a million today. The Conservatives record a rise from some 300 congregations in 1948 to 650, with an estimated membership of about 1,200,000 in August 1958 (not counting the 200 congregations which, though not dues-paying members, are closely related to the Conservative movement).⁶ The various Orthodox groups are also reaping the harvest of mounting membership, although at a slower pace. There is no question but that the majority of the Jewish population is now affiliated with the synagog, and there is every indication that the rate of affiliation will continue to rise.

Of even greater significance than the quantitative expansion of the synagog is its qualitative growth. It is scoring its greatest gains among the young native-born American Jews. In the suburbs and in the new residential settlements in the large cities, where the synagog is making its deepest inroads, few immigrants will be found in the leadership of the more liberal congregations. Second generation Jews are at the helm of these institutions, with members of the third generation broadening their participation to a very appreciable extent. It makes little difference from an ethnic point of view whether this development stems from a religious revival or represents a social process; what is important is the fact that a greater proportion of American Jews now want to assert their Jewish identification and give it organized form.

GROWTH IN JEWISH EDUCATION

Nor is the synagog the only institution that attracts sizable numbers of the younger generations. Members of these generations are the prime movers in the building and activities of the Jewish community centers, particularly in the suburbs. The grandchildren are getting in ever increasing measure something the children either missed altogether or received on a much lower scale—a Jewish education. In 1900, with a Jewish population of a little over a million, about 45,000 children were enrolled in congregational, non-congregational and private Jewish schools. In 1950, with a Jewish population of approximately 4,700,000, the enrollment was nearly 263,000. In other words, while the Jewish population increased by little more than 400 percent, enrollment in Jewish schools increased by nearly 500 percent. Considering that in 1900 the average Jewish family had twice as many children as in 1950, the proportion of Jewish families giving their children a Jewish education in 1950 as compared with 1900 becomes even greater.

Enrollment continued to increase, both absolutely and relatively, since 1950, until in 1958, it reached the figure of nearly 553,600. But here, too, quality is even more important than quantity. We are not concerned with evaluating the Jewish education children receive, but with determining trends, and the trend is toward the improvement and intensification of the Jewish educational processes. This is attested by a number of developments. At the turn of the century, most of the Jewish children receiving a Jewish education obtained it in unorganized schools—*hadarim*—where primitive conditions existed and where the instructors were rarely qualified even by the lowest teaching standards; or they received their education from private tutors who were even less qualified. Today, the overwhelming majority of Jewish pupils attend organized schools. Bar Mitzvah, to be sure, is

210

today the terminal point in Jewish education, as it had been in the past in this country; but, because of better organization and greater coordination of effort under central bureaus or boards of Jewish education, the qualifying requirements for Bar Mitzvah are higher. The progress made by Jewish day, or parochial, schools is striking. Their total attendance in 1935 was about 3,000; twenty years later the number grew to 35,000. In 1958, nearly 43,000 children were receiving their education in Jewish day schools.[7]

OBSERVANCE OF JEWISH TRADITIONAL PRACTICES

There is no evidence that the increase in synagog membership and in Jewish school enrollment has brought with it a correspondingly increased piety. On the contrary, there is every indication that American Jews are becoming more lax in their religious practices. However, certain observances are gaining wider application, and some rituals are penetrating deeper into the mores of the American Jew. We had an intimation of this development in an earlier chapter, when we discussed the trend toward more traditionalism in the Reform temples. This trend has already in some respects crystallized into a pattern which is replacing some of the innovations introduced by classical Reform into the Jewish mode of worship. Surveys made under the supervision of the Union of American Hebrew Congregations clearly demonstrate that the changes have been brought about by pressure from below, from the membership which is now in its overwhelming majority of East European origin.

Greater respect for Jewish traditional practices is also making itself felt in the home life of the Jewish young adults, especially in the suburbs. Jewish holidays are more widely observed, Jewish customs are receiving greater attention, and Jewish symbolic objects are adorning more Jewish homes. Precisely because the third generation is trying to recapture the spirit of something so many of the second generation were ready to discard, there is still much that is vague, ambivalent and contradictory in the behavior and attitudes of the young American Jew. The second generation was largely a missing link, and the third generation has to find its own way of latching on to the chain of Jewish continuity. This generation lacks a guiding philosophy, and has no accumulated body of experience to draw upon; neither has it as yet evolved a creative scale of values to direct its efforts and shape its sense of appreciation. However, when we examine closely the attitudes young American Jewry is manifesting toward things Jewish, we discern certain tendencies which will probably set the stage for future Jewish living in America.

WORLD-WIDE CONCEPT OF A JEWISH PEOPLE

The Nazi disaster aroused and intensified profoundly the national sense of kinship felt by American Jews for their fellow Jews in other lands. It magnified beyond anything previously thought possible the degree of responsibility which the American Jew had to bear for the fate of the Jewish people the world over. It was not only that he faced the task of saving hundreds of thousands of Jews from physical annihilation; he was also placed before the obligation of preserving Judaism. He was assigned a role on the scene of Jewish national survival for which he was totally unprepared and in the performance of which his psychological and spiritual capacities were taxed to the breaking point.

Hitler, almost overnight, turned American Jews into the custodians of Jewish destiny, and he did it while arousing their fears for their own position in this country. We have already seen that this resulted in the rise of community relations as a major activity in American Jewish life. At a time when American Jews were called upon to raise unprecedented sums for overseas relief and the building of Palestine-Israel, they were also forced to allot large amounts to combat anti-Semitism in this country. Between the early 1930's and the mid-1950's more than one hundred million dollars was spent by the national and local agencies on community relations. The drain on manpower and the psychological effects of this activity have weighed even more heavily on the resources of American Jewry than the financial burden.

There are no objective criteria to gauge the results of the community relations effort in terms of its basic motivation, which is the wiping out, or at least, diminution of anti-Jewish sentiment in this country. But whatever the results, there would not be so much preoccupation with community relations if there were no feeling that the position of the Jew in American society is still somewhat shaky and in need of fortification.

Helpless to prevent or halt the slaughter of millions of their kin in Europe and cruelly disappointed by the indifference of the democratic world in the face of this slaughter, American Jews sought solace in more intimate association with fellow Jews. The Nazi catastrophe reinforced the community bonds between them and the Jews in other lands at a time when the ties of individual kinship were becoming looser, thus strengthening the urge among the former to "belong." This urge was powerfully intensified by America's entry into World War II. Never before had Jews in the American armed forces been engaged in a struggle in which Jewish survival was so inextricably interwoven with the defense of their own country. Many saw action in Europe, Africa and in the Far East, and there came in direct contact with Jewish communities of which they had known next to nothing. The Jewish people as a world-wide entity ceased being an abstract concept and became a living reality. This was both a terrifying and heart-warming experience, the effects of which have followed the ex-GI's in civilian life.

THE STATE OF ISRAEL AND JEWISH "BELONGINGNESS"

Even more profound in its effect on American Jews was the emergence of the State of Israel. The State came into being at a crucial moment in the life of American Jewish youth and young adults. They had reached a crossroad in their search for emotional and moral anchorage. Pressures from without sharpened in them the need for identification with the Jewish community, but there had as yet not crystallized the inner striving to give real meaning to this identification. Arising when it did, the State of Israel turned Jewish "belongingness" into a voluntary act. The American Jew, given the choice, elected to remain a Jew because he wanted to be one and not because he was driven to it by rejection from without.

It is much too early for a categorical assertion about the effects of the existence of the State of Israel on American Jews. As we have seen earlier, the gaining of political independence by formerly subjugated peoples has invariably weakened ethnic ties among the descendants of these peoples in the United States; and some such effect, although different in form, may be discerned in limited circles of American Jewry. Paradoxically, this effect appears wrapped up in survivalist rationalizations. It is not that American Jews, with the exception of the American Council for Judaism or the Jewish communists, are disclaiming their individual responsibility for the preservation of the Jewish people whose national home is the State of Israel; it is that by overstressing the view that the primary obligation of American Jews is to strengthen Jewish life in this country, some may leave the impression that they regard Israel of secondary importance. It is a form of Jewish isolationism which is not unaffected by general American isolationism.

But infinitely greater has thus far been the ethnicizing impact of the emergence of Israel. Coinciding with the deepened urge in the young Jew to belong and with his search for a dynamic meaning for his Jewishness, the creation of the State of Israel has provided concrete form for his Judaism. Jewish music has found identifiable expression in Israeli song and dance. Jewish art has taken distinctive shape in Israeli art objects and handicrafts, and Israeli amusement patterns have become a feature in American Jewish entertainment. The use of a few Hebrew words, preferably in the Israeli pronunciation, has become a must in American Jewish homes. Israel has become both the symbol and the living demonstration of vital Judaism. Abraham G. Duker writes:

> The expression of Jewish identification through Zionism has many facets, all of them worthy of study. They range from the introduction of regular prayers for Israel in the Orthodox synagogue to the normalcy of the appearance of the Zionist or Israeli flag at Jewish gatherings whose participants cannot imagine that their Americanism thereby becomes suspect. They are seen in the little synagogue art shops, in the Israeli Seder plates and pictures in homes committed to Judaism, in the substitution of the *hora* (Israeli dance) for the *sher* (East European dance) at weddings and other *simhot* (celebrations) where notions of middle-class dignity do not inhibit Jews from expressing joy in Jewish dance forms. It is to be noted in the Yeshiva youth that does not hide its *yarmulke* (skull cap) in the subways.[8]

Nor do American Jews conceive of the State of Israel merely as a haven of refuge for homeless and persecuted Jews. Various polls taken before Israel was born showed more than 90 percent of the

Jews in this country favoring the establishment of a national Jewish homeland. By an even higher percentage do they express their solidarity with Israel and their willingness to support her constructive program. A survey conducted by the American Jewish Committee in Riverton (Trenton, N.J.), a typical Jewish community of 8,500, found 94 percent of the responding parents displaying a positive attitude toward Israel, 2 percent expressing indifference, another 2 percent having mixed feelings, and only 1 percent taking a negative position. A poll among Jewish children yielded substantially the same results.[9] A poll taken by the same committee in Baltimore in May, 1948, right after the State of Israel was proclaimed, found 95 percent of the respondents maintaining that American Jews should help the Jews of Israel even if the government of the United States did not send help.[10]

There is overwhelming recognition among American Jews that the existence of the State of Israel has enhanced the dignity of the Jew no matter where he lives and has added a new dimension to the status of the American Jewish community. The surveyors of Riverton summed up the sentiments of the Jews in that town vis-à-vis Israel in the following statement:

> Almost all Riverton Jews, even those coolest to Israel and most indifferent to Zionism as an ideological movement, feel favorably disposed toward the State. They see it, at the least, as a place of refuge for homeless Jews, and they recognize their responsibility to help their co-religionists.[11]

There is no reason to doubt that the same spirit pervades the attitudes of American Jewry generally toward the State of Israel. The rootedness of the Jew in American soil has been deepened by the realization that he is a member of a people that is no longer nationally uprooted.

12 The Self-Image of the American Jew

TRADITIONAL CONTENT IN ACQUIRED FORM

The ability to achieve through accommodation and adjustment that which other ethnic groups accomplish only through disintegration and dissolution is the secret of Jewish survival in the Dispersion. It is an emanation of the age-old Jewish capacity to transform problems into tasks, defeats into challenges and setbacks into opportunities. This ability, as we have seen, is constantly being reinforced by pressure from without, which is never completely absent even in the United States.

That Jews have not resisted the process of acculturation in America but have, on the contrary, plunged into this process with greater alacrity than others (which is another way of saying that they have submitted to assimilatory influence) has been amply demonstrated throughout this work. What is remarkable in the situation is that they have at times made acculturation serve their group ends and have in some respects converted it into an instrument for cementing ethnic solidarity. Surrendering to the tyranny of the majority and conforming to the prevailing behavior patterns and value scales, they have in many an aspect of Jewish life utilized this process as a means of avoiding a complete break with the Jewish heritage by pouring a measure of traditional content into the acquired form.

217

We have seen this in operation in the area of language, where English has become a unifying force in the Jewish community. We now see it operating in the attempts to fit the observance of Jewish holidays, Jewish ritualism and Jewish family customs into general American practices. Interestingly enough, at a time when Jews are becoming more and more lax in the observance of dietary laws, kosher processed foodstuffs are flooding the market. In addition to gefulte fish, kreplach and knishes, one may now purchase kosher bacon, egg roll or chow mein.

But the most striking illustration of assimilatory factors bolstering Jewish group cohesiveness is offered by the growth of synagog membership described in the preceding chapter. Whether this growth be viewed as an upsurge of religious feeling or a social trend, there is no doubt of its reflecting the established patterns of American respectability in which affiliation to institutional religion is an important element. As Jews become better acquainted with their neighbors, report the surveyors of Riverton, they find that "here in the United States, religion is an esteemed and enduring part of the general culture pattern." [1]

Collectively, American Jews regard themselves as first of all a religious community. Eight of ten parents in the Riverton sample defined a Jew as one who professed the Jewish religion, indicating that among first generation Jews there are still a small minority who interpret Jewishness in other than religious terms. Significantly, no such interpretation is to be found among the American-born or -reared Jewish youth: 97 percent of the adolescents in the Riverton study stated that a Jew was one who identified himself with the Jewish faith. There is every reason to believe that a national poll would result in the same findings.

SECULARIST IDEOLOGIES

Earlier we have referred to the secularist ideologies which immigration from eastern Europe had introduced into American Jewish life during the first decades of the twentieth century. It is necessary to probe deeper into these ideologies now that we are discussing the present image the American Jew has of himself.

Throughout the ages of the Diaspora and up to the time of the Emancipation, the problem confronting Jews in their relationships with Gentiles was one of adjustment rather than integration. Jews did not want to be woven into the social and cultural pattern of the lands of their abode. Quite the contrary, their transcending concern was with remaining apart from the non-Jewish world. Rather than seeking dissolution in the Gentile sea surrounding them, they bent all efforts to maintain their identity within the small island into which they either were forced or withdrew voluntarily. They wanted to live in peace with their non-Jewish neighbors without changing their own way of living. Politically and socially, the Gentile majority rejected the Jewish minority; psychologically and spiritually, the Jewish minority rejected the Gentile majority.

Jewish being was not the mystery then that it has since become. The notion that Jewish physical existence might be divorced from spiritual continuity would have been just as incomprehensible to the Jew in the ghetto as an attempt to draw a line between his belonging to the Jewish faith and his being a member of the Jewish people. To him these were not separate aspects of the "Jewish question" but one process of Jewish survival. The preservation of the Jewish body and the liberation of the Jewish spirit were both to be achieved by Messianic redemption, which was anchored on the return to Zion. Emancipation drove a wedge into the old concepts of Jewish survival and created a dualism where one did not exist before. By holding out the promise that they might live in physical security and religious tolerance in their native lands, the Emancipation for the first time presented Jews with the possibility that these lands, far from being a *Galut* (Exile), might become the permanent home of the Jewish people. The integration of the various Jewish communities into the life of the countries of which they had come to consider themselves an organic part thus became the central problem of Jewish existence in the Western World.

This revolutionary change in Jewish attitudes took place at a time when the struggle between secularism and the temporal power of organized religion was at its height among the democratic nations. The struggle revolved around two principles. The first principle was that religion is a private affair, the second, that the sphere of organized religion is limited. Spelled out politically, the two principles read the separation of church and state.

The trend toward secularism assumed different forms in Jewish life. Jews lived not in their own state but in ghettos, which were as much the product of external compulsion as of internal inclination. The dominating force in the ghettos was religion, and it imposed a rigid rule over all individual and collective acts of the Jew. Religion fulfilled many functions among Jews that government performed among territorial nations. The Torah was the constitution which shaped, regulated, and guided Jewish attitudes and behavior; and upon the constitutional foundation of the Torah, a whole superstructure of Talmudic and rabbinic literature arose—a superstructure that had to be shaken before the secularization of Jewish life could be achieved. The secularist arrows were thus directed not merely against the institutional power of the synagog; they were also aimed at the authority of religion itself. And yet we find secularism developing into a non-religious or anti-religious movement only among certain Jewish groups in eastern Europe. In western Europe, where the process of secularization had been set in motion by a growing capitalism and by the Emancipation long before it reached Tsarist Russia, no secularist ideology of Jewish survival sprang up until the rise of political Zionism. And even Zionism had a greater affinity with religion there than in eastern Europe.

Even those in western Europe to whom Jews were a people and not merely a religious group drew no line of demarcation between Jewish religion and Jewish peoplehood. Secularism did not lead to a complete break with religion in Germany because Jews learned from the experience of Protestantism that one did not have to discard religion altogether just because he could no longer accept all of its dogma or because certain of its canons could not be squared with the progress of science. It was possible, Jews discovered, to reform religion and to adapt it to the moods of modern man. Then, too, following the fall of the ghetto walls, the education of Jews was removed from the narrow confines of the Jewish community. The Jew received his general education in the public schools, along with his non-Jewish fellow citizens, and looked to the supplemental Jewish school for specialized Jewish knowledge which had religion as its core. These were two distinct types of schools, functioning on different levels, operating in separate spheres and complementing each other. It was not necessary to destroy the old institutions in order to build new ones. Those who broke with the Jewish faith—and their number was legion in western Europe—never bothered to evolve secularist programs of Jewish survival; they simply left the Jewish fold.

Conditions were radically different in eastern Europe where the church was a pillar of the reactionary regimes and where the slightest deviation from tradition was violently opposed by Jewish religious leadership. The public school was closed to the majority of the Jewish people. The average Jewish child or youth had to procure his general, as well as Jewish, education in a Jewish institution of learning or remain without such an education. Modern education could not be introduced without a fight to the finish against the religious forces which resisted reform not alone in matters of faith but in daily conduct as well. And since the contending forces met in combat at a time when the Jews were going through their greatest social and cultural upheavals, the fight between religion and secularism turned into an ideological struggle involving the basic issues of Jewish existence.

This struggle, encompassing the totality of Jewish life, followed in the wake of the social differentiation which was proceeding at an increasing pace during the second half of the nineteenth century. Secularization therefore became an inevitable step in the rise of a Jewish labor movement, something that has never developed in western Europe.

The basis of the secularist ideologies, even in their outspokenly atheistic aspects, was of course not the negation of religion but rather the recognition of dynamic Jewish culture as the most characteristic expression of Jewish peoplehood. These ideologies had their moorings in Jewish mass life and were linked to the Yiddish language, which was the living tongue of the majority of Jewish people. Stemming from the nationality status enjoyed by the Jews in eastern Europe, secularism had its stronghold in the Jewish labor movement. This is not to say that there were no groups with an exclusively secularist approach to Jewish problems among the Jewish bourgeoisie, or that there were no Hebraists who excluded all religious considerations from their philosophies of Jewish life; but there is no gainsaying the fact that secularism derived its mass following from organized Jewish labor.

At the end of the nineteenth century and the beginning of the twentieth, until the end of World War I, in fact, organized Jewish labor and the socialist movement were a decisive, if not a dominating, factor in the Jewish immigrant colonies in this country. These colonies were in some respects a replica of the thickly populated Jewish settlements in eastern Europe. Yiddish was the vernacular of the majority of the Jewish population. Yiddish literature was in its bloom. For the adult Jewish immigrant it was possible to find complete spiritual expression in modern Jewish culture inside the Jewish environment. Economic conflicts among Jews were largely fought out in a Jewish setting with Jewish workers facing Jewish employers. Insofar as the latter supplied a major portion of synagog leadership, religion also figured in the class struggles involving Jewish workers. All this created fertile ground for the secularist conceptions of Jewish national existence.

Into the new soil of America the theoreticians of progressive nationalism attempted to transplant concepts of Jewish communalism that they had brought from abroad; but the concepts began to fade the minute they touched the hard realities of American life. Unadulterated secularism thus became a one-generation phenomenon: it neither had parents nor begot children. The previously arrived German Jews, true to the tradition of western Emancipation, never took to the secularist ideologies, and the native-born sons and daughters of Polish and Russian Jews, cast in the mold of the American way of life, could not comprehend a Judaism which had neither its roots in the Jewish faith nor its trunk in the American social system.

In the artificial world which they had created, the leaders of the secularist movement were sure that: (1) American Jewry was heading toward a nationality status; and that (2) religion was dying out, among Jews faster than among others. Events proved them wrong on both scores, as we have demonstrated.

In predicting that the Jewish community would develop into a nationality in this country, secularists, not content merely to draw upon the experience of eastern Europe, reinforced their hopes by hitching

222

them to the star of the previously discussed theory of cultural pluralism. In so doing, they read into the theory something its exponents had never intended. They interpreted cultural pluralism to mean that the United States would in time develop, at least culturally, into a federation of nationalities. In their enthusiasm, they failed to detect the organic weakness of the theory—to which we have referred earlier—the fact that the cultural pluralists, envisaging this country as an orchestra in which each ethnic group represented a distinct musical instrument, had been unable to forecast in what form the instrument would be preserved in the future. Jewish secularists did not seem to realize that a nationality instrument could not help striking a discordant note which did not blend with the tunes produced by the other instruments in the American orchestra.

JEWISH FAITH AND JEWISH PEOPLEHOOD

Contrary to secularist prophecy, America, as we have seen, has manifested no desire to become a nationality state and religion has shown no inclination to die, a lesson not lost on the acculturated American Jew. However, in regarding religion as the basis of Jewish existence, he does not negate Jewish peoplehood. Quite the opposite: the concept of Jewish peoplehood is an integral part of his religious belief. American Jews can no more conceive of the Jewish faith severed from the framework of Jewish peoplehood than they can conceive of a Jewish community removed from its religious base. Hence there is a vast difference between the attitudes of the overwhelming majority of American Jews viewing themselves as fundamentally a religious community and the assimilationist theories which gave rise to groups like the Germans of the Jewish Faith and Poles of the Mosaic Persuasion in pre-Hitler Europe or to the American Council for Judaism since then. These latter groups profess a loyalty to Judaism as an abstract spiritual manifestation and reject it as a way of life. They adhere to some vague universalistic visions in Jewish prophetic faith and deny the role of the Jewish people as the repository of this faith. The assimilationist theories have found their most eloquent expression in the program advocated by Isaac W. Bernheim of Louisville, Ky., calling, in 1919, for the abandonment of the term

223

"Jew" as denoting an ethnic deflection from the rest of the American population, and urging the reconstitution of the Jewish houses of worship into "Reform Churches of American Israelites."

The fact that after fifteen years of intensive propaganda, covering the period of the greatest expansion of the synagog, the American Council for Judaism can lay claim to a membership of only sixteen thousand is most conclusive evidence of its total rejection by American Jewry. The latter is not interested in the perpetuation of a denominational sect in the United States, but in the creative preservation of the Jewish people; and we have seen how closely tied American Jews have always been to the Jews in other parts of the world not merely by the bonds of faith but by the bonds of history, culture and a common destiny as well. It is for this reason that concern with and about the fate of Jews in the rest of the world has occupied so commanding a place on the agenda of the American Jew. This concern will retain its place if the Jewish community is to survive in America.

Will it survive dynamically? If the objective conditions analyzed in this work continue to be regulated by the same subjective factors, an affirmative answer is inescapable. But such are the dialectics of the interplay of the positive and negative forces in Jewish life that the future, given the same set of circumstances, may produce results totally different from those in the past. That Jewish resistance to the disintegrating pressures in American life is bound to get weaker is attested by all evidence we have thus far been able to accumulate. Whether the existence of the State of Israel will further undermine this resistance or strengthen it is the decisive question the American Jewish community will face in the fourth century of its existence.

Conclusion

The Ethnic Individuality of the American Jew

In summing up the development of the Jewish community in the United States, we find it deviating from the course which the other ethnic groups have followed in the process of integrating themselves into the larger American society. Those groups, in contradistinction to the settlers who built a new civilization on the basis of an old culture, have discarded their old cultures in order to adapt themselves to the new civilization dominated by the Anglo-Saxon elements. The greater the distance a group has covered on the road to adaptation, the farther it has moved away from its own ethnic moorings. The Jews have proved to be an exception to this rule, and herein lies their uniqueness as an ethnic community.

Originally fragmented in their cultural views and communal activities, and subsequently achieving a high degree of acculturation in a short period of time, the Jews, had they fitted into the general patterns of integration, should have reached a state of near-dissolution as a community by the third generation. As we have seen, the opposite has indeed occurred, in contradiction to the history of the other European immigrant groups.

The contradiction consists in the growth and solidification of the

Jewish community coming about partly *because of* American assimilatory trends and partly *in spite of* them. Inner forces of cohesion within the Jewish group have turned acculturation itself into an instrument to develop and to strengthen ethnic individuality. The persistent majority attitudes peculiar to America, which we sketched in our first two chapters, resisted the complete assimilation even of those wavering Jews who may have actually desired to leave the Jewish fold. Utilitarianism, pragmatism and democracy have been transformed into factors of Jewish ethnic consolidation.

This consolidation has been reinforced by the condition of the Jewish people throughout the world. In this respect, too, the Jews have deviated from the main highway of adaptation. Not only was concern for Jews persecuted abroad a powerful stimulus for ethnic cohesion here, but the emergence of the State of Israel has so far had the effect of increasing rather than lessening the sense of "belongingness" among American Jews.

The disappearance of the Jews as a separate group is not in sight as long as prevailing social conditions in the United States and the existent world situation of the Jewish people continue. In this sense, the Jews bear a greater similarity to the colored races—the Negroes, Chinese, Japanese, Indians, and others whose status is that of castes or quasi-castes, than to the other immigrant groups that came here from Europe. But this particular status has only in part been imposed upon the Jews by the tyranny of the majority. It is also in no small measure the result of a free choice by the Jews themselves. For this reason, they may be expected to continue as a distinct ethnic group —on the level of spiritual uniqueness, religious separateness, ethnic consolidation and communal solidarity, but not in a political sense. They can have no prospective status other than that of a minority, albeit not as discriminated-against a minority as the Negroes. Within the limits in which they can function as a community, there is yet room for expansion and progress.

It is not the task of this study to decide whether or not it is good for the Jews that in time they will remain perhaps the sole exception among white ethnic groups; for the country as a whole it is certainly no disadvantage. For it is only as a community that the Jews can best and most effectively inject their tone into the American symphony

—and thus help bridge the chasm between culture and civilization. For the Jews themselves this is the fact: they exist as a separate ethnic group and will remain so in the foreseeable future. Thus, their own welfare and the best interests of the United States require that they infuse their ethnic individuality with as much positive content as possible and that they bear their ethnic identity with pride. The difference between them and a caste or quasi-caste is the voluntarism with which they approach their separateness. If they were to retain their ethnic identity solely because the majority refuses to absorb them, then their existence would be marked by all the frustrations and bitterness that naturally accompany externally imposed separateness, and their spirit would bear the imprint of the entire misfortune of marginality. If, on the other hand, their group identity is founded on their will to live and to enrich America with whatever creative originality they possess—then they will be able to make of their exceptional status a joy to themselves and a blessing for the United States.

Notes

Full information about each source cited in the notes appears with the first reference to it in each chapter. Subsequent references to a book are by short-ened title; to a periodical, by volume. To assist the reader, quotations from Yiddish works are given in English. The English translation of the title of a Yiddish source is accompanied, in the first chapter reference, by transliterated Yiddish, following the rules formulated by the YIVO Institute for Jewish Research. The following abbreviations are used: AJHS (American Jewish Historical Society); *AJYB* (*American Jewish Year Books*); *NJM* (*National Jewish Monthly*); *JR* (*Jewish Review*); *JSS* (*Jewish Social Studies*); YIVO (Yiddish Scientific Institute, now YIVO Institute for Jewish Research).

A selected list of pertinent writings, not directly cited in the Notes but found useful as background material, appears in the Supplementary Bibliography.

Chapter 1

1. Carl F. Wittke, *We Who Built America* (New York, 1939), p. 3.
2. In the Census Bureau's usage, "mother tongue" signifies the main language spoken at home during the subject's childhood. Those who in 1940 actually employed a language other than English in their daily intercourse surely constituted less than 10 percent of the population, a smaller proportion

even than in 1776. There was no mother-tongue question in the 1950 census, but it can safely be assumed that the foreign languages have lost further ground.

3. Gunnar Myrdal, *An American Dilemma* (2 vols.; New York, 1944), I, 50.
4. Richard A. Schermerhorn, *These Our People* (Boston, 1949), p. 6.
5. *Ibid.*, p. 5.
6. *One America*, ed. Francis J. Brown and Joseph S. Rouček (3rd ed.; New York, 1945), p. 6.
7. Frederick J. Turner, *The Frontier in American History* (New York, 1935), p. 3.
8. Howard K. Beale, *A History of Freedom of Teaching in American Schools* (New York, 1941), p. 79.
9. Vernon L. Parrington, *Main Currents in American Thought* (3 vols.; New York, 1930), I, 4.
10. Charles A. and Mary R. Beard, *The Rise of American Civilization* (2 vols.; New York, 1927), I, 631.
11. Alexis de Tocqueville, *Democracy in America*, trans. Henry Reeve (2 vols.; New York, 1900), I, 267.
12. *Ibid.*
13. Beale, *Hist. Freedom of Teaching Am. Schools*, p. 71.
14. V. F. Calverton, *The Liberation of American Literature* (New York, 1932), p. 232.
15. Edward Jarvis, *History of the Progress of Population in the United States from 1790 to 1870* (Boston, 1877), p. 11.
16. Marcus L. Hansen, *The Immigrant in American History*, ed. Arthur M. Schlesinger (Cambridge, Mass., 1940), pp. 24–25.

Chapter 2

1. Ber Borochov, *Nationalism and the Class Struggle* (New York, 1937).
2. Donald R. Taft, *Human Migration* (New York, 1936), p. 249.
3. In considering ethnic minorities in America, a distinction is often drawn between the "old" and the "new" immigration. In our discussion, the "old" immigration designates that which took place between the Revolution until the last third of the nineteenth century. "New" immigration refers to all subsequent immigration.
4. Caroline F. Ware, "Cultural Groups in the United States," in *The Cultural Approach to History*, ed. Caroline F. Ware (New York, 1940), p. 63.
5. Lawrence F. Pisani, *The Italian in America* (New York, 1957), p. 152.
6. Cf. Edward F. Roberts, *Ireland in America* (New York, 1931), p. 76: "The arriving Irish had to face the fact that public opinion in their new home invariably was shaped and directed by men who had inherited many of the prejudices and antipathies of their English oppressors."
7. It should be noted that their German dialect reflected the discernible influence of English. German was not a foreign tongue in the Pennsylvania

Dutch belt but, in the words of Richard H. Shryock, the "native language in those areas . . . just as much as English [was] in our adjoining counties." ("The Pennsylvania Germans as Seen by the Historian," in *The Pennsylvania Germans*, ed. Ralph Wood [Princeton, 1942]), p. 245.

8. Arthur D. Graeff, "Pennsylvania, the Colonial Melting Pot," in *Pennsylvania Germans*, p. 48.

9. *Ibid.*, p. 49. See also in the same essay the summary of a pastor's appeal for the preservation of religion, language, and agrarian social order, as quoted by Charles Maurer Lewis:

> Do you wish to leave your children a rich inheritance? Then teach them German. Do you want your children to honor father and mother? Then see that they remain Lutherans. If they are to remain Lutherans, then they must remain Germans. But why remain German Lutherans or Lutheran Germans? Because if they do not remain Lutherans they will not remain farmers, and they are nothing if not farmers. Look at your farms and then look at the others! Do you want your children to fritter away what you had earned in the sweat of your brow? How long do you think they will hold on to the family farm once they have been Anglicized? (*Ibid.*)

10. By 1834, when the fight for public school education had already assumed serious proportions, some 160 parochial schools were being maintained by the Reformed church and some 250 by the Lutheran church, sufficient to provide an elementary education for all Pennsylvania Dutch children. (Clyde S. Stine, "The Pennsylvania Germans and the Schools," in *Pennsylvania Germans*, p. 112) A year later the same schools rejected financial aid from the government because they were unwilling to open the doors of their educational system to state intervention.

11. As a group, the Huguenots most closely approximated the Anglo-Saxon elements, professing the same faith and arriving as settlers in the colonial period. They were too small in number and insufficiently compact geographically to play an important social role. In places where they did concentrate, such as Charleston, S.C., their influence was more enduring. Unlike the Pennsylvania Dutch, they had no special socio-cultural goals, and they lacked the stubborn sectarianism of religious groups that have to conduct a militant battle for their faith.

12. A factor contributing to the secularization of education was the Catholic demand for a share of tax money appropriated for education. In the end, Protestants preferred to forego religious instruction in the schools rather than allow the diversion of public funds for the subsidization of Catholic parochial schools. Thus, the Irish insistence on equal treatment to Catholics in the educational processes contributed greatly, if indirectly, to the establishment of a free public school system, which became the most important instrument of assimilation in the United States.

13. See Gerald Shaughnessy's table of Roman Catholic parochial schools

using a foreign language alone or with English in 1916, in *Has the Immigrant Kept His Faith?* (New York, 1925), p. 218. Poles and French-Canadians at that time comprised fully one-half of the membership of Catholic churches in which foreign languages were used.

14. Although no parochial schools were maintained by the Greek Orthodox church, it established many Sunday schools that were both religious institutions and islands of national tradition and culture for Greeks, Russians, Rumanians, and other ethnic groups of the same faith. Greek-Americans also maintained afternoon or supplementary schools in which Orthodox priests served as instructors.

15. In 1834, Gustave Koerner, a leader of the German immigration argued that "the Americans are in their regard for art half-barbarians, and their taste is not much better than that of the Indian aborigines, who stick metal rings through their noses." Quoted in John Hawgood, *The Tragedy of German-America* (New York, 1940), p. 41.

16. The Germania Society of New York, founded in the 1830's, is an example. Its aim was the organization of German political immigrants in the United States. See also the manifesto issued by members of the Giessen Society before leaving for America in 1834 with the intention of founding a German State, which "would naturally become a member of the American Union, but which would maintain a form of government that would guarantee the permanence of German civilization and the German language, and provide for a free and democratic existence." Quoted in *Tragedy of German America*, p. 109.

17. See Morris Hillquit, *History of Socialism in the United States* (New York, 1903), pp. 225, 258.

18. The number of German-language newspapers fell from 203 in 1926 to 82 in 1956. During the same period, the number of Polish papers dropped from 90 to 50; Italian, from 154 to 56. All of these are languages of groups that carried on important and dedicated ethnic activity. In general, the number of foreign-language newspapers dropped from 1,156 to 834 in the period 1926–1956. Owing to increased immigration from Latin America, the number of Spanish-language newspapers increased from 83 in 1926 to 130 in 1947. Since that time they too have shown a decrease: in 1956 only 76 Spanish periodicals functioned, 9 of them dailies. (Releases of the Common Council for American Unity, New York, compiled by Yaroslav Chyz, July, 1935; September, 1941; October, 1943; June, 1947; January, 1951. [Mimeographed])

19. In New Mexico, Spanish-speaking residents constitute virtually a majority of the population. In 1940 nearly as many inhabitants of that state referred to Spanish as their mother tongue as referred to English.

20. See page 16.

21. Herman Feldman, *Racial Factors in American History* (New York, 1931), p. 137.

22. Stuart Chase, *Men and Machines* (New York, 1929), p. 104. Automation, the logical outcome of the technological revolution, introduces new changes which need not concern us here, as we deal with the past rather than the future.

23. William M. Leiserson, *Adjusting Immigrant and Industry* (New York, 1924), pp. 92–93.

24. *Ibid.*, pp. 224–25.

25. For a description of the experience of the Danes in Askov, Minn., the Czechs in Virginia, and the Poles in Sunderland, Mass., see *Immigrant Farmers and Their Children*, ed. Edmund de S. Brunner (Garden City, N.Y., 1929).

26. "City College Introduces Courses in Yiddish," *News of YIVO*, No. 19 (February, 1947), p. 7.

27. See Claris E. Silcox and Galen N. Fisher, *Catholics, Jews, and Protestants* (New York, 1934), p. 211.

28. Edward F. Spiers, *The Central Catholic High School* (Washington, 1951), pp. 33, 127.

29. W. Lloyd Warner and Leo Srole, *The Social Systems of American Ethnic Groups* ("Yankee City Series," Vol. III [New Haven, 1945]), p. 241. Acknowledgment is made to the publishers, the Yale University Press.

30. Even though the Irish played a decisive role in the formation of a number of American unions, they always opposed the creation of a labor party, using their influence in the unions to strengthen their positions in the Democratic party.

31. Richmond Mayo-Smith, *Emigration and Immigration* (New York, 1890), p. 73.

32. James Bryce, *The American Commonwealth* (2 vols.; New York, 1931), II, 95.

33. Warner and Srole, *Soc. Systems Am. Ethnic Groups*, pp. 295–96.

34. *Ibid.*, p. 141.

35. Nettie P. McGill and Ellen N. Matthews, *The Youth of New York City* (New York, 1940), pp. 222–24.

36. W. Lloyd Warner and Paul S. Lunt, *The Social Life of a Modern Community* ("Yankee City Series," Vol. I [New Haven, 1941]), p. 415. The Yankees in Yankee City attended the movies 2.18 times in the course of 25 days; the members of ethnic minority groups, 2.43 times in the same period. Broken down according to individual ethnic groups, attendance during the period was:

Yankees	2.18 times	Armenians	3.60 times
Irish	2.38 "	French	2.35 "
Greeks	2.56 "	Italians	2.33 "
Jews	2.38 "	Negroes	6.0 "
Poles	2.93 "	Russians	3.0 "

37. In her *Study of Assimilation among Roumanians* in the United States (New York, 1929), "mixed marriage" denotes a marriage between spouses of different ethnic, racial or religious groups. A more precise definition distinguishes between "mixed marriage" (between spouses of different faiths each of whom retains his own religion) and "intermarriage" (implying acceptance by one spouse of the faith of the other).

38. Julius Drachsler, *Democracy and Assimilation* (New York, 1920), p. 147.

39. T. J. Woofter, Jr., *Races and Ethnic Groups in American Life* (New York, 1933), p. 207.

40. Drachsler, *Democracy and Assimilation*, p. 108.

41. *Immigrant Farmers and Their Children*, pp. 90 ff.

42. See Table 14, p. 187.

43. Bessie Bloom Wessel, *The Ethnic Survey of Woonsocket, R.I.* (Chicago, 1931), pp. 31–39.

44. Quoted by Horace M. Kallen, *Culture and Democracy in the United States* (New York, 1924), p. 175.

45. Thomas Burgess, *Greeks in America* (Boston, 1913), p. 85.

46. Drachsler, *Democracy and Assimilation*, pp. 10–11.

47. Quoted in Robert E. Park and Herbert A. Miller, *Old World Traits Transplanted* (New York, 1921), p. 99.

48. Silcox and Fisher, *Catholics, Jews, and Protestants*, p. 103.

49. Lawrence Brown, *Immigration* (New York, 1933), p. 251.

50. William I. Thomas and Florian Znaniecki, *The Polish Peasant in Europe and America* (5 vols.; Boston, 1920), I, Intro., ix.

51. Jerome Davis, *The Russian Immigrant* (New York, 1922), p. 84.

52. Warner and Srole, *Soc. Systems Am. Ethnic Groups*, p. 145.

53. *Ibid.*, p. 137.

54. "The Second Generation Immigrants," *Annals of the American Academy of Political and Social Science*, XCIII (January, 1921), 158.

55. *Soc. Systems Am. Ethnic Groups*, p. 148.

56. Franz Boas, *The Mind of Primitive Man* (rev. ed.; New York, 1938), p. 266.

57. Hannibal G. Duncan, *Immigration and Assimilation* (Boston, 1933), p. 827.

58. Mayo-Smith, *Emigration and Immigration*, p. 73.

59. Federal Writers Project: *The Italians of New York* (New York, 1938), p. 224.

60. Samuel Koenig, "Second- and Third-Generation Americans," in *One America*, ed. Francis J. Brown and Joseph S. Rouček (3rd ed.; New York, 1945), p. 473.

61. *Ibid.*, p. 484.

62. Quoted in Kallen, *Culture and Democracy*, pp. 131–132. See also Joseph

Rouček, and others, "Summary of the Discussion," in *Cultural Approach to History*, pp. 88–89:

> Today New England culture is not Plymouth Rock culture, with transitional French, Portuguese, Polish, Italian, Greek, Syrian, Irish, and other group cultures held, as it were, in suspension within. New England today *is* French, Portuguese, Polish, Italian, Greek, Syrian, Irish—American. These *are* the New England people—who vote in elections, work in mills and offices, pay taxes, support churches, listen to radios, drive over highways, stage Fourth of July carnivals, St. Patrick's Day parades and Our Lady of Mt. Carmel celebrations, and bring up the next generation of Americans. They *are* the American people.

63. Kallen, *Culture and Democracy*, p. 42.
64. *Ibid.*, pp. 62–63.
65. "Cultural Diversity in American Life," in Alain Locke and Bernard J. Stern, *When Peoples Meet* (New York, 1942), p. 717.
66. Maurice R. Davie, "Our Vanishing Minorities," in *One America*, p. 551.
67. Warner and Srole, *Soc. Systems Am. Ethnic Groups*, p. 295.
68. *Ibid.*, p. 155.

Chapter 3

1. Samuel Joseph, *Jewish Immigration to the United States from 1881 to 1910* (New York, 1914), p. 132.
2. Liebman Hersch, "Jewish Emigration in the Past Hundred Years," *General Encyclopedia* (2nd ed.; New York, 1941), I, 465–66. Totals in original text not 100 percent. ("Yidishe emigratsye far di letste hundert yor," *Algemayne Entsiklopedye*, Yidn, Alef.)
3. *Ibid.*, I, 464.
4. Joseph, *Jewish Immigration to the U.S.*, p. 137.
5. Hyman B. Grinstein, *The Rise of the Jewish Community of New York, 1654–1860* (Philadelphia, 1945), p. 169.
6. Anita Libman Lebeson, *Jewish Pioneers in America, 1492–1848* (New York, 1931), p. 173.
7. Lee J. Levinger, *A History of the Jews in the United States* (Cincinnati, 1931), p. 181.
8. Louis Wirth, *The Ghetto* (Chicago, 1928), p. 183.
9. Rudolph Glanz, "The Immigration of German Jews up to 1880," in *The History of the Jewish Labor Movement in the United States*, ed. Elias Tcherikower (2 vols.; New York, 1943), I, 59. ("Di aynvanderung fun di daytsche yidn biz di 80-er yorn," *Geshikhte fun der Yidisher arbeterbavegung in di Faraynikte Shtatn.*)
10. Elias Tcherikower, "How the American Jews Received the Russian

Jewish Immigrants," in *Hist. Jewish Labor Movement*, I, 202. ("Vi azoy hobn Amerikaner Yidn oyfgenumen di rusish-yidishe imigratsye.")

11. Stuart E. Rosenberg, *The Jewish Community in Rochester, 1843–1925* (New York, 1954), p. 66.
12. Isaac Mayer Wise, *Reminiscences*, trans. David Philipson (Cincinnati, 1901), p. 21.
13. Grinstein, *Rise of the Jewish Community of N.Y.*, p. 172.
14. Everett V. Stonequist, *The Marginal Man* (New York, 1937), pp. 121–22.
15. Heinrich H. Graetz, *History of the Jews*, ed. and in part trans. Bella Lowy (6 vols.; Philadelphia, 1895), V, 587.
16. Uriah Z. Engelman, *The Rise of the Jew in the Western World* (New York, 1944), p. 191.
17. Quoted in Edwin Wolf 2nd and Maxwell Whiteman, *The History of the Jews of Philadelphia from Colonial Times to the Age of Jackson* (Philadelphia, 1957), p. 297.
18. Wise, *Reminiscences*, p. 211.
19. David Philipson, *My Life as an American Jew* (Cincinnati, 1941), p. 96.
20. Quoted in Rosenberg, *Jewish Community in Rochester*, p. 68.
21. Leonard Bloom, "The Jews of Buna," in *Jews in a Gentile World*, ed. Isacque Graeber and Steuart H. Britt (New York, 1942), p. 186. Acknowledgment is made to the publishers, The Macmillan Co., for permission to quote from *Jews in a Gentile World*.
22. Quoted in Ismar Elbogen, *A Century of Jewish Life*, ed. Solomon Grayzel (Philadelphia, 1944), p. 130.
23. Rosenberg, *Jewish Community in Rochester*, p. 100.
24. Adolph Krause, *Reminiscences and Comments* (Chicago, 1945), pp. 151–52.
25. Herbert T. Ezekiel and Gaston Lichtenstein, *The History of the Jews in Richmond* (Richmond, Va., 1917), p. 225.
26. Barnett A. Elzas, *The Jews of South Carolina* (Philadelphia, 1905), p. 152.

Chapter 4

1. Quoted in Isaac A. Hourwich, *Immigration and Labor* (New York, 1912), p. 370.
2. Samuel Joseph, *Jewish Immigration to the United States from 1881 to 1910* (New York, 1914), p. 191.
3. Hyman B. Grinstein, *The Rise of the Jewish Community of New York, 1654–1860* (Philadelphia, 1945), p. 129.
4. Joshua Trachtenberg, *Consider the Years* (Easton, Pa., 1944), p. 125.
5. Ben B. Seligman and Harvey Swados, "Jewish Population Studies in the United States," *AJYB*, L (1948–49), 651–90.
6. "Jewish Population of the United States, 1955," *AJYB*, LVII (1956), 119–30.

7. Henry Cohen, "Jewish Population Trends in New York," Federation of Jewish Philanthropies of New York, 1955. (Mimeographed)
8. Morris C. Horowitz and Lawrence J. Kaplan, *The Jewish Population of New York Area, 1900–1975,* (Federation of Jewish Philanthropies of New York [New York, 1959]), Table 7, p. 17.
9. "Who Belongs to What Churches," *Catholic Digest,* XVII (January, 1953), 3.
10. U.S. Bureau of Census, *Seventeenth Census of the United States: 1950,* Current Population Reports, Population Characteristics Series P-20, No. 79, p. 1.
11. Ben B. Seligman, with the assistance of Aaron Antonovsky, "Some Aspects of Jewish Demography," in *The Jews, Social Patterns of an American Group,* ed. Marshall Sklare (Glencoe, Ill., 1958), p. 67. Reprinted with the permission of the publishers, The Free Press.
12. Edward P. Hutchinson, *Immigrants and Their Children* (New York, 1956), pp. 24–26.
13. Nathan Reich, "Economic Trends," in *The American Jew, a Composite Portrait,* ed. Oscar I. Janowsky (New York, 1942), p. 173.

Chapter 5

1. Jacob Lestchinsky, "The Economic Development of the Jews in the United States," in *The Jewish People–Past and Present,* (Jewish Encyclopedic Handbooks, Central Yiddish Cultural Organization [CYCO]), I (New York, 1946), 392.
2. Nathan Goldberg, "Occupational Patterns of American Jews," *JR,* III, No. 4 (January–March, 1946), 275.
3. Nathan Goldberg, "Occupational Patterns of American Jews," *JR,* III, No. 3 (October–December, 1945), 172.
4. *Jewish People–Past and Present,* I, 399.
5. General population figures are from the U.S. Bureau of the Census, *Seventeenth Census of the United States: 1950,* Vol. II, *Population,* Tables 73 and 75. Figures for the Jewish population are from the following surveys conducted by the Council of Jewish Federations and Welfare Funds and local community councils: Camden, N.J. (1948); Charleston, S.C. (1948); Indianapolis (1948); Miami (1949); Newark (1948); Portland, Ore. (1947); Utica (1948); Gary (1949); Nashville (1949); Trenton, N.J. (1949); Los Angeles (1950); Passaic (1949); Port Chester (1950); New Haven (1950); New Orleans (1953); Newark suburbs (1948).
6. Henry Cohen, "Population Trends in New York," Federation of Jewish Philanthropies of New York, 1955. (Mimeographed)
7. The cities studied were: (1935–45) Buffalo, Detroit, Erie, Grand Rapids, Jacksonville, New Orleans, Passaic, Pittsburgh, San Francisco, Trenton, N.J.; (1948–1953) Camden, N.J., Charleston, S.C.; Gary, Indianapolis, Los

Angeles, Miami, Nashville, New Orleans, Newark, Passaic, Port Chester, Trenton, N.J., Utica.

8. H. Dewey Anderson and Percy E. Davidson, *Occupational Trends in the United States* (Stanford University, Cal., 1940), pp. 16–17. Tabulation of census errors, revisions, and years 1880, 1890, 1910 omitted. Reprinted with the permission of the Stanford University Press.

9. Lewis Corey, "The Middle Class," reprinted from *Antioch Review,* Spring, 1945, p. 6.

10. Joel Seidman, *The Needle Trades* (New York, 1942), p. 13.

11. Nathan Goldberg, "Occupational Patterns of American Jews," *JR,* III, No. 1 (April, 1945), 14.

12. Hertz Burgin, *History of the Jewish Labor Movement* (New York, 1915), p. 103. (*Di geshikhte fun der yidisher arbeter-bavegung in Amerika, Rusland un England.*)

13. Corey, *Antioch Review,* Spring, 1945, p. 4.

14. Anderson and Davidson, *Occupational Trends in the U.S.,* pp. 436–37.

15. *U.S. Census:* 1950, Vol. II, Part I, Table 53.

16. *Ibid.,* II, Part I, Table 125.

17. *Ibid.*

18. *The Immigrant Jew in America,* ed. Edmund J. James (New York, 1907), p. 190.

19. Nettie P. McGill and Ellen N. Matthews, *The Youth of New York City* (New York, 1940), p. 62.

20. Benjamin B. Goldman and Alvin Chenkin, *The Jewish Population of New Orleans: 1953* (Jewish Community Surveys, Council of Jewish Federations and Welfare Funds [New York, 1954]), p. xxxiv.

21. Robert Shosteck, *The Jewish College Student* (B'nai B'rith Vocational Service [Washington, 1957]), p. 49. Totals are not 100 percent.

22. Robert Shosteck, "Our Youth in College," *NJM,* LXXI, No. 3 (November, 1956), 9.

23. Frank Lorimer and Frederick Osborn, *Dynamics of Population* (New York, 1934).

24. Samuel Koenig, "Ethnic Groups in Certain General Cultural Activities in Connecticut," *YIVO Bleter,* XXV, No. 3 (May–June, 1945), 380. ("Etnishe Grupes in gevise algemayne kulturele tetikayten in Connecticut.")

25. W. Lloyd Warner and Leo Srole, *The Social Systems of American Ethnic Groups* ("Yankee City Series," Vol. III [New Haven, 1945]), p. 59.

26. *Ibid.,* p. 61.

27. Goldberg, *JR,* III, No. 4, 277.

28. Samuel Koenig, "Socioeconomic Structure of an American Jewish Community," in *Jews in a Gentile World,* ed. Isacque Graeber and Steuart H. Britt (New York, 1942), p. 211.

29. Bessie Bloom Wessel, "A Comparative Study of the Jewish Communities of New London and Norwich, 1938," in *Jewish Population Studies,* ed. Sophia M. Robison and Joshua Starr (New York, 1943), pp. 66–78.
30. Bessie Bloom Wessel, "The Jewish Population of Trenton, 1937," in *Jewish Population Studies,* p. 16.
31. Goldberg, *JR,* III, No. 4, 265–66.
32. Goldman and Chenkin, *Jewish Population of New Orleans,* p. xxviii.

Chapter 6

1. Julian B. Feibelman, *A Social and Economic Study of the New Orleans Jewish Community* (Philadelphia, 1941), p. 136.
2. Isaac Mayer Wise, *Reminiscences,* trans. David Philipson (Cincinnati, 1901), p. 57.
3. Quoted in Louis Wirth, *The Ghetto* (Chicago, 1928), pp. 139–40.
4. N. W. Ayer and Sons, Philadelphia, Pa., Directory of Newspapers and Periodicals, 1948–57.
5. Editors of Fortune, *Jews in America* (New York, 1936), p. 78.
6. Everett V. Stonequist, *The Marginal Man* (New York, 1937), p. 82.
7. Raymond Kennedy, "The Position and Future of the Jews in America," in *Jews in a Gentile World,* ed. Isacque Graeber and Steuart H. Britt (New York, 1942), p. 420.
8. Horace M. Kallen, *Culture and Democracy in the United States* (New York, 1924), p. 113.
9. Gerald Shaughnessy, *Has the Immigrant Kept His Faith?* (New York, 1925), p. 268.
10. Stonequist, *Marginal Man,* Intro., p. xviii.
11. Waldo Frank, *Our America* (New York, 1919), p. 85.
12. Releases of the Common Council for American Unity, New York, compiled by Yaroslav Chyz, 1956. (Mimeographed)
13. Quoted in Hyman B. Grinstein, *Rise of the Jewish Community of New York, 1654–1860* (Philadelphia, 1945), p. 376.
14. *Ibid.,* p. 379.
15. Charles R. Snyder, "Culture and Jewish Sobriety: The Ingroup-Outgroup Factor," in *The Jews, Social Patterns of an American Group,* ed. Marshall Sklare (Glencoe, Ill., 1958), pp. 560–92.
16. Sophia M. Robison, "A Study of Delinquency Among Jewish Children in New York City," *The Jews,* p. 538. Quoted with the permission of the publishers, The Free Press.
17. Howard W. Polsky, "A Study of Orthodoxy in Milwaukee: Social Characteristics, Beliefs, and Observances," in *The Jews,* pp. 325–35.
18. Marshall Sklare, "Aspects of Religious Worship in the Contemporary Conservative Synagogue," in *The Jews,* pp. 357–76.

19. Harry S. Linfield, "The Jewish Population of the United States," *AJYB*, XLVII (1956), 644.

20. Maurice J. Karpf, *Jewish Community Organization in the United States* (New York, 1938), pp. 75–76.

Chapter 7

1. W. Lloyd Warner and Leo Srole, *The Social Systems of American Ethnic Groups* ("Yankee City Series," Vol. III [New Haven, 1945]), p. 60.

2. Editors of Fortune, *Jews in America* (New York, 1936), p. 42.

3. *Rights*, Anti-Defamation League of B'nai B'rith Reports on Social, Employment, Educational, and Housing Discriminations, II, No. 8 (November–December, 1959).

4. *Jews in America*, p. 42.

5. Ismar Elbogen, *A Century of Jewish Life*, ed. Solomon Grayzel (Philadelphia, 1944), p. 584.

6. Everett V. Stonequist, *The Marginal Man* (New York, 1937), p. 102.

7. Raymond Kennedy, "The Position and Future of Jews in America," in *Jews in a Gentile World*, ed. Isacque Graeber and Steuart H. Britt (New York, 1942), p. 423.

8. John Higham, "Social Discrimination Against Jews in America," AJHS *Publications*, XLVII, No. 1 (September, 1957), 4–5.

9. Claris E. Silcox and Galen N. Fisher, *Catholics, Jews, and Protestants* (New York, 1934), p. 36.

10. New York *Herald Tribune*, October 30, 1947.

11. *Jews in America*, p. 76.

12. *Ibid.*, p. 31.

13. W. Lloyd Warner and Paul S. Lunt, *The Social Life of a Modern Community* ("Yankee City Series," Vol. I [New Haven, 1941]), p. 290.

14. W. Lloyd Warner and Paul S. Lunt, *The Status System of a Modern Community* ("Yankee City Series," Vol. II [New Haven, 1942]), p. 75.

15. Donald Young, *American Minority Peoples* (New York, 1932), p. 318.

16. Stuart E. Rosenberg, *The Jewish Community in Rochester, 1843–1925* (New York, 1954), p. 18.

17. Albert I. Gordon, *Jews in Transition* (Minneapolis, 1949), pp. 279–96.

18. Young, *American Minority Peoples*, p. 296.

19. Anti-Defamation League of B'nai B'rith, "A Survey of Resort Admission Policies in Respect to Jews," prepared by Albert Weiss, Albert and Harold Braverman, under supervision of Arnold Forster, 1954. (Mimeographed)

20. Robert S. and Helen M. Lynd, *Middletown* (New York, 1929), p. 479.

21. Robert S. and Helen M. Lynd, *Middletown in Transition* (New York, 1937), p. 408.

22. Leonard Bloom, "The Jews of Buna," in *Jews in a Gentile World*, p. 181.
23. Young, *American Minority Peoples*, p. 396.
24. Samuel Koenig, "The Socioeconomic Structure of an American Jewish Community," in *Jews in a Gentile World*, p. 217.
25. Louis Wirth, *The Ghetto* (Chicago, 1928), pp. 254–55.
26. William H. Whyte, Jr., *The Organization Man* (New York, 1956), p. 374.
27. Herbert J. Gans, "The Origin and Growth of a Jewish Community in the Suburbs," in *The Jews, Social Patterns of an American Group*, ed. Marshall Sklare (Glencoe, Ill., 1958), pp. 205–48.
28. *Ibid.*, pp. 228–29.
29. John R. Seely and others, *Crestwood Heights* (New York, 1956), p. 238.
30. *Ibid.*, p. 307.
31. Albert I. Gordon, *Jews in Suburbia* (Boston, 1959), p. 170.
32. *Ibid.*, p. 231.
33. The immigration of refugees from Nazi persecution may in some respects be considered a fourth wave; however, this immigration was too varied culturally to affect the course followed by the Jewish community in this country. Only the ultra-Orthodox Jews identified with the Williamsburg district in Brooklyn have made an impact.
34. Higham, AJHS *Publ.*, XLVII, No. 1, 28.
35. Wirth, *The Ghetto*, pp. 264–65.
36. Horace M. Kallen, "The National Being and the Jewish Community," in *The American Jew, A Composite Portrait*, ed. Oscar I. Janowsky (New York, 1942), p. 271.
37. Salo W. Baron, *The Jewish Community* (3 vols.; Philadelphia, 1945), II, 146.

Chapter 8

1. The Jewish Colonization Association (ICA) was established by Baron de Hirsch in 1891, with the aim of helping Jewish immigrants from Tsarist Russia. It was incorporated under English law and had its seat in London.
2. Gabriel Davidson, *Our Jewish Farmers and the Story of the Jewish Agricultural Society* (New York, 1943), pp. 11–12. See also Leonard G. Robinson, *The Agricultural Activities of the Jews in America* (New York, 1912), p. 51.
3. Maurice J. Karpf, *Jewish Community Organization in the United States* (New York, 1938), p. 5.
4. Bernard Weinstein, *Jewish Unions in America* (New York, 1929), p. 45. (*Di yidishe yunions in Amerika*)
5. *Ibid.*, p. 50.

6. Max Pine, "Days Gone By," in *United Hebrew Trades 1938 Jubilee Book* (New York, 1938), p. 43. ("Teg vos zaynen shoyn lang avek," *Gewerkschaften.*)

7. Weinstein, *Jewish Unions in America*, pp. 65–66.

8. Elias Tcherikower, "The Occupation of the Wage Earners; the Sweatshops," in *The History of the Jewish Labor Movement in the United States*, ed. Elias Tcherikower (2 vols.; New York, 1943), I, 255. ("Di arbeter-parnoses; der shvitshop," *Geshikhte fun der Yidisher arbeterbavegung in di Faraynikte Shtatn.*) Quoted with the permission of the publishers, YIVO Institute for Jewish Research.

9. Herman Frank, "The United Hebrew Trades and the Jewish Labor Federation," in *Hist. Jewish Labor Movement*, II, 409. ("Di faraynikte yidishe geverkshaften un di yidishe arbeter-federatsye.")

10. Joel Seidman, *The Needle Trades* (New York, 1942), p. 225.

11. *Ibid.*, p. 226.

12. *Ibid.*

13. *Ibid.*

14. Frank, "United Hebrew Trades . . . ," in *Hist. Jewish Labor Movement*, II, 418.

15. *Ibid.*

Chapter 9

1. Max F. Baer, "Counting the Jewish College Students," *NJM*, LXII, No. 3 (November, 1947), 92.

2. "Our Youth in College," *NJM*, LXXI, No. 6 (February, 1957), 32.

3. Melvin M. Fagin, "The Status of Jewish Lawyers in New York City," *JSS*, I, No. 1 (January, 1939), 103.

4. "Employment Discrimination against Jews in the United States," American Jewish Congress, 1955. (Mimeographed)

5. Jacob A. Goldberg, "Jews in the Medical Professions," *JSS*, I, No. 3 (October, 1939), 332.

6. Alfred I. Shapiro, "Racial Discrimination in Medicine," *JSS*, X, No. 2 (April, 1948), 106.

7. Lee J. Levinger, "Jews in the Liberal Professions in Ohio," *JSS*, II, No. 4 (October, 1940), 401–34.

8. Julius Drachsler, *Democracy and Assimilation* (New York, 1920), p. 128.

9. Claris E. Silcox and Galen N. Fisher, *Catholics, Jews, and Protestants* (New York, 1934), p. 264.

10. Bessie Bloom Wessel, *The Ethnic Survey of Woonsocket, R.I.* (Chicago, 1931), p. 109.

11. Bessie Bloom Wessel, "A Comparative Study of the Jewish Communities of New London and Norwich, 1938," in *Jewish Population Studies*, ed. Sophia M. Robison and Joshua Starr (New York, 1943), pp. 66–67.

12. Samuel Koenig, "The Socioeconomic Structure of an American Jewish Community," in *Jews in a Gentile World*, ed. Isacque Graeber and Steuart H. Britt (New York, 1942), pp. 235–36.

13. Aaron Antonovsky, "Aspects of New Haven Jewry: A Sociological Study," *YIVO Annual of Jewish Social Studies*, X (1955), 139.

14. Samuel Moment, "A Study of San Francisco Jewry, 1938," in *Jewish Population Studies*, p. 176.

15. Julian Feibelman, *A Social and Economic Study of the New Orleans Jewish Community* (Philadelphia, 1941), p. 22.

16. Benjamin B. Goldman and Alvin Chenkin, *The Jewish Population of New Orleans: 1953* (Jewish Community Surveys, Council of Jewish Federations and Welfare Funds [New York, 1954]), p. xxxiv.

17. Jacksonville Jewish Community Council, *All About Us! 1954 Census* (Jacksonville, Fla., 1954), p. 11.

18. Los Angeles Jewish Community Council, *Preview of the Greater Los Angeles Jewish Community* (Los Angeles, Cal., 1951).

19. Stanley K. Bigman, *Jewish Population of Greater Washington in 1956* (Jewish Community Council of Greater Washington [Washington, D.C., 1957]), p. 125.

20. Charles Reznikoff, with the collaboration of Uriah Z. Engelman, *The Jews of Charleston* (Philadelphia, 1950), p. 239.

21. Benjamin Kaplan, *The Eternal Stranger* (New York, 1957), pp. 85, 99, 124.

22. Hershel Shanks, "Jewish-Gentile Intermarriage," *Commentary*, XVI, No. 4 (October, 1953), 370.

23. U.S. Bureau of Census, *Current Population Reports*, Population Characteristics Series P-20, No. 79, p. 8.

24. Uriah Z. Engelman, *The Rise of the Jew in the Western World*, (New York, 1944), pp. 192–201.

25. Jacob Lestchinsky, *The National Physiognomy of Diaspora Jewry* (Buenos Aires, 1955), pp. 234–80. (*Dos natsionale ponim fun golus-yidntum.*)

26. Louis Rosenberg, "Canada," *AJYB*, LIX (1958), 229–30.

Chapter 10

1. David de Sola Pool, "Judaism and the Synagogue," in *The American Jew, A Composite Portrait*, ed. Oscar I. Janowsky (New York, 1942), p. 48.

2. Hyman B. Grinstein, *The Rise of the Jewish Community of New York, 1654–1860* (Philadelphia, 1945), p. 19.

3. These are the American Jewish Committee, the Anti-Defamation League of B'nai B'rith, the American Jewish Congress and the Jewish Labor Committee. The last two, with the Jewish War Veterans, central religious bodies

and 51 local community councils form the National Community Relations Advisory Council (NCRAC).

4. Selig Adler, *The Isolationist Impulse* (New York, 1957), p. 9.
5. *Ibid.*, p. 306.
6. Gustavus Myers, *A History of Bigotry in the United States* (New York, 1943), pp. 127–28.

Chapter 11

1. Charles A. and Mary R. Beard, *The Rise of American Civilization* 2 vols.; New York, 1927), II, 750.
2. Samuel Koenig, "The Socioeconomic Structure of an American Jewish Community," in *Jews in a Gentile World,* ed. Isacque Graeber and Steuart H. Britt (New York, 1942), p. 227.
3. Samuel Moment, "A Study of San Francisco Jewry, 1938," in *Jewish Population Studies,* ed. Sophia M. Robison and Joshua Starr (New York, 1943), p. 180.
4. Nettie P. McGill and Ellen N. Matthews, *The Youth of New York City* (New York, 1940), p. 241.
5. "Brooklyn Protestantism, 1930–1945," Brooklyn Church and Mission Federation, 1946, p. 19. (Mimeographed)
6. The figures for both religious bodies were obtained from their respective national offices.
7. Alexander M. Dushkin and Uriah Z. Engelman, *Jewish Education in the United States,* I (New York, 1959), 48.
8. Abraham G. Duker, "The Impact of Zionism on American Jewry," in *Jewish Life in America,* ed. Theodore Friedman and Robert Gordis (New York, 1955), p. 316.
9. Marshall Sklare and Mark Vosk, *The Riverton Study* (American Jewish Committee [New York, 1957]), p. 21.
10. Marshall Sklare and Benjamin B. Ringer, "A Study of Jewish Attitudes toward the State of Israel," in *The Jews, Social Patterns of an American Group* (Glencoe, Ill., 1958), p. 440.
11. Sklare and Vosk, *The Riverton Study,* p. 22.

Chapter 12

1. Marshall Sklare and Mark Vosk, *The Riverton Study* (American Jewish Committee [New York, 1957]), p. 22.

Supplementary Bibliography

SOCIAL AND CULTURAL DEVELOPMENT OF THE UNITED STATES

Adams, Thomas S. and Sumner, Helen L. *Labor Problems*. New York, 1905.

Boone, Richard G. *Education in the United States*. ("International Education Series," Vol. XI.) New York, 1890.

Boorstin, Daniel J. *The Americans; the Colonial Experience*. New York, 1958.

Chase, Stuart. *The Road We are Traveling, 1914–1942*. New York, 1942.

Corey, Lewis. *The Crisis of the Middle Class*. New York, [1935].

Dewey, John. *Characters and Events*. Edited by Joseph Ratner. 2 vols. New York, [1929].

———. *Freedom and Culture*. New York, [1939].

Faulkner, Harold U. *American Economic History*. ("Harper's History Series.") Rev. ed. New York, 1931.

Federalist, The. Sesquicentennial ed. With an introduction by Edward Meade Earle. Washington, [1938].

Grant, Madison. *The Conquest of a Continent*. With an introduction by Henry Fairfield Osborn. New York, 1933.

Hillquit, Morris. *Loose Leaves from a Busy Life*. New York, 1934.

James, William. *Pragmatism*. New York, 1931.

Jenkins, William S. *Pro-Slavery Thought in the Old South*. ("University of North Carolina Social Study Series.") Chapel Hill, N.C., 1935.

245

Jones, Howard M. *American and French Culture, 1750–1848.* Chapel Hill, N.C., 1927.

Lee, Everett S. and others. *Population Redistribution and Economic Growth, United States, 1870–1950.* 2 vols. Philadelphia, 1957.

Lerner, Max. *America as a Civilization.* New York, 1957.

Merriam, Charles E. *A History of American Political Theories.* New York, 1928.

Noble, Stuart G. *History of American Education.* New York, 1938.

Riesman, David, and others. *The Lonely Crowd.* (Yale University "Studies in National Policy," No. 3.) New Haven, 1950.

Schlesinger, Arthur M., Jr. *The Age of Jackson.* New York, 1945.

Thompson, Warren S. *Population Problems.* 3rd ed. New York, 1942.

Zucker, Morris. *The Philosophy of American History.* 2 vols. Long Island City, N.Y., 1945.

IMMIGRANTS AND MINORITIES IN THE UNITED STATES

Benson, Adolph B. *Americans from Sweden.* ("Peoples of America Series.") Preface by Carl Sandburg. Philadelphia and New York, 1950.

Berkson, Isaac B. *Theories of Americanization.* (Teachers College, Columbia University, "Contributions to Education," No. 109.) New York, 1920.

Bossard, James H. S. and Boll, Eleanor S. *One Marriage, Two Faiths.* New York, 1957.

Brown, Francis J. and Rouček, Joseph S., eds. *Our Racial and National Minorities.* ("Prentice-Hall Education Series.") New York, 1937.

Burma, John H. *Spanish Speaking Groups in the United States.* (Duke University Sociological Series, No. 9.) Durham, N.C., 1954.

Capek, Thomas. *The Czechs in America.* Cambridge, Mass., 1920.

Carpenter, Niles, and Katz, Daniel. *A Study of Acculturization in the Polish Group of Buffalo, 1926–1928.* ("University Monographs in Sociology," Vol. VII, No. 3.) Buffalo, 1929.

Catholic Colleges and Schools in the United States. (Dept. of Education, National Catholic Welfare Conference.) Washington, 1940.

Catholic Colleges and Schools in the United States. (Summary of Catholic Education, 1955–56, National Catholic Welfare Conference.) Washington, 1958.

Commons, John R. *Races and Immigrants in America.* New ed. New York, 1920.

Ellis, John T. *American Catholicism.* ("Chicago History of American Civilization.") Chicago, 1956.

Fairchild, Henry P. *Immigration*. Rev. ed. New York, 1925.

Federal Writers. Project. *Louisiana*. ("American Guide Series.") New York, 1941.

———. *New Mexico*. ("American Guide Series.") New York, 1940.

———. *New Orleans City Guide*. ("American Guide Series.") Boston, 1938.

———. *New York Learns*. ("American Guide Series.") New York, [1939].

Handlin, Oscar. *Boston's Immigrants*. Cambridge, Mass., 1959.

Jenks, Jeremiah W. and Lauck, W. Jett. *The Immigration Problem*. 6th ed., rev. and enl. by Rufus D. Smith. New York, 1926.

Lengyl, Emil. *Americans from Hungary*. ("Peoples of America Series.") Philadelphia and New York, 1948.

Mulder, Arnold. *Americans from Holland*. ("Peoples of America Series.") Philadelphia and New York, 1947.

Simpson, George E. and Yinger, John M. *Racial and Cultural Minorities*. New York, 1953.

Smith, Bradford. *Americans from Japan*. ("Peoples of America Series.") Philadelphia and New York, 1948.

Thompson, Frank V. *The Schooling of the Immigrant*. New York, [1920].

Wittke, Carl F. *The Irish in America*. Baton Rouge, La., 1956.

THE JEWS

Cohen, Israel. *Jewish Life in Modern Times*. 2nd ed., rev. and enl. London, 1929.

Duker, Abraham G. "Emerging Culture Patterns in American Jewish Life," *Publications* of the American Jewish Historical Society, XXXIX, No. 4 (June, 1950), 351–88.

Engelman, Uriah Z. *Jewish Statistics in the United States Census of Religious Bodies*. (Conference on Jewish Relations.) New York, 1947.

Friedman, Lee M. *Jewish Pioneers and Patriots*. With a preface by A. S. W. Rosenbach. Philadelphia, 1943.

Fuchs, Lawrence H. *The Political Behavior of American Jews*. Glencoe, Ill., 1956.

Glanz, Rudolf. *Notes on Early Jewish Peddling in America*. (Conference on Jewish Relations.) New York, 1945.

Glazer, Nathan. *American Judaism*. ("The Chicago History of American Civilization.") Chicago, [1957].

Goldberg, Israel (Rufus Learsi, pseud.). *The Jews of America*. Cleveland, O., 1954.

Goodman, Abram V. *American Overture.* Philadelphia, 1947.

Gordis, Robert, *Judaism for the Modern Age.* New York, 1955.

Grayzel, Solomon. *A History of the Jews from the Babylonian Exile to the End of World War II.* Philadelphia, 1947.

Gutstein, Morris A. *The Story of the Jews of Newport.* With an introduction by David de Sola Pool. New York, 1936.

Herberg, Will. *Protestant, Catholic, Jew, an Essay in American Religious Sociology.* Garden City, N.Y., 1955.

Jewish Communal Register of the *Kehillah* (Jewish Community) of New York. New York, 1918.

Jewish Occupational Council. *Patterns of Jewish Occupational Distribution in the United States and Canada.* Report No. 6. New York, 1940.

Kaplan, Mordecai M. *The Future of the American Jew.* New York, 1948.

———. *Judaism as a Civilization.* New York, 1934.

Kohn, Eugene, ed. *American Jewry.* New York, 1955.

Korn, Bertram W. *American Jewry and the Civil War.* Introduction by Allan Nevins. Philadelphia, 1951.

———. *Eventful Years and Experiences, Studies in Nineteenth-Century American Jewish History.* (Publications of the American Jewish Archives, No. 1.) Cincinnati, 1954.

Lebeson, Anita Libman. *Pilgrim People.* New York, 1950.

Levinger, Lee J. *A History of the Jews in the United States.* 4th ed., rev. Cincinnati, 1949.

Lewisohn, Ludwig. *The American Jew.* New York, 1950.

Marcus, Jacob Rader. *Early American Jewry.* 2 vols. Philadelphia, 1951–53.

———. *Memoirs of American Jews, 1775–1865.* ("Jacob R. Schiff Library of Jewish Contributions to American Democracy.") 3 vols. Philadelphia, 1955–56.

Mopsik, Samuel. *The Jewish Population of Worcester.* (Conference on Jewish Relations.) New York, 1945.

Ruppin, Arthur. *The Jewish Fate and Future.* ("Studies in Modern History.") Translated by E. W. Dickes. London, 1940.

Schappes, Morris U., ed. *A Documentary History of the Jews in the United States, 1654–1875.* Preface by Joshua Bloch. New York, 1950.

Sklare, Marshall. *Conservative Judaism: An American Religious Movement.* Glencoe, Ill., 1955.

Steinberg, Milton. *The Making of the Modern Jew.* Indianapolis, 1934.

Straus, Oscar S. *Under Four Administrations, from Cleveland to Taft.* Boston, 1922.

U.S. Bureau of Census. *Census of Religious Bodies,* 1936. Bulletin No. 72. (Jewish congregations, statistics, history, doctrine and organizations, prepared under the supervision of T. F. Murphy. History, doctrine and organizations furnished by H. S. Linfield.) Washington, 1937.

Waldman, Morris D. *Nor By Power.* New York, 1953.

Wiernik, Peter. *History of the Jews in America.* 2nd ed., rev. and enl. New York, 1931.

Wolf, Simon. *Presidents I Have Known from 1860–1918.* Washington, [1918].

Index

Jewish Tidings, 76, 77
Jewish War Veterans, 243
Jewish youth, 46, 109, 110, 130, 175, 178, 186, 213, 215
Joseph, Jacob, 76
Joseph, Samuel, 60, 61, 235, 236
Judaism, 70-72, 75-77, 124, 126, 127, 154, 167, 193, 212, 214, 222, 223. *See also* Jewish religion

Kahol Kadosh Beth Elohim, synagog, 72, 80
Kallen, Horace M., 51, 121, 154, 234, 235, 239, 241
Kaplan, Benjamin, 186, 243
Kaplan, Lawrence J., 237
Kaplan, Mordecai M., 126
Karpf, Maurice J., 135, 240, 241
Kashruth. See Dietary laws
Katz, Daniel, 43
Kehilla, 201
Kennedy, Raymond, 121, 142, 239, 240
Kennedy, Ruby J. R., 185
Kilpatrick, William, 51
Kishinev pogrom, 198
Koenig, Samuel, 48, 49, 113, 115, 149, 185, 208, 234, 238, 241, 243, 244
Koerner, Gustave, 232
Kohler, Kauffman, 73
Kosher food, 43, 115, 218
Krause, Adolph, 77, 236

Ladino, language and press, 78, 79
Landsmanschaften, 40, 81, 83, 155, 159, 162, 163
Latin, classical, 31
Latin America, 232
Lebanon Lodge. *See* B'nai B'rith
Lebeson, Anita Libman, 65, 72, 235
Leeser, Isaac, 74-75, 118
Leiserson, William M., 27, 28, 233
Lestchinsky, Jacob, 99, 182, 188, 237, 243
Levantine Jews, 79
Levinger, Lee J., 65, 180-81, 235, 242
Lichtenstein, Gaston, 236
Lilienthal, David, 73, 74
Lindbergh, Charles A., 203
Linfield, Harry S., 88, 208, 240
Lithuania, 87, 192; Jews from, 73, 192

Little Holland, 30; *See also* Dutch
Locke, Alain, 235
London, England, 198, 241
Lorimer, Frank, 112, 238
Los Angeles, Cal., 90, 91, 186, 237, 238
Louisiana, 159, 186
Louisville, Ky., 133, 223
Lunt, Paul S., 36, 233, 240
Lutheran church, 21, 22, 231
Lynd, Robert S. and Helen M., 36, 147, 240

MacIver, Robert M., 51
Macy's, 139
Marginality, 70, 72, 123, 125, 126, 128, 154, 227
Marranos, 69, 154
Marx, Marxism, 104
Maryland, 71
Massachusetts, 93, 179
Matthews, Ellen N., 36, 109, 233, 238, 244
Mayo-Smith, Richmond, 34, 48, 233, 234
McGill, Nettie P., 36, 109, 233, 238, 244
Melting pot, 53, 54, 55, 85, 118
Mennonite church, 21
Merriam, Charles E., 6
Merzbacher, Leo, 72-73, 74
Methodist, 204
Mexicans, 183
Meyers, Lena, 115
Miami, Fla., 90, 237, 238
Miami Beach, Fla., 57
Michigan, 30, 48, 93
Middletown, 36, 147
Miller, Herbert A., 234
Milwaukee, Wis., 130
Minneapolis, Minn., 91, 145
Minneapolis Athletic Club, 145
Missouri, 14
Moment, Samuel, 243, 244
Montefiore, Moses, 198
Moravian church, 21; Moravians, 87
Mormons, 57
Moslems, 58
Mother tongue, 2, 30, 31, 41, 79, 120, 162, 174, 229-30, 232
Mutual aid associations, 23, 168, 172
Myers, Gustavus, 204, 244
Myrdal, Gunnar, 3, 8, 64, 230

Edited by Barbara C. Woodward
Designed by Richard Kinney
Set in Linotype Garamond
Printed on Warren's Olde Style Antique White Wove
Bound in Joanna Mills, Natulin cloth
Manufactured in the United States of America

Date Due

JAN 5 '62			
DEC 1 4 '62			
NOV 8 '63			
SEP 3 '65			
OCT 1 9 '66			
DEC 4 1967			
DEC 15 1967			
JAN 1 3 1969			
JAN 28			
MAR 2 0 1970			
MAR 2 2 1971			
MAY 1 2 1973			
	PRINTED	IN U. S. A.	